Strong Starts, Supported Transitions and Student Success

Strong Starts, Supported Transitions and Student Success

Edited by

Andrew Funston, Miguel Gil and Gwen Gilmore

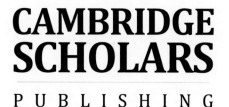

Strong Starts, Supported Transitions and Student Success,
Edited by Andrew Funston, Miguel Gil and Gwen Gilmore

This book first published 2014

Cambridge Scholars Publishing

12 Back Chapman Street, Newcastle upon Tyne, NE6 2XX, UK

British Library Cataloguing in Publication Data
A catalogue record for this book is available from the British Library

ISBN (10): 1-4438-5499-9, ISBN (13): 978-1-4438-5499-3

CONTENTS

LIST OF TABLES AND ILLUSTRATIONS

Tables

Illustrations

FOREWORD

PROFESSOR MARIE BRENNAN
PROFESSOR OF EDUCATION, COLLEGE OF EDUCATION
VICTORIA UNIVERSITY, MELBOURNE

This book asks academics in higher education to rethink how they understand the role of the university and how the university might be re-imagined. Written by authors all located in one Australian university—characterised by high levels of culturally and linguistically diverse students, often from areas of high poverty—the book's challenge is profound. What does massification of the university mean for students, for student support and all disciplinary areas?

In a society characterised by growing inequality and social stratification, such as (but certainly not only) Australia, the "good" of formal tertiary education is valued within a range of often competing discourses, where the dominant policy good is economic: that the individual will contribute to the national economic success through gaining qualifications. Around the world, initially through policies sponsored by the member states of the OECD, the economic purposes of education (from early childhood, through schooling to further and higher education) have been put in place through a wide range of steering techniques by governments and by institutions which they fund. Often these purposes have sat uneasily alongside more traditional concerns of equality and citizenship. As these wider changes to educational institutions have been taken up, strategies for inclusion of new groups of students have been explored in new ways. It is in exploring this challenge through both theoretical and case-study examples that the book works beyond its own institution.

Much of the new higher education policy discourse uses terms like "flexibility", "knowledge economy" student induction, transition and retention, and "unbundling" the university experience; responses often proceed by tagging particular groups in "equity categories" as "under-prepared". There is a small but growing scholarship around the world that problematises such concepts and bureaucratic procedures, to which this book contributes. Miguel Gil's tour of 30 years of scholarly debates around retention and transition identifies a wide range of issues, particularly for institutional action, and is thus helpful to other scholars of teaching and learning. His historical tour links a range of debates about first-year experience programs, changes in support services, and services integrated with academic disciplinary areas. However, many common institutional problems tend to impede systematic work: lack of leadership, poor coordination and short-term project-based approaches, alongside a tendency towards deficit assumptions that underpin expectations that students will have to learn to "fit in"—i.e. assimilation into an unproblematised status quo. Piecemeal approaches are common, focused on single dimensions of identified problems, undermining any systematic effort. The majority of chapters in the book provide detailed case studies of particular initiatives—some over 20 years old—as they grapple with evolving pedagogies, organisational arrangements, approaches to partnership and/or external policy shifts, using a range of conceptual resources to support understandings of the changing terrain. While there are commonalities which show evidence of longstanding conversations among the authors across their diverse functional "homes" within the university, each chapter also brings diverse theoretical resources to bear, ranging from Indigenous standpoints, postcolonial critique, theories of language and learning, and critical multiculturalism, to mention only a few. The initiatives are varied, ranging from Foundations Programs, to placements in early childhood teacher education, listening to first-year students, Students Supporting Students and Core Units in bachelor's degrees. What is particularly interesting is the partnering work across disciplinary fields and those in units responsible for academic support and development, language, literacy and learning units, library and ICT support—what the authors call "co-curricular" groups. Such joint approaches, argues the book as a whole, need to be integrated for "Strong Starts" to higher education to be supported. There are no recipes here but plenty of efforts to learn through systematic collaboration. In demonstrating multiple efforts to address "transition pedagogies" (Kift *et al.* 2010) within a single institution, each chapter provides testimony to the effect of ongoing coordination— and that coordination is possible.

However, standardised accountability and reporting tend to impede innovations. Given the performativity that frames institutional self-representations in the market and centralised accountability in many countries (Ball 2006; Power 2003), institutional isomorphism often works against innovation and its embedding. Innovation may appear counter-productive to institutional efforts to manage risk. In such a context, making systematic efforts to coordinate across the institution is rarer than it should be. It is easier to work within existing frames than to take on a longer-term, whole-of-institution approach. A relatively resource-poor institution, such as Victoria University, Melbourne, working with students from marginalised social groups, may find it easier to take the risks of innovating, whereas more elite universities may see themselves as having too much to lose. The case studies of partnering within the institution, described here, may offer clearer directions than does policy towards future developments that are effective in transitioning students and reinventing the university across a sector.

I commend this book as an important intervention into current debates about how to enable successful transition of new student groups into the university. Each chapter provides a practitioner's researched account of their practice; each adds important dimensions to understanding what is at stake—for staff and students—in meeting the challenges of university massification. Taken as a whole, the book makes a case that it is possible to undertake systematic conversations and research for developing new approaches to the problem of transitions.

Marie Brennan

Reference List

Ball, Stephen J. 2006. "Performativity and Fabrications in the Education Economy: Towards the Performativity Society", in *Education, Globalisation & Social change*, edited by H. Lauder, P. Brown, J.-A. Dillabough and A.H. Halsey (eds)., Oxford: University Press, 692–701.

Kift, Sally, Karen Nelson, and John Clarke. 2010. "Transition Pedagogy: A Third Generation Approach to FYE—A Case Study of Policy and Practice for the Higher Education Sector." *The International Journal of the First Year in Higher Education* 1 (1) (July 21): 1–20. doi:10.5204/intjfyhe.v1i1.13.

Power, M. (2003) "Evaluating the Audit Explosion", *Law & Policy* 25(July): 185–202.

INTRODUCTION

SUPPORTING STUDENTS' TRANSITIONS IN CHALLENGING TIMES

ANDREW FUNSTON, MIGUEL GIL AND GWEN GILMORE

As editors of this book we feel we have a good story to tell about the higher education transitions of students at one of Australia's newer universities. Victoria University is a multi-sector institution based in Melbourne. The institution distinguishes itself as the *University of Opportunity* with a "vision to be excellent, engaged and accessible and to be internationally recognised for our leadership in empowering diverse groups of students to grow their capabilities and transform their lives" (www.vu.edu.au).[1]

The university is "proud of its leadership role in the west of Melbourne", historically the industrial heartland of the metropolis, and serves "a very diverse student cohort with a wide range of countries, cultures, and educational backgrounds represented". One of Australia's 39 public universities, Victoria University has more than 50,000 enrolled students, including over 12,000 international students, and offers programs at all levels of the Australian Qualifications Framework (AQF). The focus of this book is students in the first year of their diploma or undergraduate degree-level courses. We are concerned with both their campus-based experiences but also the larger ways education features in their lives and connects to their aspirations and career plans.

We do not report here on all of the transition strategies employed across our large university or within our own colleges, and we do not speak on behalf of the institution. The authors of this book are academics and professional staff working with students enrolled in humanities and social science courses, including the Liberal Arts Diploma which operates as one of Victoria University's important internal pathways into degree courses. We benefit from our participation in a lively "first year in higher education" (FYHE) or "first-year experience" (FYE) community of practice which is active at Victoria University and connects us to Australian and international networks.

Sustaining Inclusive Learning Communities

Victoria University claims a "reputation for increasing opportunity for participation in tertiary education among students from low socioeconomic backgrounds, which is now regarded as a major national priority". Around 22 percent of our domestic students come from the bottom SES (socioeconomic status) quartile (as measured by the Australian Bureau of Statistics based on household postcode). That is above the 20 percent target set by the previous federal government.

The fate of our students and this publically funded institution is determined to a considerable degree by government funding levels. Particularly relevant was the federal Labor government (2007–13) policy response to its review of higher education, commonly referred to as the Bradley Review (2008) and a later review of base funding, referred to as the Lomax-Smith Review (2011). Contrary to that report's recommendation, base funding was not increased. The incoming federal Coalition government (2013–) is yet to make explicit its higher education policies and funding commitments although a \$2.3 billion cut in the Labor government's 2013 Federal Budget, prior to losing the election, is likely to stand for the new government's first term.

The outgoing government's policy achievements should be acknowledged here. According to the Australian Council for Education Research (ACER, March 2013), "in the past five years the number of students in higher education has increased by 25 percent" (11). Australia now has above-OECD (Organisation for Economic Co-operation and Development)-average bachelor-degree attainment levels (13). The proportion of students from low-SES backgrounds has increased from around 16 to 20 percent. That has been without a substantial increase in Australia's total expenditure on tertiary education as a proportion of GDP (13), which sits at around 1.5 percent (compared to, for instance, US at around 2.7 percent and Canada at around 2.5 percent). However, we also note that ACER (2012) reported that much of the increase in growth of 25 to 34-year-olds with degree qualifications has been driven by skilled migration.[2]

It is against this backdrop of financial constraints and swelling student numbers that this book deals with some of the challenges students face when they start their course at the university and our strategies to support their transitions. We do not buy into "deficit" views of our students, including those who arrive with low university entrance scores. The diversity of backgrounds is the wellspring of aspirations, knowledge and capacities our students bring to their new learning communities and something we keep in mind in designing our curriculum. Many of our most successful graduates in the humanities and social sciences courses commenced their studies with a low Australian Tertiary Admission Rank (ATAR). Their chances of "making it" would have been seriously compromised had their access been based on "strict academic merit".

While ACER (February 2012) reported that university retention and completion rates have been improving, "the engagement of low-SES groups will be crucial to ensure the Australian Government achieves the target of 40 percent of all 25–34-year-olds having a qualification at the bachelor level or above by 2025" (3). ACER Senior Research Fellow Julie McMillan called for close monitoring, and while her research indicated that "students from low socioeconomic status (SES) backgrounds persist in their studies at rates similar to, or slightly lower than, high-SES students" (3), she also observed:

> As the participation of students from disadvantaged backgrounds increases, it will be necessary to continue to monitor their retention and completion rates closely. Among those who discontinue their studies, low-SES students are more likely to cite academic and financial difficulties as a consideration for non-completion of their degrees. (3)[3]

Attrition among both low-ATAR students and among students from lower-SES backgrounds is a persistent problem across Australia and within our own institution. Many of the transition strategies and research programs discussed in this book take up the challenge of improving retention and course completions. This work starts with the students' orientation, carries through the first year and beyond, and requires a "whole-of-institution" approach.

At Victoria University, leadership is provided by our Centre for Collaborative Learning and Teaching (CCLT) and by management teams in each of our seven colleges, including directors of teaching and learning (T&L) and a range of specialist and professional staff who work alongside the academics. We also benefit from Victoria University's Centre for Cultural Diversity and Wellbeing and an education research body, the Victorian Institute for Education, Diversity & Lifelong Learning.

In a recent article by the Victorian Institute's director, Professor Roger Slee (2013), we are reminded that exclusion "is ingrained into the global fabric in general and education in particular" (3) and as educators we need to be wary of rhetorical claims of inclusionary practices, especially when they entail crude tests or measures. As we attempt to demonstrate in this book, we do more than talk:

> The rhetoric of inclusion is strong but conceptions and practices of inclusive education are inconsistent and disconnected from other aspects of social and education policy that drives exclusion in stark and subtle manifestations. (3)

We turn now to discuss one of the most pressing issues facing all Australian universities and the wider society, which is the persistently low level of participation in higher education by Indigenous Australians which connects in part to the comparatively lower levels of school completion to Year 12 and also to failures by the tertiary education sector. We follow this by describing some of the important programs at Victoria University including work undertaken by the Moondani Balluk Academic Unit where we focus on transition pedagogies and co-curricular supports for students enrolled in the Bachelor of Arts (Kyinandoo). To provide context and background for that discussion we begin by talking about the federal Labor government's 2011 review in this area.

Higher Education Access for Indigenous Australians

Chaired by Professor Larissa Behrendt, *The Review of Higher Education Access and Outcomes for Aboriginal and Torres Strait Islander People Final Report* (2012) described the current situation where Aboriginal and Torres Strait Islander students "made up 1.4 percent of all enrolments in university in 2010, yet made up 2.2 percent of the working population" and only one percent of all full-time equivalent staff in universities. In their background paper, prepared for the review, Ekaterina Pechenkina and Ian Anderson (2011) provide a fairly grim picture of the current situation:

> Despite various efforts made by Australian universities to tackle issues behind low education participation of Indigenous Australians, the state of Indigenous education can be currently described as being in crisis. Based on the analysis of Indigenous student data in higher education, Indigenous institutional outcomes can be categorised crudely (with a couple of exceptions) into two categories: those with high enrolment and low completions and those with low enrolments and high completions... Indigenous completion rates are relatively lower than those of non-Indigenous students across all institutions. By comparison students from low socioeconomic backgrounds perform nearly as well as students coming from other socioeconomic groups (with the exception of those

from remote and regional areas). Accordingly, the pattern of Indigenous outcomes that is described here also reflects a system-wide issue: the relatively small pool of Indigenous Australians with adequate preparation for tertiary education. (1)

In their *Final Report* (2012) Behrendt *et al.* take a more optimistic view, in providing the following vision:

> While the ultimate aim of the Review is to achieve parity in higher education for Aboriginal and Torres Strait Islander students and staff, the Panel's vision is much broader. In coming years the Panel wants higher education to become a natural pathway... Success in higher education will lay the foundations for an Aboriginal and Torres Strait Islander professional class that can contribute to closing the gap and to Australia's broader wellbeing and economic prosperity. The Panel also wants to see more high-quality Aboriginal and Torres Strait Islander researchers in universities and research agencies contributing to a national research agenda that values Aboriginal and Torres Strait Islander perspectives and reflects Indigenous development priorities. The Panel ultimately hopes to see the higher education sector playing a leading role in building capacity within Aboriginal and Torres Strait Islander communities, and making meaningful contribution to closing the gap between Indigenous and non-Indigenous Australians. (xi)

To this end Behrendt *et al.* (2012) make a set of recommendations which we summarise below (and we return to some of these in our later discussion of Indigenous programs at Victoria University). The report recommends that:

- the population parity rate should be defined and regularly revised according to Australian Bureau of Statistics population statistics and then used to set national targets (Rec 1)
- these targets and timeframes should be for the proportion of total domestic students "focusing initially on priority disciplines that support the Closing the Gap agenda, retention and completion rates, proportion of university general and academic staff, reflecting geographic and demographic catchments" (Rec 2)
- government should engage universities in discussions about achieving targets through compacts and rewards for achieving or moving beyond targets (Rec 3)
- government should work with state and territory education departments to ensure careers advisers and teachers are equipped to encourage higher education (Rec 4)
- government should revise the Higher Education Participation and Partnerships Program (HEPPP) to refocus, to support students'

academic skills development, aspirations to go to university, support peer and family networks, better mentoring in Years 10 to 12 with pathways support, more relevant information (Rec 5)

- universities and the vocational education and training (VET) sectors should work with employers and professional associations around issues such as cadetships, scholarships, flexible leave arrangements, and with professional bodies to extend alternative pathways between VET and higher education (Rec 6 and 7)
- the reach and effectiveness of "enabling courses for disadvantaged learners" and "dedicated contact points and Aboriginal and higher education advisers located within universities" should be improved (Rec 8 and 9)
- there should be a whole-of-universities approach..."backed up by Indigenous Education Units..." (Rec 10)
- Indigenous Education Units should be supported to provide a "culturally safe environment" and reviewed as to whether they have "appropriate objectives, funding, structures and accountability measures to ensure quality student outcomes" and with a focus on "outreach work with schools and other sectors; improvements in retention and completion rates; access to quality tutoring services..." (Rec 11)
- there should be better support for communities "by refining university planning processes to take account of the likely future needs... for a professional workforce... and innovative local partnerships" (Rec 12)
- funding should be reformed for the Indigenous Support Program and the Indigenous Tutorial Assistance Scheme Tertiary Tuition (ITAS-TT), to "allow universities greater flexibility to provide locally relevant, tailored support... to achieve an improvement in current enrolment levels but also with greater emphasis on retention and completion rates... and to ensure that funding would be simpler to administer" (Rec 13)

Indigenous standpoints

In "Negotiating University 'Equity' from Indigenous Standpoints: A Shaky Bridge", Tracey Bunda, Lew Zipin and Marie Brennan (2011) offer a critique of how "dominant notions of 'equity' subordinate or cannibalise possibilities for what higher education could mean for Indigenous peoples" (941). They explain how, despite the push for curricula inclusions having resulted in the setup of Indigenous Studies courses and programs at Australian universities, this "has not significantly affected wider academic and professional studies programs which are the main game of the university" (942). They locate this within a "compensatory logic" which "projects a *deficit* view of Indigenous cultures, contradicting impulses to recognise Indigenous cultural perspectives in university teaching and learning" (942). Referencing Fazal Rizvi and Bob Lingard (2009), the authors find that "impulses of cultural recognition and inclusion have largely been lost in the ascendance of "equity" as a justifying keyword for increasing Indigenous (and other 'less advantaged') presence in universities" (942), and blunting "the critical-ethical force of justice discourses that speak in terms of redressing *inequalities*" (942).

For universities to become institutions that "support collaborations among Indigenous people, hopefully with others, to build new and better bridgeworks" (943), Bunda, Zipin and Brennan (2011) believe "we need to establish critiques, from Indigenous perspectives, of how in crossing the 'equity' bridge, Indigenous people run up against forbidding walls of university whitestream 'normality'" (943). Drawing on Bunda's doctoral study, based in part on interviews with staff at a number of Australian universities, they report on "a systematic process of absencing Indigenous ontologies, epistemologies, cultures and values" (944), and the challenge of "re-educating whitestream assumptions and judgements" (945). However, this is often for Indigenous academics and centres a "one-way burden" on top of "negotiating institutional expectations of filling 'difference' gaps without unsettling institutional norms" and which "adds greatly to the workload, and work stress of Indigenous academic and administrative staff" (946). In "re-imagining universities as places for Indigenous bridgework" from Indigenous perspectives, universities need to re-educate themselves, and need a lot more than tokenistic inclusions:

> Indigenous standpoint work needs to cultivate both *critical* and *(re)imaginative* capacities, and to bring both to bear upon an institution that does the reciprocal work of learning how to listen and engage (952).

Bunda, Zipin and Brennan describe the "fraught ambivalence" of Indigenous centres offering a "formal space for developing Indigenous community within the university... enclaves of protection from dangerous whitestream effects" yet risking marginalisation from the centres of power at the university, and typically having "overwhelming responsibility and labour" (947). Their critique reminds us that different cohorts of students have particular needs and these are not "deficits" but, rather, aspects of identity and the responsibilities and knowledges that go with our identities:

> Indigenous students are more likely to have community obligations— including the mourning of deaths—than other students; more likely to have financial problems; and, like Indigenous staff, structurally more likely to

find the university alienating to cultural knowledges and values. Thus the level of support required, even for relatively small numbers, can be very substantial; but recognition of this is often deflected through deficit views of Indigenous "inability" to perform up par with "normal" students. (947)

Moondani Balluk

Victoria University, officially through its statutes and in other ways, "acknowledges and recognises Aboriginal and Torres Strait Islander peoples as the first peoples of Australia and the Kulin as the traditional owners of university land" (www.vu.edu.au). One of the university's successful and inclusive programs is operated by the Moondani Balluk Academic Unit. That unit delivers the Bachelor of Arts (Kyinandoo) and an Indigenous Foundation Program, Mumgu-Dhal, as well as assisting Indigenous Australian students on a range of matters: "ABSTUDY (the government allowance); academic support; social support; referrals and support in housing and finance matters; enrolment and course advice; counselling and discrimination advice; access to the Indigenous Resources library".

The name Moondani Balluk means "embrace people" in the Wurundjeri language of the people who first lived in the western region of Melbourne. The stated vision of the unit is to create and foster:

- a culturally safe environment that welcomes, nurtures, and recreates community
- a community that is embedded in relationship to land, culture, law and Elders
- sharing of Indigenous knowledge, and translating and embedding Indigenous practices into all its work, research, and curricula
- respect for all people within and without Moondani Balluk through mutually engaged relationships
- a commitment to pursuing political and social justice, equity and access to education of Indigenous people
- accountability to Indigenous cultural values, protocols, and norms

The director of the Moondani Balluk Academic Unit, Karen Jackson, in an interview with Andrew Funston (August 2013), discussed several issues directly related to the themes of this book, including an interest in sustaining inclusive learning communities and the importance of strong starts and supported transitions. For Jackson, an essential aspect of successful higher education transitions for Indigenous students relates to respect for Indigenous knowledge and links into community.

Moondani Balluk Academic Unit was named after extensive consultation with Indigenous staff and permissions from the Wurundjeri Tribal Council. Subject guides across the colleges and most other important university publications include an acknowledgement to the Kulin as the traditional owners of the university. Karen Jackson spoke of the significance of the five language groups and important cultural sites in the western region. She welcomes requests by members of the university to explore ways of extending acknowledgments for particular purposes or situations. Important events such as conferences at the university commence with the traditional Welcome to Country from traditional owner Aunty Joy and other Elders.

Moondani Balluk evolved over the past two decades from a unit in the Equity and Social Justice branch of the university, to an academic unit delivering courses. In earlier times this was a Bachelor of Education for Indigenous students in the Echuca area (in the state's north). Later offerings have included courses designed and taught by Indigenous academics and other professional staff based at the St Albans campus of the university.

The BA (Kyinandoo), as described to prospective students on the university website, is "aimed specifically at Indigenous Australians and for non-Indigenous people interested in working with or for Indigenous communities or groups". Students are selected into the course by "direct entry" and the course is open to applicants with high school (VCE) or Vocational Education (VE) backgrounds or on the basis of working-life experience rather than formal education or training qualifications. It draws students from a number of pathways, including from the community services and education areas, and links students to a range of government traineeships and internships. New students may be eligible for "recognition of prior learning" or "advanced standing" credits, allowing some students to accelerate through the degree.

Jackson, underscoring the importance of successful transitions, explains that building relationships is vital, and this starts well before a student enrols in the course:

> When we are out in community talking to people who are prospective students one of our first conversations is about who you are, "Who are you? Where's your family from? Who's your mob?" With that you create a connection with them, which is the start of your relationship. And then you can have the conversation, "So, you're from that country, from this mob, you're Yorta Yorta" and so forth. That's really a good conversation and people feel really comfortable with you.

The BA (Kyinandoo) entails six core Indigenous Australian units and six core Global Indigenous units, as well as 10 elective units chosen from across the university. There are two core foundation units: Managing Learning and Inquiry, and Indigenous Career Development. The course includes the study of Indigenous traditions and cultural heritage, Indigenous organisations and communities, contemporary issues and Indigenous leadership. The course encourages community-related research projects and community placements. This includes work the students do in their Oral Traditions unit, where students interview someone they know and admire from their community, reflect on what they hear in their journals, and report back often through digital media recordings.

Jackson described the importance of Moondani Balluk as a "safe cultural space" for commencing Indigenous students, some of whom come to Melbourne to study from rural or remote areas or other smaller regional cities and towns. She explained an approach taken in the foundation units—and this connects to several other chapters in this book—where commencing students are encouraged to find their voices and confidence in an academic setting by telling their stories and keeping reflective journals. For many of the Indigenous students this involves the impacts on their parents and grandparents of appalling treatment at the hands of the state and institutions:

> We get lots of stories about grandparents and parents, about what happened in their lives, and not only in education. We find that a lot of our students' parents were from the Stolen Generation, and their grandparents were too, and so there are a lot of issues there about parenting, about taking care of each other, about understanding the connection to country. Some of them know only that they are Aboriginal, and other ones have really good connections to community and understand which language group they are from, and know ceremony and story. That is a tension in itself... and that's why we spend a lot of time in that first couple of weeks, so students can tell each other their stories, and then talk about how everyone of us is different.

Many commencing students feel disoriented, and simple but important processes such as getting passwords and university email accounts can be defeating unless support is provided in a timely manner. As well as helping to orient students with these important but basic steps, Moondani Balluk also advises students about their eligibility for ABSTUDY and the Commonwealth Government Scholarship for Indigenous students. Staff at Moondani Balluk advise students as they take up non-core or elective units outside of the centre (from second semester of the first year), to make sure they are likely to have the necessary prerequisite knowledge or skills and not be at risk of academic failure or disappointments so early in their course. Indigenous students are encouraged, where possible, to move out into the larger courses in pairs or with groups, to support one another.

Many of the Indigenous students have a range of non-academic matters to contend with, and many of the issues raised here connect to Andrew Funston's case study later in the book. Jackson described herself "cringing" when she hears successful leaders in the university refer to their own "first in the family" experience of higher education transitions, to which she feels compelled on occasion to respond:

> I say, "You probably had a family that had income, and had employment, and a safe place to live". And a lot of our students come from regional and rural areas, some come from interstate, some from close by, but their housing is always a tension, whether they can afford to stay in that house. Most of them have a number of kids so they've got to get kids to school. They've got to be able to pick kids up. They've got to pay for their child-minding fees. So we never start our classes until 10 am and finish by three so that parents can drop off and pick up their kids, rather than having to pay for after-school care.

Financial matters are significant for the Indigenous students, just as they are for most Victoria University students. Jackson describes a recent case where a student who was on an ABSTUDY allowance and in receipt of the re-location scholarship was struggling to make ends meet after paying $300 a week in rent for a furnished room close to the university. The student was studying full-time, and was considering dropping to part-time study. This would have meant losing her allowance and scholarship (for students to be officially full-time they must be enrolled in a minimum of three units per semester):

> We told her to come to St Albans and we'd help out. We went through her assessments, and helped her work out a plan to do all that extra work. We haven't got money to pay for tutors so we have to do that ourselves which is another extra bit on top of our workloads. A lot of our students are "first in family" to come to university but they also have parents who have never been through much schooling. So for them actually to write something and then hand it in is really hard, especially when they are very unsure or have low self-esteem or are lacking in confidence.

This level of close support, and a scaffolded approach to curriculum design, and providing a "safe cultural space" for Indigenous students are important features of Moondani Balluk and link to the significance the BA (Kyinandoo) curriculum attaches to work with communities; through field work and the networking with other Indigenous students and leaders across Australia and internationally. Students for the past few years have attended the Dreaming Festival in Queensland where activists, musicians and artists share their stories and career advice. In 2012 a group of students and staff visited Hopi and Navajo lands in USA and were able to experience at close range the very different approaches to cultural maintenance and governance arrangements. Another important field-work element embedded in the course relates to the triennial World Indigenous People's Conference on Education (WIPCE). The last conference was in Peru and the next will be held in Hawaii, in 2014. In anticipation of participating in that conference the students in 2013 have been fundraising and researching grant application processes as part of their capacity-building, while keeping journals.

In reporting on the progress students make through their degree course, Jackson referred to the satisfaction that some later-year students report as they approach completion of their degree studies. She also spoke of some graduates who had gone on to further studies:

> One is at RMIT, one at Melbourne Uni and looking to do some more postgraduate work. Groups of students are going through doing their honours. So there are some really good stories there, and you have that conversation with them in third year and they tell you, "Oh my god, I'm nearly finished, when I was in first year I never thought I'd make it through, but here I am, and I've just got this and this to do, and I can see it". Their writing is sometimes really touching. Some people have also had had a death to deal with, or something happened to their kid, and you read their third-year writing and you know we've made a leader out of that person and they are going back to their community.

Of course, these are challenging times for universities in Australia, and we referred earlier to federal government budget cuts and unclear policy settings for higher education with the incoming federal Coalition government, where there has been talk of reining in the growth in student numbers made possible when the previous government uncapped supported places for domestic students, allowing universities to attract as many students into their courses as they could manage. Within our own institution there have been some unsettled times as the university grappled with ongoing funding challenges, including difficulties created by cuts to TAFE funding by the Victorian State Government, and a drop in international students coming to Australia (a situation which has only been reversed in the last 12 months). At the same time, and in part as a means of repositioning itself in an under-funded field, the university has undertaken a massive restructure; collapsing the sectors and old faculties into seven new colleges. With this backdrop of funding constraints and institutional restructure, Jackson reports on her continued advocacy for Moondani Balluk retaining its separate-entity status within the university structure, and this is very much in keeping with recommendations 10 and 11 of the federal government review (2012).

The Learning Commons

Before we offer an outline of the remaining chapters in this book, and some "take out" messages for educators and administrators to conclude this chapter, we want to highlight the vital role of our university librarians and the Victoria University Learning Commons (LC). Many of our academic–professional partnerships are enacted in or through the Learning Commons which in turn works closely with the university's Centre for Collaborative Learning and Teaching.

In preparing the book we sought advice from the Senior Librarian for the College of Arts, Mark Armstrong-Roper. He started by speaking about initiatives emerging from "more progressive thinking on learning behaviours at the start of the 21st century", and librarians' determination to move "from stewardship of books and journal collections as the main role to one of providing skills that allow students to find, evaluate, use and manage information".

Armstrong-Roper described the important role of the university librarians and the Learning Commons in helping set students up for lifelong learning. He referred to principles developed at Victoria University by Shay Keating and Roger Gabb (2005) for the new student learning spaces:

- *learning oriented*: facilitates active, independent and collaborative learning
- *learner centred*: focuses on student needs, preferences and work patterns
- *university wide*: part of university-wide development of learner autonomy
- *flexible*: responsive to the changing needs of learners for resources and support
- *collaborative*: based on collaboration between different learning-support areas in the university and Faculty/Division staff
- *community-building:* provides a hub for physical and virtual interaction for staff and students

The Learning Commons model based on these principles "moves the library from being a service provided at the periphery of the student experience to being at the hub of campus life and aligns it with the University's shifting pedagogy from teacher-centre to learner-centred curricula". Connected to this has been the co-location of a range of services including library, careers advice, the Writing Space and "latest technologies to create a learning environment focusing on how students learn, how they use information, and how they participate in the life of a learning community".

The librarians are routinely involved in "learning, teaching and research initiatives including the development of the LC, transitioning programs, and the overall focus of the student experience". The librarians also take leadership roles in "knowledge and data management, institutional repositories, the open access movement, and the Victoria University Research Data and Materials Plan".

While libraries across this multi-campus university are as old as the institution itself, the Learning Commons has existed as an entity for around five years. In that time Armstrong-Roper reports that the visits per student has continued to go upwards, the number of print loans has receded, while the demand for online resources has increased. Opening hours have been greatly extended and various new services have come on stream, including the Writing Space, Maths Help and Student Rovers:

> Although the Learning Commons (LC) is good at offering students these "point-of-need" services, most students come in and work independently in groups or alone with "help in the background". In the LC face-to-face library services to students have been largely replaced by a mix of self-service and advice/problem-solving services. This frees up librarians to work more collaboratively with the colleges to support the academic program.

Armstrong-Roper also spoke about ways the role of librarians has changed. The world wide web is one of the more obvious areas where the research skills needed by students for success at university has required librarians to use "the burgeoning variety of web 2.0 tools to develop e-learning objects that can be integrated into the curriculum and support blended learning". The popularity and increased capability of mobile devices has "accelerated the demand by students for the librarians to communicate and work with them online, via blogs, Skype, chat, Twitter, and cloud services such as Dropbox and Endnote web".

Armstrong-Roper spoke about the librarians' and the Learning Common's contribution to student transitions. This extends well beyond

Orientation Week and the "transition to university" programs, and entails close collaboration, ideally starting with the curriculum design of foundation units: "The first year is critical in this process as most students need to acquire new research skills to survive at university".

Examples of this collaboration are the humanities foundation unit Knowing and Knowledge and the social sciences foundation units Critical Literacies in the Social Sciences and Foundations of Social Science Research Knowing and Knowledge, where the librarians work with the unit coordinators to design assessment tasks that require students to find, use and evaluate information:

> The students are then assisted with these aspects of their assessment tasks face-to-face in tutorial time, but increasingly with online assistance in the form of purpose-built videos, animations and web pages. A benefit of the face-to-face time in K&K is the opportunity for librarians to build a relationship with the students, and by bringing them into the library and teaching them essential research skills, challenge and transform their expectations of a university library which is quite different from the role school or public libraries have played in their lives.

Overview of Later Chapters

In "Approaches to Retention and Transition: An Antipodean Perspective" (chapter one), Miguel Gil starts by mapping the emergence in Australia of more sophisticated approaches to retention and transition. Our universities in the past tended to roll out perfunctory orientation programs and reserve most co-curricular support services for students with skills deficits, services that were for the most part away from classrooms and outside of the core curriculum. This changed with an emerging appreciation from the mid-1990s that it was time to replace rather piecemeal approaches to retention and transition with more executive-led and holistic approaches to curriculum reform that take account of student diversity and the complex multiplicity of factors affecting students. Gil explains that policies can frustrate when they are short lived, or produced "top-down", or not matched by sufficient resources, or fail to set out responsibilities or accountabilities. He sees the benefit of additional documentation including "models and overarching frameworks" which make clear people's roles and responsibilities, planned actions and projected outcomes.

Gil welcomes the concept of "transition pedagogy" first formalised by Sally Kift *et al.* (2010) which acknowledged the "totality of the students' learning experience" and the value of credible coordinating bodies within the institution. He extends his analysis of strategic frameworks and models by drawing a distinction between an *integrative* (or assimilative) model of the university—which imagines its role as integrating students into the existing "culture, ethos, habitus and modus operandi" and, if required, providing students with "remedial teaching, extended orientation, and learning-support programs"—and an *adaptive* model which "assumes that students come with different degrees of cultural and social capital that need to be valued and fostered as true strengths".

Gil characterises Victoria University as fostering a "culture where student-centred practices take the lead" and where "virtually all processes are given impetus by a retention and transition mandate". He highlights recent initiatives including the Student Experience Strategy (2011), Students Supporting Student Learning program (2011), Language Literacy and Numeracy Strategy (2011), and a reinvigorated Orientation Program in 2010, the creation of Retention and Transition Coordinator positions, and the Flag and Follow Project to contact students who had missed more than a few weeks of classes. He also highlights the range of foundation units to induct students into their courses (and two of these are discussed in later chapters in this book). The university's new Strategic Plan (2011) and Victoria University's Agenda (2012) set out a refined mission, values, goals and "strategic pillars", providing the broad framework for these innovations, and included an important benchmarking exercise to capture best practice across the "student lifecycle" at the university.

When pondering the question of what constitutes "student success", Gil quotes visiting American transition and retention expert Joe Cuseo who said, "We shouldn't define quality b on who we let in but on the students we turn out relative to the way they were when they came in".

Knowing our students better

In "Getting to Know Our Students Better through a Mixed-Methods Case Study of their First-Year Experiences" (chapter two), Andrew Funston describes his mixed-methods case study of a cohort of commencing humanities and social science undergraduate students. This in-depth research allowed us to get to know better our non-traditional students, taking into account their educational aspirations, expectations and first-year experiences.

Funston reported that the majority of first-year students he surveyed were generally well pleased with their first year at university. The majority had performed academically at the level they had expected or exceeded that level and most felt they had acquired substantial knowledge and skills. However, Funston's analysis of this first-year cohort's academic results and re-enrolment patterns (for the second year) indicated that around 25 percent of the large cohort had not returned to their courses at Victoria University. Most perplexing, a significant minority of those who did not re-enrol had passed all or most of their subjects.

The in-depth interviews helped Funston appreciate some possible causes of attrition. Most students faced some challenges, especially in the early weeks, disorientation and extreme loneliness for some. Some students spoke of their confusion or anxiety about knowing what was expected of them in lectures and tutorials. Several expressed anxiety about academic writing and their first assessments although these same students tended to say that they were well supported and instructed and felt happy with the results of those early assignments.

Funston's case-study interviews also made visible some of the very difficult circumstances many of these "non-traditional" students were facing off campus. Some students were "doing it tough", living on low incomes, travelling long distances to get to university, struggling to balance study with paid work which many needed badly to keep themselves afloat financially.

More optimistically, Funston discovered that many of these students—even some of the younger ones, aged 18 or 19—were arriving at the university with significant knowledge, life experiences and capacities which the students could draw on as they faced daily challenges on campus and off campus. He found his research participants to be, generally speaking, aspiring and idealistic. They also tended to be pragmatic about why they were studying, what they were studying, and why they had come to university now. He was concerned to discover that several of the young women he interviewed were struggling to juggle a "triple shift" of full-time study, paid work and onerous household duties as well as other responsibilities.

Scaffolds and pathways

In "Rethinking Engagement and Transition: The Case of Liberal Arts" (chapter three), Michael Hallpike suggests it is time to "shift the discussion from the current preoccupation with "operational" issues to an "ontological" conception of student engagement". Hallpike promotes course design "that will provide a scaffolded induction into the discourses of the humanities and social sciences" and not make presumptions about the scholarly orientations, knowledge and literacies of students. Indeed, he advocates approaches that encourage students "to draw on the rich cultural resources and alternative knowledges and ways of knowing that they bring with them to the course". While some of the Liberal Arts Diploma students will go on to engage successfully in particular disciplinary fields, many on commencement find specialist discourses quite estranging. They benefit from a multidisciplinary curriculum that is culturally inclusive of all students in the classroom.

Hallpike explains how students are invited to engage with the "culture of argument" and the "culture of interpretation" in scaffolded ways that allow them write themselves into what Charles Bazerman refers to as the professional "networks of literate practices". They are supported to "try on" different subject positions and value-orientations in their speaking and writing, in what amounts to a kind of explicit academic *socialisation* process that allows for degrees of identity shifting. This process of "staged induction", which encourages critical reflection, might occur through biographical writing, semiotic analysis of family photos and so forth in which the contingent nature of the subject positions the students "try on" is made explicit.

Hallpike argues that institutions are increasingly concerned with "operational engagement" arising from the expansion of intrusive accounting regimes on the one side, and market-driven strategic management on the other. He calls for a "counter-discourse... needed to rethink student engagement in *ontological* rather than *operational* terms" and Hallpike argues that this requires rethinking the public mission of the university. He describes how the Liberal Arts course was informed by the idea that there are vital connections between public and academic discourses, and between the modern/postmodern university and democracy as a form of life. Drawing on Nick Zepke and Linda Leach (2010) he recommends a re-imagined curriculum in which students learn to negotiate challenges to their knowledge claims, acquire autonomy and a fine sense of judgement in the moral-practice sphere, and develop "a strong capacity for reflexivity and creative self-alteration".

In his postscript, Hallpike draws on Simon Marginson (2000) to raise the problem of corporatised university cultures where strategic leadership detaches from the academic units below, where academics lose status, and where disruptive conditions make long-term, whole-of-university collaborative projects hard to achieve.

Core foundations

In "Embedding a Third-Generation Transition Pedagogy: The Role of Core Foundation Units" (chapter four), Brian Zammit reminds us of why we want to improve participation rates as well as equity and social inclusion outcomes, thereby creating a more participatory democratic society that deals with the demands and opportunities of a globalised economy. He also reminds us that student attrition remains stubbornly high in Australian tertiary education (albeit fluctuating across the sector), with significant personal costs to those students who forgo tertiary education and with negative impacts on the institutions.

Zammit draws on studies to indicate the range of intersecting factors contributing to attrition (commuting difficulties, balancing study with paid work and family commitments, financial difficulties, lack of preparation, unsociable campuses, disconnects between course and career goals, bad experiences in the course, wrong choice of course, personal factors). He describes a broad consensus that the first weeks and the first year are critical, and that challenges are pronounced where students come from low-SES backgrounds and where they arrive on campus with low entry scores.

Marcia Devlin (2011) speaks of "sociocultural incongruence" and Zammit works with this notion to introduce us to the challenge for students when they are less attuned to "implicit expectations and tacit understandings" of what university study requires of them, and proceeds to make the ethical case for the universities recognising their obligations and responding to the needs of these and other students. Zammit shares Vincent Tinto's recognition that universities are finding it hard to translate an expanding body of research findings into substantial gains for student retention, with Adams *et al.* (2010) suggesting that a significant challenge lies with academic issues only accounting for a minority of withdrawals. Clearly, "external factors" need to be taken seriously and universities— often struggling with resource allocation—need to avoid rash decisions about the sustainability of particular courses and programs based on simplistic assumptions about the causes of high attrition from a particular course or student cohort.

Following from Tinto and Brian Pusser's (2006) arguments that institutions need to move from research and theories about retention into definable courses of action, Zammit returns to the notion of an intentional first-year curriculum design and support that carefully scaffolds and mediates the first-year learning experience for contemporary heterogeneous cohorts and which requires and relies upon "a partnership between academic, support and professional staff". In discussing Kift and others' pioneering work Zammit reminds us of some pitfalls and challenges when attempting a "whole-of-institution" approach, such as "tensions between centralised programs and traditionally autonomous faculties.... less than genuine consultative processes... gaining consensus from stakeholder... long-term commitment".

Zammit presents a case study of a core foundation unit (CFU) at Victoria University, Knowing and Knowledge A (K&K A), a compulsory credit-bearing unit for students from several different degree courses. The unit has a key responsibility for providing academic literacy support to students who are new to tertiary study. Taking an interdisciplinary approach, with content focusing on questions of Australian identity, the unit encourages students to draw on their existing knowledge and experiences while refining their critical thinking and a range of academic skills including referencing and note-taking. The course is designed to develop a broad appreciation of academic integrity. Academics work with Language and Learning Unit staff, and Library (Learning Commons) staff who assist with the design of weekly activities, sourcing teaching materials, including online academic skills modules, and participating in workshops scaffolded to individual assessment tasks.

A key feature of K&K A is its three-pronged approach to identifying and intervening where students are "at risk". Another key feature is its peer mentoring component, which entails the ongoing collaboration between academic staff, the Students Supporting Student Learning (SSSL) program, the Learning Commons Rovers program, and the Writing Space program. In supporting the dictum that "retention is everybody's business", Zammit argues strongly that retention strategies should not be located at the margins of university life. Indeed, Knowing and Knowledge A (K&K A) exemplifies the sorts of curriculum design and partnerships that can be forged between academic, support and professional staff in order to explicitly engage first-year students and help them feel they belong in higher education.

In "'Come As You Are': Inclusive, Transitional and Multicultural Pedagogy in a First-Year Foundation Unit" (chapter five), Julie Fletcher focuses on the importance of first-year students developing a sense of belonging and engagement with the university, which is frequently an "unknown land". She outlines ways in which "inclusive and transitional pedagogies and an inter-disciplinary, multicultural curriculum" can be successfully incorporated into foundation units. Drawing on Trevor Gale's (2009) historical account of the democratisation of university education, and the growing numbers of "non-traditional" students on campuses across the country, Fletcher describes some of the scholarly literature particularly relevant to the First-Year Experience (FYE), and like several of the authors in this book draws on Sally Kift's (2009) work on "transition pedagogy", and Vincent Tinto's (2009) discussions about the value of deeply integrated strategies to build and sustain "learning communities" that recognise and work with students' expectations and need for support, feedback and involvement or engagement. Fletcher also draws on Kinnear's (2008) and Leach's (2013) work to explain the significance of students' "quality day-to-day interaction with approachable and enthusiastic teaching staff" and peer-support networks amongst students; all essential in encouraging students' help-seeking and other self-management behaviours.

Fletcher reminds us that transition strategies and approaches should be based on a "deep recognition of, and response to, student difference" in terms of English language skills levels, social or cultural background and other aspects of identity, which if not recognised may leave students potentially or effectively marginalised. She draws on the work of Rashne Jehangir (2009) who explains just how large is the gulf often experienced by non-traditional students between the "home worlds" and the university which has tended in Australia to pressure students to—according to Jehangir—"shed part of themselves" (34). Similar arguments are made by Trevor Gale who draws on Raewyn Connell's (2007) ideas in his call for a "Southern Theory of higher education" to "unsettle" the "centre–periphery relations in the realm of knowledge" in ways that recognise students as "insiders" and central to the knowledge system and knowledge production. For Fletcher, this requires that "curriculum not only teach about difference, but also provide room for different ways of thinking, knowing and engaging to shape the ways that teaching and learning is done", and it is here that she engages with Jehangir's (2009) concept of "full academic citizenship".

These ideas inform Fletcher's Critical Literacies in the Social Sciences foundation unit (which parallels Knowing and Knowledge, the foundation unit for humanities students discussed by Brian Zammit in chapter four). This unit embeds and integrates skill-building, support services, staged formative assessment with "learning community principles and a themed multicultural curriculum designed to foster voice, experience-based learning, inclusion, participation, peer support", while also aiming to "challenge/dissolve/soften/render more porous" barriers to inclusion which might otherwise exist for her non-traditional students. In the early weeks of semester students start their journey by exploring ideas of being at home, of feeling displaced or unsettled by the university, as if it were "a foreign land" and one where the students might benefit from something of a "travel guide" which makes explicit "many of the implicit rules and expectations".

Two case studies

In "Exploring First-Year Transition Pedagogy: Indicators of Enhanced Transition and Retention in an Experiential Early-Years Teacher- Education Setting" (chapter six) Gwen Gilmore advocates more experiential curriculum and pedagogy. She sees this as an essential aspect of Victoria University's Early Childhood Pre-service Teacher (PST) development program, where students undertake a mix of theoretical and practical studies. PST student groups, from different year levels, are placed in community settings where they facilitate children's playgroups for a few hours each week throughout their first semester. This *KindaKinder* program, established in 2005, expects these PST students to work with a mentor teacher to design and deliver numeracy, literacy and play elements, organise attendance of children and parents, participate in the activities, then take time to reflect on what has happened.

Gilmore discusses transition pedagogy, focusing on the importance of university students being both challenged and feeling well-supported in their learning. She argues that engagement is more likely when teachers and students have opportunities to co-construct their learning in mutually respectful ways. She suggests that students need to be given the freedom to make choices and do things for themselves, even in the early stages of their degree studies. Gilmore is particularly interested in the uniqueness of people, as manifest in their use of language and production of meaning within particular social settings and physical environments, and by virtue of their particular relationships, and ways in which people's identities change, and in part through their educational experiences and reflections.

Gilmore reports on what students said about their learning experiences, and observes their dynamic, relational and reflexive meaning-making, and in particular the fluid ways they support one another in these KindaKinder settings. Her focus-group conversations confirmed the value of the experiential learning for giving students opportunities to build on their strengths, develop new skills and discover talents, boost self-confidence and feelings of competence. The students spoke of enjoying their role in designing the curriculum for their site-based placements, and linking what they experienced to the theories they were learning about elsewhere in their course. They felt like knowledge creators and active participants rather than observers acquiring information. The students also valued the relationship-building that occurred, with several people in the focus groups describing how they felt they now belonged to a *Kindacommunity*.

In "Becoming a Community of Readers: Academic Literacies in the Social Work Classroom" (chapter seven) Juanita Custance, John Fox and Pauline O'Maley discuss their team-teaching project which embedded academic language and learning (ALL) in key units of the social work course. This project involved identifying and testing action in order to change pedagogical practices. The project worked with an expectation of transforming both researchers and research participants. This project worked from an understanding that students were often reluctant to take up external ALL supports even when they were intimidated by the reading and analytic demands that are integral to the course.

In the first cycle/semester the project focused on how to structure the team teaching and embed integrated activities in response to the students' ALL needs. In the second cycle/semester, closer attention was given to investigating why students were not engaging with the readings, leading to the design of a group presentation (the first assignment) about the difficulties members of the group were having with set readings, and how the students had helped one another to tackle the problem. Supporting this approach, tutorial activities involved the team working in class with small groups, discussing the readings and discussing *how* students were reading. Three questionnaires sought information about students' reading strategies, about their appreciation of how texts they considered worked, and about their perceptions of being in the class. Students' assignments were selected to see if the students were foregrounding their reading.

In the third cycle/semester the team continued its approach, "but with greater emphasis on drawing out the connections (or indeed disconnections) students were able to identify between the texts and their own experience and cultural understanding". Advice from students lead to teaching strategies such as providing focus questions for the weekly readings, close readings in small groups, providing more time to explore different cultural perspectives, and the use of comparative and evaluative graphic organisers.

In discussing their findings, Custance, Fox and O'Maley highlight the "importance of normalising difficulties", including the challenge of reading in the discipline, and building a "learning community" that is inclusive and enabling and safe, and which allows students to "bring their own expertise, perspectives and strengths with them", which paralleled the emergence of the research team itself becoming a learning community. The specific reading strategies were linked to the assignments and assessments, offering the students "tangible incentive to engage in the labour of reading". This project found that students were becoming "strategic readers" who felt empowered and adept, especially at concept mapping and contextualising information, and taking on responsibility for their contribution to their groups.

Students supporting student learning (SSSL)

Our book concludes with Gill Best's "Students Supporting Student Learning (SSSL) and Practices of Empowerment", which reports on a suite of student–peer mentoring programs at Victoria University. The wider professional context and network for these programs is the Association of Academic Language and Learning (ALL), established in 2005 whose members see their role as "initiation, not remediation" (Beasley, 1988) and geared towards "scaffolding" the process of student learning by embedding skills in the curriculum, amongst other means. Gill maps changes in institutional approaches, including at Victoria University from the late 1990s, and locates these changes in growing acceptance of the essentially social nature of learning that suits student–peer learning and peer support. She argues that in SSSL programs "students are the knowledge-holders and knowledge-sharers, meaning there is the capacity to open new ways of knowing". Gill illustrates how SSSL programs "not only have an impact on students' academic success but foster a greater student connection and engagement with the university in general". This also helps to achieve what William Tierney (2000, 219) felt would see students' diverse identities on campus "affirmed, honoured and incorporated into the organisation's culture".

Gill outlines the range of SSSL programs at Victoria University, describing first the student mentors (generally high-achieving students competitively selected and paid for their advanced learning from other mentors and SSSL staff) whose mission is to "assist students with their learning and to impact positively upon students' academic, social and emotional wellbeing".

There are three SSSL programs *connected to units of study*, including weekly group-based review sessions (PASS), peer-assisted tutorials (PAT) and Trident (created specifically for first year Engineering students and incorporating PASS and PAT methods). Approximately 35 high-achieving students are currently employed across four campus Learning Commons sites.

A second centrally delivered program engages student writing-mentors who are "students who like writing and who have learned about the challenges and joys of academic writing and who wish to take on a role to assist other students with their writing development". They work in the Writing Spaces of the Learning Commons; "drop-in" spaces based at the two larger campus libraries.

Finally, Gill describes the Senior Mentors program, with one senior rover. These are students who have been selected to paid positions based on a detailed written application and their experience as SSSL mentors.

She concludes by describing the palpable "energy, commitment and enthusiasm" of the SSSL participants.

Reflections and Directions

As indicated in our beginning remarks, the chapters in this book constitute a significant but by no means exhaustive account of our institution's efforts to understand and improve students' transitions and success. We hope that this book has cast its net wide enough to give a snapshot of the linkages connecting the work of academics and professional staff with the major preoccupations identified in the title of the present volume, *Strong Starts, Supported Transitions and Student Success*. Underlying all this is our stubbornly optimistic spirit, seasoned with some disappointments and defeats, and rooted in the authors' rich personal, professional and institutional trajectories. We make our respective practices very explicit. Not surprisingly, we use terms such as "reflexivity", "criticality" and "meta-cognition" quite extensively in our writing and our conversations about higher education transitions. These conceptual tools are useful for thinking about our own practices and some of the dilemmas we face as educators.

The emergence or popularity of certain phrases and concepts indicates some significant shifts in thinking in this field. To begin with, the concept of "transitioning", with its associations with rites of passage and rituals, was fundamental in the first conceptualisations of retention as articulated by Vincent Tinto. Equally important were notions of "learning communities", "involvement" and "retention" which have been partly superseded at present by conceptions of "engagement" (George Kuh) and "student success". Sally Kift's notion of "transition pedagogies" is now widely used, and associated with a "whole-of-institution" approach, "intentional curriculum design", and an understanding that "the student experience" extends to the whole range of interactions between students, academics and other members of the university community. As Kift says, "transition and retention should be everybody's business" in the contemporary Australian university. An even more nuanced view of student transitions is conveyed by Marcia Devlin's concern for "inclusive curriculum" and Devlin's (2012) more recent ideas about successful transitions being a "joint venture" to be managed and operated by students, academics, professional staff and wider communities.

"Student success" in the past was quite narrowly conceived. Entry to a limited number of university places was supposedly based on "strict academic merit", and under such a system "success" was fairly predictable, with high-score entrants fulfilling their "promise" and confirming conventional wisdom about who belongs at university and who does not. Clearly this restrictive view has shifted somewhat, although "success" is still tightly coupled to concerns about retention, course completions and graduate employment destinations. In any case, there is an uncomfortable truth for those favouring more restrictive entry and that is the significant proportion of supposedly "academically under-prepared" students who are aspiring to try out higher education, are getting accepted into degree-level courses, are making their way through the course, and finding their way into professional careers, albeit with less-linear and secure life-course transitions than a university-educated person might have expected in the past.

Our "real life" test leaves us in no doubt that something is going right for many of these "under-prepared" students, and to such an extent that this widely circulating construct of "unpreparedness" probably needs to be challenged more rigorously. So, too, should we be questioning alarmist claims and innuendo (rife, it seems, in the conservative media) about "falling standards" or "dumbing down" at our universities because of "mass" access to courses. This rhetoric is sometimes linked to other visions of our higher education malaise which present the sector as a near-comatose patient soon to be dealt a final blow by a Brutus-like MOOC disruptor.

Of course these concerns fly in the face of the experiences of many of us working in Australian universities. It is also questionable given Australia's continued popularity as a destination for international fee-paying students (tertiary education is often hailed as the country's third or fourth biggest "export" earner). And, while attrition remains a persistent problem, the situation has not been deteriorating markedly in recent years and that is despite the considerable growth in numbers of "first in the family" and "under-prepared" students. The sky is not falling.

Just as unhelpful are clichés conveyed by uncritical "success stories" about "equity groups" powering through higher education, replete with heroic lecturers and resilient and persistent students working "against the odds". These clichés rarely acknowledge just how difficult it is for some groups to find their way to university and finish their courses. Nor do these stories sufficiently acknowledge the institutional policies and strategies that have been put in place, or the carefully designed transition pedagogy with its extensive co-curricular supports. Some of the authors in this book acknowledge persistent attrition problems, and identify where our approaches are not working as well as we hoped or expected. Indeed, the book describes some "unexceptional", even faltering educational outcomes.

As academics and other professionals working with commencing students—some of us for more than 20 years—we are alert to dismissive language that surrounds our efforts and those of colleagues at other universities. Three learning metaphors in particular tend to polarise and restrict discussions about retention, transition and success. We hear people lament "hand-holding" and "spoon-feeding" as they champion the virtue of self-directed or even "autonomous learning" (as if that ever really existed). This language often nips in the bud discussions about "support", with its insinuation or explicit claims that students are becoming lazy and over-reliant on handouts, leg-ups, life-respirators. In opposing these unhelpful and platitudinous metaphors, we recommend Vincent Tinto's cautionary maxim, "Access without support is not opportunity". We would also evoke the literary figure of the "imbecile" as one who falters because they insist on walking without a staff even when one is at hand.

Our students should not be expected to "make it" without supports, as if there was virtue in that autonomy or self-sufficiency. Related to this, we have attempted in a range of ways to eschew some indefinable image of "the student". We hope to have conveyed here the diversity of our student cohorts, and we wanted to make tangible or visible some of challenges they face. We do not see our students as figures in some "retention puzzle". We do, however, see them—in all their diversity and capacities—as part of the solution, and we hope to reinforce this idea by putting last in the book, but not least, Gill Best's chapter on Students Supporting Student Learning.

Since this is a book by practitioners in the field, all chapters speak to a dimension of university work that reflects in various degrees what each of us think and breathe, virtually on a daily basis. This book has afforded us, editors and authors alike, an opportunity to share insights that are usually inaccessible or compartmentalised. The mere sharing of these experiences has created a momentum of its own, if you will, "a community of practice", "a learning community". Indeed, our collaboration on this book has helped us reaffirm collegial values in keeping with Jaspers' conception of the university as a "community of scholars and students engaged in the task of seeking truth" (Jaspers 1960) and in keeping with Habermas's characterisation of our efforts as "the egalitarian and universalistic content of their forms of argumentation" (Habermas 1987) or Gouldner's "culture of critical discourse" (Gouldner 1982)

We think that there is merit in letting fellow-colleagues and readers judge if our stories and experiences resonate with them. At any rate, we think that no sense of direction, common destination or collective wisdom can be achieved unless we educators and professionals take the time to explain ourselves and deconstruct some of our embedded tacit understandings. We feel that the addition of this one work to the growing literature devoted to student transitions and success is justified not only because of its local testimonial value—our students' voices and our voices matter, our stories should be told and heard—but also because the book points to a range of considered approaches which we feel are effective and worth sharing. Finally, we signal here our intention to work swiftly on a new book focusing more closely on academic writing—from foundations to final-year capstone projects—in the era of mobile social networks, blended learning and MOOCs.

Notes

[1] In his "Message from the Vice-Chancellor and President" (November 2013) Professor Peter Dawkins describes the university's refreshed Strategic Plan 2012–2016 and the designation of Victoria University as *The University of Opportunity* explaining that: "This focus challenges traditional notions of what defines a great university, acknowledging that Victoria University has a broader role to play than educating the academic elite. We are here to help students from diverse backgrounds to achieve true success. The ability to enter and exit at different levels in the AQF, with seamless pathways and strong support, from broad access programs to more selective programs in some of our flagship areas, will distinguish the Victoria University model of education, from our competitors".

[2] See, for instance, Australian Council for Education Research (ACER) *Higher Education Update*, February 2012, which quotes Dr Daniel Edwards, Senior Research Fellow, as stating that the "clear growth in attainment over the past decade cannot be attributed to increased participation of domestic students... more likely that growth in higher education attainment levels has been the result of a strong skilled migration program... " (2).

[3] Similar observations are made by Ameera Karimshah *et al.* (2013) in "Overcoming Adversity Among Low SES: A Study of Strategies for Retention", *Australian Universities Review* vol. 55, no. 2: 72–9.

Reference List

ACER. 2012. "University Retention and Completion Rates Have Improved." *Higher Education Update February 2012*. Alexandria, NSW: Australian Council for Educational Research.
—. 2013. "Comparing accessibility and funding of Australian higher education." *Higher Education Update March 2013* page 12. Alexandria, NSW: Australian Council for Educational Research.

Australian Government. 2012. *Review of Higher Education Access and Outcomes for Aboriginal and Torres Strait Islander People Final Report.* Canberra ACT: Commonwealth of Australia.

Beasley, Vic. 1988. "Developing Academic Literacy: The Flinders Experience." In *Literacy by Degrees,* edited by Vic Beasley, Gordon Taylor, Brigid Ballard, Hanne Bock, John Clanchy and Peggy Nightingale. Milton Keynes: SRHE & Open University Press.

Bunda, Tracey, Lew Zipin, and Marie Brennan. 2011. "Negotiating University 'Equity' from Indigenous Standpoints: a Shaky Bridge." *International Journal of Inclusive Education.* 16 (9): 941–957.

Bradley, Denise and Peter Noonan, Helen Nugent, and Bill Scales. 2008. *Review of Australian Higher Education – Final Report.* Canberra ACT: Commonwealth of Australia.

Devlin, Marcia. 2013. "Bridging Socio-Cultural Incongruity: Conceptualising the Success of Students from Low Socio-Economic Status Backgrounds in Australian Higher Education." *Studies in Higher Education,* 38 (6): 939-949. doi: 10.1080/03075079.2011.613991.

Edwards, Daniel. 2013. *Growing Attainment in Higher Education.* Alexandria, NSW: Australian Council for Educational Research. [Accessed October 2, 2013]. Available from http://rd.acer.edu.au/article/growing-attainment-in-higher-education.

Gouldner, Alvin Ward. 1982. *The Future of Intellectuals and the Rise of the New Class: A Frame of Reference, Theses, Conjectures, Arguments, and an Historical Perspective on the Role of Intellectuals and Intelligentsia in the International Class Contest of the Modern Era.* New York: Oxford University Press.

Habermas, Jürgen. 1987. "The Idea of the University: Learning Processes." Trans., John R. Blazek, *New German Critique,* Special Issue on the Critiques of the Enlightenment, 41: 3–22.

Karimshah, Ameera, Marianne Wyder, Paul Henman, Dwight Tay, Elizabeth Capelin, and Patricia Short. 2013. "Overcoming Adversity Among Low SES Students: a Study of Strategies for Retention." *Australian Universities' Review* 55 (2): 5–14.

Keating, Shay and Roger Gabb. 2005. *Putting Learning into the Learning Commons: a Literature Review.* Melbourne: Victoria University. Retrieved 10 October 2013 from http://eprints.Victoria University. edu.au/94/

Kift, Sally, Karen Nelson, and John Clarke. 2010. "Transition Pedagogy: A Third Generation Approach to FYE - A Case Study of Policy and

Practice for the Higher Education Sector." *The International Journal of the First Year in Higher Education* 1 (1) (July 21): 1–20. doi:10.5204/intjfyhe.v1i1.13.

Jaspers, Karl. 1960. *The Idea of the University*. London: Peter Owen.

Lomax-Smith, Jan, Watson, Louise and Beth Webster. 2011. *Higher Education Base Funding Review - Final Report* DEEWR. Canberra ACT: Commonwealth of Australia.

Pechenkina, Ekaterina and Ian Anderson. 2011. *Background paper on Indigenous Australian Higher Education: Trends, Initiatives and Policy Implications*. Canberra ACT: Commonwealth of Australia.

Rizvi, Fazal, and Bob Lingard. 2009. *Globalizing Education Policy*. New York: Routledge.

Slee, Roger. 2013. "Meeting Some Challenges of Inclusive Education in an Age of Exclusion." *Asian Journal of Inclusive Education* 1 (2): 3–17.

Tierney, William. 2000. "Power, Identity and the Dilemma of College Student Departure." In *Reworking the Student Departure Puzzle*, edited by Braxton, John, 203-234. Nashville, TX: Vanderbilt University Press.

Tinto, Vincent. 2012. *Completing College*. University of Chicago Press.

Victoria University, refreshed Strategic Plan, 2012-2016.

CHAPTER ONE

APPROACHES TO RETENTION
AND TRANSITION:
AN ANTIPODEAN PERSPECTIVE

MIGUEL GIL

The problems of the real-world-practice do not present themselves to practitioners as well-formed structures. Indeed, they tend not to present themselves as problems at all but as messy, indeterminate situations. (Schön 1983)

Introduction

In the sections that follow I will review the lessons of the past 30 years of experience in retention, transition and first year in tertiary education as learnt and received from an Antipodean perspective. They provide some justification for the optimism implicit in the conviction that our collective experiences are heading us in the right direction. At the same time they highlight some of the known unknowns and blind spots that continue to beleaguer us.

This chapter, like the rest of the book, combines general thematic syntheses with insights from Victoria University's more recent experience. As such, they seek to encapsulate the thinking and action (and thinking-in-action) that keeps motivating practitioners in the field.

Victoria University, it should be noted from the outset, is a dual-sector "new university" which has decided to approach its dual character in an integrated fashion by blurring the boundaries across sectors, effectively embracing a perspective on transitions that to a large extent does away with the vocational and university divide. In this process, the university has brought to the fore, and indeed laid open for public discussion and scrutiny, a re-configured understanding of the first-year experience(s) for both staff and students. This is reflected in a new restructuring of schools, an overhaul of course offerings now underway, and a commensurate renewal of the curriculum, which brings into play a new responsive language as well as a sense of mission, place and time. None of these processes come free from uncertainties nor are immune to the strictures of budgetary balancing acts.

Theorising First-Year Initiatives

By and large, tertiary institutions in Australia have historically responded to retention and transition concerns through the prism of perceived student needs and expectations. This has meant that innovations in this field have often taken on a mediated character, emanating less from retention and transition considerations than from derivative analyses. New elements have thus been thrown into the mix in a more or less organic fashion, principally in three main areas: support services (co-curriculum), curriculum/course offerings, and first-year experiences, with the latter area becoming somewhat of a last frontier where the other two have found a liminal point of contact. In this respect, the concept of a "transition pedagogy" can be regarded as the clearest example so far of a genuinely Antipodean, whole-of-university approach to retention and transition.

In an oft-quoted article, higher education specialist Kerri-Lee Krause (Krause 2003) identified a number of key issues that are the staples of retention and transition practitioners in Australia. On the basis of her own experience and research expertise, she identified a pattern of growth in first year in higher education retention initiatives that seems to lead to the adoption, sooner or later, of explicit retention and transition policies and, ultimately, to a corresponding institutional location. Krause illustrated this process with a useful linear outline, reflective of the still-prevalent indebtedness of retention and transition models to their origins in skills, language and orientation support programs. It also showed, at least indirectly, the intimate connection between these programs and the various extended orientation/transition strategies that have taken root in most Australian universities over time.

The linear image suggested in Krause's continuum, however, needs not to be taken literally. The coordination of "learning and teaching processes contexts" may not have resulted necessarily from, or been historically preceded by, orientation and support-service initiatives. In fact, the continuum should be read more as part of a convergence of relatively parallel processes originating in the two largely autonomous spheres of student services (student affairs in the US) and learning and teaching, glued together at the ideal end by a tighter, but again often independent, connection with policy and overseeing institutional bodies, including governmental agency controls.

The expansion and subsequent convergence of the supplemental and extended orientation programs has been possible in large part thanks to a growing acceptance of the intrinsic educational value of programs provided by support services, both specialised and non-specialised; a typical example being the trajectories of "language centres" and their language support programs. Just as the student does not come to university as a "student", but rather as a person with other identities and agency claims, support services are no longer there to provide "fixes" of one sort or another.

Tom Prebble *et al.* (2004) have pointed out that programs attached to support-services areas have moved progressively from being conceived as remedial or supplemental in intent, to articulate themselves into non-deficit co-curricular or developmental initiatives. The key point in this shift of perspective has been an accepting recognition of the enrolled student as he or she is, and an institutional commitment to provide them with commensurate learning experiences that will take them to a new level of success. The process is in essence a transformative one whereby, through institutional experiences that are intentional and purposeful, students are assisted in mastering disciplinary knowledge and related skills as well as a set of corresponding attitudes. This process can be expressed in terms of the 3P model proposed by John Biggs and Catherine Tang (2011). Thus, in addition to an acknowledgement of the obstacles standing in the way of students, institutions also need to better understand the makeup and phases students go through in their journeys, what makes them "tick", what gives them a sense self-worth and enhanced agency (see Funston, chapter two).

At the same time, all support programs are being subjected to stringent rationalisation and accountability requirements, some to be axed for good, others resized to reflect consumer demand. Student unions, once powerful points of reference for service provision and student activism, have all but disappeared under the effect of new volunteering student unionism policies (effective since 2005–06), with surviving pockets of their traditional services re-allocated to student services units.

Seen from this kaleidoscopic perspective, poor or conflicted student performance takes on very different dimensions. Stories emerge of long commuting times, family disruptions, weak internet connections, job juggling, erratic attendance patterns, recurrent ill-health, career changes, anxiety and time-management problems, reconstructed identities, lack of cultural and social capital. Combinations of any of the above in turn are reshaped by the quality and nature of the interactions with staff, as well as with academic settings and institutional arrangements, much of which is also a function of multiple crossovers of benchmarking exercises, good and best practice, evidence-based practice, anecdotal evidence and even stereotypical characterisations. Studies highlighting the fact that cross-institutional variation may indeed be less than internal variation further suggest the obvious: one-size-fits-all solutions are unlikely to work in contexts where internal conditions are bound to differ, sometimes even dramatically.

First-year initiatives and overarching frameworks

What does this all mean for retention and transition? In comparing the current situation with the relatively straightforward experiences of some 20 or 30 years ago, one can see that helping students to settle into their studies requires nowadays a far more sophisticated approach to how anxieties, expectations and needs are identified, let alone navigated. Settling by itself does not equate with the sense of belonging and resilience that persisters, as opposed to non-persisters, seem to be able to develop even in the face of unsettling circumstances such as long commuting hours, unworkable timetables, ill-health bouts, and a host of similar disrupting situations.

It is not just the diversity of students, but also their increasing numbers and the multiplication of points of entry, together with the shifting sands of new knowledges and new paradigms, that has a dramatic effect on how retention and transition interventions are framed. Add to this the fact that tertiary teaching staff may lack specific tertiary teaching qualifications, and one may start to understand the desperation and even scepticism with which this whole area is contemplated from both afar and close range. One can also understand the proneness of retention and transition practices to re-appear and disappear in and out of focus, as well as from actual reality.

Despite this, an institutional response to most of the above seems to have been crystallising for the past 10 or 15 years in Australian universities around a number of main vectors: a) introduction of first-year initiatives; b) reviews of retention literature; c) tracking and monitoring of at-risk students; d) development of overarching frameworks; e) implementation of transition pedagogies, supported by a demand of specific tertiary teaching qualifications from academic staff. As a result, programs with a degree of validity in their own right, such as the one-off initiatives identified by Krause as originators of first-year experiences, can now be regarded increasingly as isolated exponents of good practice that need to be married to something far larger and encompassing. For these initiatives to transcend "feel-good" tokenism and work synergistically there is a crying need for systemic approaches that draw effectively on the human and material resources available to the university, in a holistic way.

Introduction of first-year initiatives

The first in the series of four iterations of the First-Year Experience Survey in Australia, conducted by Craig McInnis and Carmel McNaught (1995), was a major contribution to changing the perception of what universities do to their students. Running every five years, the reports have yielded a series of snapshots representative of the bulk of the Australian tertiary system from 1995 to 2009 (Krause and University of Melbourne Centre for the Study of Higher Education 2005; James *et al.* 2010). More important, perhaps, than the data contributed through this series is the now firmly established notion of a "first-year experience" as key to the success of university programs in terms of retention, transition and completion rates. It was no coincidence that the First Year in Higher Education international conferences, also starting in 1995, saw the concept further normalised and given strong impetus by providing a highly respected forum for practice-sharing and renewal.

From the four outstanding reports evidence has been mounting of an increasing trend on the part of students to devote less and less time to study, to spend more time on part-time work (15 hours per week) and to make career choices based on more pragmatic and vocational outcomes. Yet, a unilateral and prescriptive reading of this data should be avoided, as aptly pointed out by Michael Hallpike in chapter three. Learning habits and campus climate have changed considerably, in part as a result of new communication technologies, now ubiquitous in wireless campuses and elsewhere. Students study more in front of a computer and tend to socialise less with their classmates than with their own previous networks. Australian universities have been compensating for some of these "losses" by creating shareable "award-winning" learning spaces, fostering collaborative work, providing opportunities for block scheduling (common lunch hours), and maximising whenever possible disciplinary progression and connections between subjects (McInnis and James 2004); all these measures often try to bring into the campuses some of the elements that set the "old" residential universities apart from their commuting counterparts .

Parallel processes in the international arena saw the publication of key reports highlighting the significance of the first-year experience as an engine for transformative growth. The Boyer Report (The Boyer

Commission on Educating Undergraduates in the Research University 1998) and the Kellogg series of reports (Kellogg Commission on the Future of State and Land-Grant Universities 1997–2001) set the tone for much of what was to come in the United States and beyond. In the land of first-year seminars, extensive course-advising, residential campuses, and writing across the curriculum, the gap between the aims and analytical descriptions in the above-mentioned reports and the real application of some of its insights and recommendations has proved greater than anticipated, yet progress towards the implementation of its key recommendations has also been noticed (Katkin 2003).

While an intellectual acceptance of first-year experiences in Australia can be taken as a given, the implementation of first-year initiatives has been in practice piecemeal, short-lived, heroic and of the garden variety (Burnett 2006). Equity-enabling programs have also faced important conceptual, practical and organisational obstacles, compounded by much uncertainty around the value proposition of "investing in students from equity groups" (Silburn and Box 2008). Furthermore, while coordinating roles in the areas of retention, transition and first-year experience have been created in a number of universities, their functions have tended to mutate, finding too-narrow niches of application (student services, enrichment and engagement programs; learning and teaching centres; faculty or school supports), most of them located in the more unstable terrain of the extra- and co-curricular. Exceptions such as Queensland University of Technology's holistic approach have still to prove that they are sustainable in the long-term and more fully integrated into a broadly defined renewed curriculum.

Dissatisfaction with this state of affairs has given rise to more executive approaches, as drastic as eliminating or downgrading what is perceived as a further layer of bureaucracy altogether, or as bold as elevating the student experience concept to a new level of synthesis, usually through a rethink of its developmental contribution, as in Queensland University of Technology's case. The no-frills approach can find some justification in the fact that customary support and transition practices exert only a moderate impact on retention. Part-timers, de facto distance students, and many mature-age students find little justification in paying for extra services they are highly unlikely to use precisely because of their busy conflicting agendas.

The next three sub-sections illustrate what is more likely to be the dominant pattern in the shifting sands of transition in tertiary education.

Reviews of Retention Literature and Distillations of First Principles

Characteristically, initiatives around retention have often originated in a mix of institutional realisations: 1) the drainage of resources entailed by departing students; 2) an acknowledgement of how little is known about the students' perspectives (their expectations and needs); and 3) a reaffirmation of the centrality of learning to the student experience, which usually leads back to further reconceptualisations of the curriculum, student experience and student success

The need to do something about any of the above aspects has led to the setup of small special units, or, more often, to the commission of internal studies with a brief to provide workable recommendations. Selections and digests of representative articles have been advanced in the hope of generating momentum, while reviews of the literature are fully available (Harvey *et al.* 2006; Prebble *et al.* 2004; Whittaker 2008; Nicol 2009; Troxel and Cutright 2008). As a result, there has been a growing if somewhat mystified acceptance of the inherent complexity involved in any retention/transition strategies, usually underscored by the maxim that "retention is everyone's business".

The perspective afforded by major reviews and thematic syntheses has thus contributed to the questioning of facile assumptions based on privileging a limited number of "retention factors" or "predictors" that may apply, or not, in certain contexts (Yorke and Longden 2004). Instead, universities have learned to recognise the inherent diversity and multiplicity of those factors and their corresponding realities; which usually leaves begging the question of which ones need prioritising for practical purposes. This includes elementary discriminations between types of students (international, Indigenous, mature-age, school leavers, gap-year students), fields of study and modes of study (part/full-time); tertiary institutions (commuting/non-commuting, vocational/higher education, single campus/multi-campus, sandstone/brick university, rural/urban). A simple recombination of these factors gives an idea of what kind of delicate balance is needed to channel resources in ways that would maximise benefits for all, especially for students from low socioeconomic status backgrounds. In line with this understanding, engaged personnel have been given more scope for experimentation and attempts at oversimplification have been discarded in the process of analysis and synthesis of retention and transition interventions. Thus, more holistic strategies tend to determine:

- which factors may be amenable to some type of action or intervention by the institution (for instance by identifying discrete at risk factors);
- which outcomes may result from such efforts and what type of lessons will more likely be learnt if the expected results do not materialise (most plans leave this door open as if it would be in bad taste to suggest that things may not go as expected);
- which factors belong in a policy and institution-wide strategy category;
- which factors have moved beyond the pale to enter into the realm of high politics or long term investment–disinvestment strategies (amalgamation of campuses, changes in the brand, moving off-shore, etc);
- which key elements and principles will need to enter into the equation for the plan/strategy/framework to hold together.

Table 1-1: Key guiding principles in a retention and transition policy/strategy

Universal encapsulations of experience	Heuristic principles (Cuseo)	Overall psycho-pedagogical principles (Cuseo)	Properties/principles of effective First Year Student Support programs (Cuseo)
• retention is everyone's business • good teaching equals retention (Cuseo) • success is measured by the outcomes achieved by the student relative to their situation at entry (Cuseo) • retention equals challenge and support (Upcraft) • access without support is not opportunity (Tinto)	• how intentional are we about this? • how well we model what we teach/do?	• personal validation • self-efficacy • personal meaning • active involvement • social integration • personal reflection • self-awareness	• mission-driven (institutional commitment to students [Tinto, 1992]) • intentional • developmental (Educational commitment [Tinto, 1992]) • social and intellectual community (Tinto, 1992) • student-centred • pro-active • diversified • comprehensive • collaborative • systemic • durable • empirical (evidentiary)

Failing a degree of explicitness about these elementary questions, retention and transition may simply go unnoticed, or be counted as of secondary importance in the large scheme of things. Lack of explicitness in this regard may also fuel the impression that the main drivers for retention efforts are chiefly rhetorical at best, while at worst they may be perceived as discretionary ammunition in the argy-bargy of budget talk and managerial blame-games (Hill 2012).

Literature reviews as well as distillations from the cumulative knowledge in action gathered by reputable theorists/practitioners have resulted in the identification of a series of retention/transition/success principles. They can be used as prompters for quality assurance purposes, policy drafting, and strategic planning. We have grouped them above in Table 1-1 for ease of reference.

Monitoring of students at risk of disengaging

The need for a systematic approach to retention and transition has found a strong ally in the changes that have been occurring in the area of online learning and ITC development. Greater access to faster internet connections, the irruption and dominance of social media, new and more powerful student management systems, video-capturing recording of lectures, and further improvements in e-learning mean that virtual realities now blend with the physical reality in a number of ways previously thought of as impossible. The combined impact of these developments in the physical university can be observed in the provision of new formal and informal learning spaces where computers, books and modular spaces reflect a wide range of uses, and in the more intensive use of learning management systems.

But, just as profoundly, the ability of electronically tracking all interactions between the university and the students, through their electronic imprint, currently allows universities to devise pro-active interventions on the basis of the three-dimensional images of students (biodata, diagnostic tests and academic results, interactions with the system). Partly as a result of this new prowess, universities have turned to exploiting all opportunities for the tracking of students' interactions with the university systems. Retention follow-up programs of "at risk" students (that is, students at risk of failing), rebadged in Australia as Monitoring of Student Learning Engagement, are perhaps the latest addition (Nelson and Creagh 2013).

The "at risk" category is a construct made up of a number of pre-defined student "behaviours"—accessing of email; accessing of student management systems; attendance; and academic results, among others—that trigger an intervention, usually a follow-up call by a friendly student advisor. As such category it is clearly indebted to Vincent Tinto's vision of the student as coming to the tertiary environment with a set of attributes (family background, personal traits, academic preparedness) that interact with the institution's characteristics.

Offers of assistance and referrals may vary in accordance with the response and time of the year. Relevant information is noted and further follow-up actions are instituted when warranted. Monitoring systems of this nature can be restricted to all first year students, or to specific units that attract lower retention rates. Some monitoring systems combine enrolment information (biodata/demographics) with other data (diagnostic tests, pre-entry tests, hurdles) and behaviours in order to further refine targeted interventions.

Yet, the increasing resort to this type of heavily mediated interactions is not without its own risks. The use of enrolment information to create student profiles has been objected to as a case of profiling (Harvey 2012). The very language used by Alan Seidman, perhaps the strongest of its proponents (Seidman 2005), belies a tendency to assimilate this kind of activity with medical diagnosis, thus endowing it with an aura of predictive power likely to appeal to university managers in their quest for "interventions" and solutions that work. The efficacy of the system depends to a great extent on the ability to connect information systems operating in the background (such as RIGHT NOW, Starfish, Callista) with a well-oiled team of callers (trained senior students or student advisors), and data collection at the coal-face (lecturers, tutors).

At least three such systems featured at the First Year in Higher Education Conference held in 2012 (Murdoch University, Edith Cowan University and La Trobe University), and a book-length report has been produced documenting a wider array of similar experiences in Australia (Nelson and Creagh 2013) collectively gathered under the rubric of Monitoring Student Learning Engagement (MSLE). The efficacy of the system can be measured by looking at improvements in overall satisfaction and retention, which Queensland University of Technology claims to be a significant "nearly 13 percent" amongst first-year students [enrolled in 2012] compared to "16.7 [percent] for the previous year" ("Student Success Program Boosts Retention Rates" 2012).

Some universities are relying on these schemes to achieve ongoing improvements in key performance indicators such as sustained yearly increases in retention of one percent or thereabouts. The initial investment may not pay for itself, however, if any of the conditions falter or if there is but little cooperation from academic or other key administrative staff. Karen Nelson and Tracy Creagh's report (Nelson and Creagh 2013) has provided a more credible rationale for this type of initiatives by resting it on a recognition that the "at risks" category affects more severely students from low socioeconomic backgrounds, culturally and linguistically diverse students, and Indigenous students.

A general description of the main features of monitoring systems, such as the above, cannot cover the practical details involved in their actual implementation, yet it is at this practical level that some of the institutional and human constraints are usually put to the test more clearly. Benefits become also more obvious when the phenomenon is observed in its ramifications. For instance, if class attendance is monitored, some of the flow-on effects of such activity are that:

- a strong signal is sent to students about the value of contact hours
- people's names are more easily retained and used in class and outside class contacts
- group learning opportunities are effectively fostered (no use for it, though, if only a tiny minority attends classes)
- withdrawal-prone situations are more easily detected
- students and fellow students provide reasons for their absences

But by the same token, all these benefits become questionable if the adopted model sees no additional or little actual value in class attendance per se, as this may be compensated by virtual lectures or can be rationalised as one more choice to be made by the student-consumer.

Development of policies, models and overarching frameworks

The need to streamline and accelerate progress, achieve economies of scale and stipulate degrees of cooperation between university agents and stakeholders may explain the push towards policy approaches that prescribe how things are meant to be done at university, as well as the corresponding mechanisms for compliance and quality control. Over time, a number of universities in Australia have developed a number of policies that govern such aspects as orientation, transition, first-year/student experience, student engagement, etc. Yet, a feature commonly reported by practitioners is that policies and strategies may fall in abeyance, be non-existent, exist only partially (as recommendations by another name), be unenforceable due to under-resourcing or to lack of clarity as to who will take responsibility for what and how the process will be evaluated or managed.

Another hindrance commonly found is that changes to existing organisational arrangements at the top level may call into question perfectly viable and productive programs that lack "fit" into fresh organisational parameters. Under these conditions, policies may enjoy only a limited lifespan and a more restricted scope of application than initially contemplated. Lack of funding and a filtering down of key accountabilities often result in the undermining of the original intentions and in a growing dissatisfaction, if not frustration, with the quality of leadership this usually entails.

A way of overcoming the descent of top-down policy approaches is the provision of models and overarching frameworks. Like mind-maps and Gant representations, models and overarching frameworks afford a much needed clarification as to how to operationalise and visualise a number of defined themes (retention, transition, first-year experiences, student support, and graduate capabilities). This allows for a clear identification of the actions and people responsible for them, either in the abstract or over a timeframe. Such frameworks, and their visual representations, can be more easily assimilated by all university areas than single policies or detailed plans because they map out, at a glance, multiple levels of information. Uncluttered by complex representations of relationships and locales, they are the equivalent of a good map for a driver, or a blueprint for an architect. Responsibilities are more easily identified, expanded and contracted, while movable pieces can be replaced or reallocated to match.

Models and frameworks are no substitutes for policies and strategies, and their underlying assumptions, but provide a degree of explicitness that, paradoxically, policies and strategies tend to bury in their own linear detail.

A framework can thus situate in a particular context (retention, transition, first-year experience) elements, programs, actions and agents that may also feature in a varied number of other contexts. Tinto and Pusser's model of institutional action (Tinto and Engstrom 2008; Tinto and Pusser 2006) supplies a model of institutional action that identifies such main elements. Both authors attach great importance to the provision of institutional leadership and to a commensurate commitment. This is a recognition that strategic guidelines and resource allocations are needed to glue together a wide range of major areas of institutional action that otherwise may drift away or remain as disjointed circles. Kuh (2005) and Cuseo (2011), for instance, attach considerable importance to the generating of an appropriate climate through a tightening of the relationship between mission, vision and values articulated in a strategic plan that resonates powerfully with the university community. It should be noted that Tinto and Pusser's model is abstract enough to be applied to all kinds of higher- education institutions, and sufficiently dynamic to identify the various key influencing factors and their logical interactions.

In the Australian context, Deakin University can be mentioned as offering a highly visual and current example of a systemic transition framework (Deakin University 2012) that self-defines as a "holistic approach to course design, skills development and student support".

Good frameworks presuppose a solid experiential base. They also promote further clarification of existing policies and strategies, which may be simplified as a result of the connectedness and trust that the framework itself may foster. Examples of policies that evidence a framework quality can be found, in particular, in Queensland University of Technology's Protocols (Queensland University of Technology 2009), and La Trobe's Transition Plan (La Trobe University 2012).

The systemic quality revealed by most of these approaches reflects a progression of sorts. According to Tinto (2005), during the 1980s the concept of student "involvement" was explored in depth (Pascarella 2006): "We learned that involvement matters and that it matters most during the critical first year of college" (3). Attention was, accordingly, largely focused on transition, first year at college, and the provision of retention activities carried out by "student affairs professionals"; "most retention activities were appended to, rather than integrated within, the mainstream of institutional academic life. Retention activities were then, as they are in some measure today, add-ons to existing university activity" (3).

Transition pedagogy

As indicated, the need for a holistic approach to "course design, skills development and student support" explains a further promising development in the form of transition pedagogy, a concept first formalised by Sally Kift (Kift *et al.* 2010a; Nelson *et al.* 2012) but pre-formed in a number of works (Nelson *et al.* 2005; Kift 2008) calling for a transfer of retention, support services and co-curriculum from the periphery to the very core of curriculum design and innovation.

Generally, the first-year experience (FYE) work and research that has occurred to date has centred around the curriculum, or in aid of it, but has not come in from the curriculum's periphery to focus on what intentional and holistic first-year curriculum design, which is at the centre of the student FYE, might optimally entail. This requires a shift from primarily co-curricular "first-generation FYE approaches" to second and third-generation FYE strategies (Wilson 2009, 10) that focus squarely on enhancing the student learning experience through pedagogy, curriculum design, and learning and teaching practice in the physical and virtual classroom ("Transition pedagogy" 2011).

Transition pedagogy is the formalisation of a trend towards further integration of first-year initiatives, monitoring of at-risk students, integration of support *services*, policies and frameworks, and curriculum renewal. It is not simply an umbrella concept, but an attempt at harnessing the complexity of university processes from a perspective that is more empowering than customary top-down approaches. The concept is an acknowledgement of the totality of the students' "learning experience" from a perspective that privileges the processional aspect of the student journey/experience (now the standard guiding metaphor in the field). Here a multiplicity of duly identified key entry and exit points becomes the object of strategic/standard interventions. Teamwork and open lines of communication between university sections are recognised as fundamental to the success of any transition pedagogy, as made apparent in Queensland University of Technology's approach (Nelson *et al*. 2007).

The broad principles of transition pedagogy as identified by Kift and her colleagues include: transition, diversity, design, engagement, assessment, and evaluation and monitoring (Nelson and Clarke 2010b). Each of these principles in turn is subdivided into sub-principles and scalable programs and projects. Thus, for instance, a broad principle subsumable under the transition category dictates that there should be consistency of communication, language and expectations. This may imply typically that information previously disseminated through various outlets and areas is vetted, subjected to corporate brand rules, re-aligned with the university's strategic plan, and reintegrated into multi-channel (print, online, phone, human) communication packages that deliver key messages at appropriate times (or just in time) while minimising information overload. Easier said than done, certainly, yet pivotal to a fully-fledged transition pedagogy.

Communication of expectations is also a main focus of "orientation", understood as a period, rather than an event, where the student interacts with peers and staff, and starts to absorb the university's culture through a series of carefully designed experiences.

Similarly, under the principle of "engagement", it is argued that a holistic curriculum means "bringing together the academic administrative and other support programs available under the organising device of the curriculum" (Nelson and Kift 2005). The implicit assumption here is that the curriculum not only recognises pedagogical value in what support programs bring in, but actually unpacks those values and redefines them in light of the university's overall intentions. The notions of embedment and scaffolding here become standard to understanding this multi-vocal process: all areas must contribute to the modelling of a global learning experience.

The intentionality of the process is also underscored by another key element: its explicitness. Intentions are spelled out so as to ensure that clarity is achieved and tests for compliance are more easily devised. Intentionality, for instance, is fundamental in the way expectations by all parties (students and staff) are recognised, validated, and responded to; for instance, during the critical orientation period, or during the first weeks of transition, when assessment and feedback are discussed with students.

As it stands in its formulation and actual implementation at Queensland University of Technology, much of the success of the principles, strategies, programs and lines of action included within this transition pedagogy depends on the existence of a credible coordinating body that ensures effective steps are taken across the university. This coordinating entity embodies the high priority accorded to transition pedagogy by the university leadership and hence may exert direct responsibility for a number of strategic projects, as well as enjoying supervisory and advising roles in most other areas.

It is not clear, however, how senior leadership arrangements may allow for the creation of such a high profile role with such a broad mandate. Furthermore, trends in higher education provision may divert attention and resources to the parallel development of blended-learning approaches that feed into platforms such as Coursera. In the process, university decision-makers are caught in the dilemma of unbundling components of the traditional university business model, turning the non-negotiables of the past into optional or debatable elements: entry scores, student–staff ratios, the future of tenure, the trinity teaching-research-service, the year-round utilisation of teaching spaces, the further casualisation of teaching staff, the shift towards accreditation and self-regulation in a freer higher education market; all these elements become again matters for further instability. The "disruptive" university may not have yet materialised in Australia, but the signs are unmistakably there (Ernst and Young 2012).

The integrative and the adaptive models

The above outline describes a clear trend towards integrated approaches to retention, transition and first-year experience, or in the words of Kift, "second [now third] generation FYE strategies" (Australian Government, Office for Learning and Teaching 2009). Whether the six FYE principles identified by Kift and colleagues can translate into standards, as suggested, is perhaps less significant than the broad consensus they are starting to enjoy Australia-wide. Given, however, the somewhat idiosyncratic nature of any taxonomy of principles, the term "adaptive model" is proposed here to reflect the broader characteristics and features common to many of the approaches already described.

Although the term "adaptive" is used in contrast with the "integrative or assimilative" approaches largely identified with Vincent Tinto's original model and its variations, there is no suggestion of an abrupt opposition but rather one of progression within limits and tensions that call for endurance and coping skills rather than drastic resolutions. In fact, Tinto and Pusser's (2006) above-mentioned model of institutional action is a clear example of the "adaptive" model, with its greater emphasis on what the institution needs to do in order to accommodate the growing reality of a diversified student population.

In the integrative or assimilative model, students are induced into university life (culture, ethos, habitus, modus operandi) in an effort to expedite the students' transitioning to and from university. The main aim is to facilitate academic and social integration as a means to ensure retention, completion and success. In addition to the application of remedial teaching, extended orientation, and learning-support programs, the integrative model favours the application of cooperative and collaborative learning through the provision of learning communities and peer and staff-mentoring initiatives.

In this model the university is seen as a community of learners committed to preserving and advancing the values of higher learning through a conscious cultivation of science and its underpinning values. The integrative model believes in the inherent good of a university education, and espouses a combination of excellence, merit and success strategies as key to its own development, including self-marketing. The integrative model often fuses the ethics of self-improvement and democratic citizenship/service (especially important in the American tradition) into pre-existing elite and hierarchical tendencies. In stressing the importance of community and rituals to foster belonging and *esprit de corps*, there recurs the archetype of the university as a microcosmos, perhaps the hard core of a "university town" or one of the main drivers of an entire economy. In this imagined community, students are absorbed or co-opted into this culture, apply it and transmit it after a long protracted induction/initiation process (the student lifecycle), culminating in various degrees of success. The integrative–assimilative model of retention tends to implicitly place the university (institution) at the centre even as it strives to be student-centred.

By contrast, the adaptive model assumes that students come with different degrees of cultural and social capital that need to be valued and fostered as true strengths. It sees access to university as a process distinct from mere entry and dependant on variables that are simultaneously societal, institutional and personal and hence less amenable to simplifications. In this context, how a sense of self-efficacy and agency is or has been developed by the student can exert an enormous influence on how risk factors and stressors interact to inform persistence and decisions to withdraw (Karimshah *et al.* 2013). The adaptive model provides a "re-colonising" (rather than alternative) perspective into what really happens and should happen in tertiary education. It brings more self-awareness and a more critical perspective to university practices. For example, it calls into question the assumptions built into routine givens such as "plagiarism", "assumed previous knowledge", "transferability or generalisability of basic skills", all of which are known to cause puzzlement among students as well as staff. It sees universities as compounds of different cultures, with differing academic approaches and disciplinary "tribes" that apprentice students into their respective fields of practice and academic discourses.

The adaptive model requires, if not demands, that universities live up to their own values and expectations (which can indeed be lofty ones); it also identifies and privileges areas of strength as foci for shared actions, and seeks to renegotiate win-win style, the contradictions between the various co-existing paradigms (organisational, disciplinary, professional) while acknowledging, without naivety, the difficulties in doing so (Zipin and Brennan 2003).

Its student-centredness is driven less by a user-pays mandate than by a developmental focus that has students' diversity at heart. This diversity is re-fed into the curriculum and the way the university organises its space, learning resources and strategies. The "shape" and "face" of the university changes as a result. Students' needs, expectations and perceptions become the focus of renewed teaching practices. The student voice is not simply heard, but consciously placed where it can make a difference.

In an adaptive context, transition is reframed as the expression of the student journey/lifecycle/experience. Transitioning is thought of as a continuum punctuated by key transition points, the sum of which may lead to different and sometimes divergent ends. Successful transitions are, therefore, not only those that retain students by engaging them in their learning, but crucially those that assist students to succeed in their goals as independent learners along an otherwise tricky continuum.

Retention and transition at Victoria University

Elements of Tinto's learning communities and of Kuh's culture of excellence and engagement can be clearly recognised at Victoria University. Initiatives such as the Student as Staff and the Leadership programs, peer mentoring schemes, orientation volunteers/hosts, library rovers, and community work placements all bear witness to the university's capacity to use the students' own potential in situations that clearly go beyond the occasional tokenistic feel-good "enrichment" programs.

The retention imperative has become all the more demanding given that Victoria University caters to a large extent for: students from low socioeconomic status (around 23 percent); a high proportion of culturally and linguistically diverse students (around 40 percent); the largest cohort of non-school leavers of all higher education institutions in Victoria; a significant proportion of students articulating from the vocational sector, many of whom may require considerable levels of support to succeed in their studies (Messinis, Sheehan and Miholcic 2008).

Major university changes now underway are set to lead to a concentration of interdisciplinary research and partnerships with key sectors. Implicit in this impetus are analyses of current trends, threats and opportunities. Changes in the socio-demographic base of Melbourne's western suburbs, in particular, are bound to alter the face of demands and reputational expectations by prospective students, community and industry.

Like most other tertiary institutions in Australia, Victoria University has contended with issues of transition since its re-birth as a university in 1990, perhaps even more so given its multi-sector and multi-campus nature and its long-standing commitment to serve the needs of the western suburbs in Melbourne. These concerns have figured prominently in the university's agenda, leading to the gradual introduction of a wide range of approaches and strategies known for reducing attrition and promoting successful transitions. Some of the most effective strategies implemented at present originated in well-tested experiences with various starting points in the late 1980s up to the present. Award-winning initiatives such as the student mentoring and leadership programs (see Gill Best chapter in this book), complemented with the introduction of foundation units have gone a long way towards fostering a university culture where student-centred practices take the lead. This only confirms the trend among most Australian universities towards the creation of a retention culture (McInnis and James 2004) in which virtually all processes are lent impetus by a retention and transition mandate.

In keeping with this, and informed by an assortment of surveys (Student Barometer, Course Experience Questionnaire, Australasian Survey of Student Engagement, Graduate Exit Survey, University Experience Survey) and internal studies aimed at gauging fundamental components of the student experience (key demographics, pathways, course advising), Victoria University embarked upon new initiatives such as the Student Experience Strategy (Caldwell 2011), the Students Supporting Student Learning and the Language Literacy and Numeracy Strategy (2011), all while learning commons and informal learning spaces were underway in an effort to better meet the needs of students.

A reinvigorated orientation program, introduced in 2010, was followed in the two subsequent years by ever-improved university-wide orientation programs that in 2011 included welcome sessions as well as short introductory courses to the university's IT environment and to academic skills (UniReady 1 and 2). In parallel, a new impetus to retention and transition efforts was communicated through the creation of Faculty Retention and Transition Coordinating positions, followed or preceded by the allocation of retention/transition workload points to academic school staff. Two pilot projects for flagging at-risk students were launched in 2011 (Flag and Follow Project; and Starfish Project). Foundation units were also established as a way of ensuring that embedded literacies would induct students into their courses.

Concurrently, two university-wide, externally commissioned reports (Adams *et al.* 2010; Adams *et al.* 2011) provided in-depth analyses pertaining to retention and transition issues. The launching of the latter was timed to coincide with the visit of Emeritus Professor Joe Cuseo for a series of workshops focusing on all aspects of the first-year experience. Also in 2011, and under the new leadership of Vice-Chancellor Peter Dawkins, the university embarked on an ambitious strategic review that led to the publication of a Strategic Plan (September 2011), and finally to the Victoria University Agenda (September 2012). In addition to identifying a new vision, mission and set of values, the new plan has also articulated a number of goals, distinctive specialisations (majors) and strategic pillars that will support the required restructuring. During the period intervening between the two documents, pressing financial needs, aggravated by state government budget cuts to the funding of vocational courses, further brought home the need to undertake an even firmer realignment of all university processes.

Meanwhile, the work carried out by the Curriculum Commission, itself defined as one of the university's six key "strategic pillars", led to the adoption of a number of guiding principles of action that, together with the Research and Knowledge Exchange Strategy, will inform the core business of the university. A "transition pedagogy", successfully trialled in 2013 in the College of Business, is now recognised as fundamental to the curriculum review, and so is the distinctive contribution of the Workplace Learning strategy. The university's colleges, which replaced the original three faculties, have engaged in reframing their own missions, which include a firm commitment to providing "seamless transitions".

While it is simply too soon to determine how the above positioning will eventuate in practice and how the proposed transition pedagogy will adapt to and transform the contours of the student experience, the main principles and components are clear enough to inform current and renewed practices. The makings of an integrated approach to retention are evident, not only in the articulation of a Victoria University-specific transition pedagogy, but also in the reintegration of existing strategies into it.

Students have been engaged as ambassadors, volunteers, peer mentors, and advisors in an attempt to allow them to become role models who can ease fellow-students into their own transitions. Re-engaging the student with their learning has, in a number of instances, led to a complete re-thinking of what it means to learn in a "knowledge economy": whether it is learning by doing, problem-based learning, learning in the workplace, or big-wicked issues learning, the realisation is there that learning is less about the mediation itself and more about the capacity to "value-add" to the student experience.

Picturing the student lifecycle

As indicated, synchronising with the restructuring of Victoria University's senior management and the consultative processes leading up to the final Strategic Plan, a parallel process of consultations crystallised in the Tony Adams & Associate's report on retention (2010). This was a sequel to the Hobsons Retention Project and Factor Analysis Report (October 2010), whose general benchmarking exercise was taken one further step up by clearly positioning Victoria University relative to other 16 tertiary universities in terms of retention difficulty factors and retention performance factors.

For the purposes of its benchmarking exercise the report translated the "common features of best practice" identified in the Hobsons report (28–9) into actual "retention performance factors", which were then reconverted into broad recommendations (4-6). Table 3 summarises main phases of the student lifecycle identified in the report (each briefly described) together with the corresponding retention factor.

Table 1-2: Best practice across the student lifecycle

Student lifecycle	Description	Related retention performance factor
• Prospect Management • Potential enquirers are driven to the web site	• Dynamic web site, web positioning, web marketing, fairs, school based activities, agents and agent based activities, print materials • Handling of enquiries, marketing communication strategies campaigns, follow-p activities • Use of Customer Relationship Management technologies • E-newsletters and e-newspapers	
• Application • Period from the moment an application is being provided through to acceptance or rejection	• Personalised responses • Specific offer follow up, regular contact through marketing communications (e-newspaper) • Counselling and interviewing of applicants (course advisory service; early diagnosis)	
• Enrolment processes and orientation • From acceptance of an offer to enrolment, including arrival and orientation	• Compulsory and lively orientation, socialisation activities, access to academic and support staff, allocation of students to advisors, mentor programs, online orientation	• Screening for early detection • Self identification • Orientation compulsory • Counselling for course choice
• Semester / Year Transitions • Touch points through cycle, inclusive of at risk detection and managing of communications	• At risk identification through the term; monitoring of first and later assignments, practical periods, learning and language difficulties; at risk scale and enforceable staged interventions	• Non attendance monitored • Measures of student engagement • Assignment submission monitored

	• Compulsory attendance of counselling/learning advisory meetings, peer mentoring schemes universally implemented; celebration of students achievements; monitoring of placements through regular reporting; further communication with students through Facebook, SMS and emails, e-newspaper.	• Performance monitored prior to end of first semester • Performance monitored on completion of semester • Program for at risk students
• **Final Semester /Year** Preparation for graduation, further studies, career prospects	• On campus and virtual advising, access to experienced staff	• Satisfaction surveys • Exit surveys compulsory • Grievance process informs retention policy/ process • Results inform retention policy/ program
• Alumni • Creation of a strong alumni community	• Word of mouth, referrals, role models, guest lecturers, ongoing testimonials ; use of CRM system	

Source: Adapted from Adams report (7–11)

The rationale behind the benchmarking exercise was predicated on a basic calculation of the costs of attrition and the imputed effect of poor retention performance against a scale of difficulty factors. The case for a purely pragmatic reconsideration was based on the strength of the high costs of attrition. As claimed in the Hobsons report, a one percent drop in attrition would save an estimated $2.6 million per university on average, roughly $100 million for Australia (see Table 1-3). In essence, the Adams report advocated a systemic approach to retention which included:

- a "retention culture"
- central funding
- an "agreed university-wide approach to retention"
- the introduction of principles of accountability (retention key performance indicators, performance reviews)
- the institutionalisation of working arrangements (creation of a "new small centre or unit, supplemented by the empowering of the Education, Retention and Transition Committee with decision-making capacity)

This representation can be particularly useful when considering the implications of re-engineering the student lifecycle into matching descriptions and retention performance factors. University strategists may take this as a useful "to-do list" that may inform their more elaborate frameworks and models.

The report concludes that on both counts—retention difficulty and retention performance—Victoria University is found at the respective lower ends of both scales. Unsurprisingly, this is matched by higher levels of attrition than those obtaining at other average Australian universities, a phenomenon equally confirmed by universities in the same scoring league.

Table 1-3: Institutional costs of attrition

	International students	Domestic students	Total Average University Intl. students	Dom. students
Lost tuition fees per year	$17,000	$8,000	$11 million	$27 million
Recruitment costs	$3,288	$500	$1.7 million	$3.3
			Total av. $42.6* *1 percent attrition: $2.6 per University	

Source: Adapted from Hobsons report (16–18)

Yet, as noted by Joe Cuseo (in Trounson 2011), when these broad results are considered, assumptions about quality may need to be turned on their heads: "We shouldn't define quality based on who we let in but on the students we turn out relative to the way they were when they came in". A similar position has also been taken by Jamil Salmi, the World Bank's coordinator of tertiary education professionals (Kelly 2011), when he ranked Victoria University at the top of any equity ranking precisely on the grounds of how well it performs in bringing up students. A recent opinion piece by the university's vice-chancellor (Dawkins 2013) also highlights the importance of these outcomes when ranking universities, a point illustrated with an extended reference to the outstanding sixth position achieved by the University of Texas at El Paso (UTEP) in the Washington's Monthly National University Rankings of US Institutions, which ranks universities according to their contribution to the public good (Harvard comes next in the seventh position). Links between Victoria University and UTEP, it should be noted, have been strong and continue to be a source of emulation for both universities. It is in the light of these considerations that student success becomes a far more elastic category than previously acknowledged.

Redefining Student Success

Redefining student success requires us to pose a deeper question at a number of levels. Elite tertiary institutions have traditionally built up their "solid" reputations based on selectivity. Students admitted into courses on the "sole basis of academic merit" are thus more easily retained without the institution having to make any special investment in terms of support and developmental programs. Students tend to do well regardless because they are already "integrated" into the culture and expectations associated with their studies, as one and very often both of their parents are already higher-degree holders. These students are in the main the Suzannes who, as described by John Biggs and Catherine Tang (2011), require little external guidance or motivation to perform well. They are largely studying at the university of their first choice and tend to be school-leavers who are inclined to see a university career as the natural extension of their school years.

By contrast, non-elite institutions, and especially dual-sector and regional universities, provide education to a far more variable student body that, as in the case of Victoria University, is largely comprised of mature-age, non-traditional, and culturally and linguistically diverse (CALD) students. In this type of tertiary institution the school-leaving population may be only a fraction of the total. Students may come to a university that is not their first or second choice, and may undertake courses of studies that are intended as bridges to other preferred options, often located elsewhere. A variety of pathways may assist the students to wend their way through their studies. Family, job and health commitments may fill the experience with interruptions and zig-zagging turns that educational authorities may read as either "unconventional", or, as Victoria University staff will do, as examples of a special kind of resilience in the face of adverse circumstances. In these contexts the experience of being a tertiary student often becomes more conflicted and more prone to self-doubt. Students in these categories may be more like the "Roberts" in Biggs and Tang's description and, as a result, may require more guiding attention. Being "first in the family" in gaining a tertiary education, these students may not only lack any referents to turn to among their family and friends, but are often forced to overcome contradictory perceptions of opportunity costs along with feelings of declassing and status alienation, as well as their opposites (doing well, moving up the ladder, etc). No matter how clearly university maps locate and tell students "you are here", the student's own sense of orientation seems to detect the presence of other coordinates at work.

Perhaps in a crude Rumsfeldian way, the politically incorrect truism about students "not knowing what they do not know" applies to students in this expansive bracket. So much so, that a major difficulty identified by administrators and teaching staff refers to a certain lack of "administrative literacy" displayed by students (Lawrence 2005) . Different treatments are usually proposed to remedy this weakness ranging from a streamlining of services along well-identified transition points, down to a forthright no "hand-holding" shock therapy, possibly accompanied by great reservations about the rights of student as consumers, all of which are conditions less applicable to the well-established research universities (Sharrock 2013).

Under these conditions, defining student success is less a matter of student completions, important as this is, than of successful transitioning to completion. Indeed, if the meandering trajectories of the new lifelong learners are more typical of the "average student", the metaphor of the student journey may require readjusting, reflecting more clearly the three-dimensional and existential components of the learning experience involved. Coastal navigation rather than a long one-way voyage with a set final destination becomes the norm. Distances mediating between the starting point, when the student enrols, and the finishing line, signalling completion, are rarely the same any more. Students come from very different educational and professional coordinates, and are more and more immersed in other lives or identities that may run parallel, overlap or intersect in different ways with their own student selves. Unfortunately, as Andrew Funston warns us (Funston 2012), the students' voices are often surveyed, but not heard in the richness of their own stories. Some of the laments deploring our lack of knowledge about what makes students withdraw or persist could be more easily addressed if the trajectories of students are followed and acted upon beyond the limited scope of regular student experience surveys. Knowing about which factors are more likely to influence retention does not necessarily entail willingness to act on them. In the words of Johnston *et al.*: "This underlines the importance of complementing such developments with richer accounts of student experience, written in the students' own words" (Johnston and Kochanowska 2009).

Perceptions of the learning experience as a whole, therefore, do reflect a wide variety of vital and professional situations that are less amenable to homogenising. Under these conditions, "success" takes on a more nuanced meaning encompassing the attainment of satisfactory outcomes all along the way; outcomes that apart from the issuing of a degree award, may include potent intangibles such as a sense of empowerment and agency (being in charge of one's future), professional currency, being treated with respect (not as a number), establishing lasting friendships, and so on. Universities are aware that expectations about these intangibles may reflect the moods and fads of the market, including belated and or exaggerated responses to the spectre of recession and job losses.

Conclusion

Given the need for tertiary institutions to maximise their own resources, retention and transition strategies have become a must, dictated by an uneasy mix of both self-interest and sound pedagogical grounds. In the process of understanding the reasons for retention and attrition, universities and theorists around the world have virtually exhausted all approaches to the so-called retention puzzle, which explains the increasing search for other foci of attention that may prove more productive of student outcomes, namely assessment in the developmental culture and blended learning in the managerial and virtual cultures (Bergquist and Pawlak 2008).

To the older American tradition of research into the area goes the credit of having established the parameters that have helped define the problem, largely in terms of a process of adaptation, integration and enculturation. The legacy of this rationale is still very much alive in the form of now-standard support services, with its increasing focus on student engagement and the discovery of the first year in tertiary education.

The Australian experience, for its part, has been clustering around four main distinct foci of reflection and renewal, which includes the Student Experience Survey, the Course Experience Questionnaire the First-Year Experience in Higher Education Conference and, finally, government-backed research into key areas of tertiary education.

The word "experience" in association with surveys of one kind or another, as well as with exchanges of professional practice around the first year can be taken as fairly suggestive of a down-to-earth and matter-of-fact approach that takes the student side of things very seriously. Yet, the transfer of the knowledge gathered from these various sources has been slow and rather ad-hoc.

Inducing a "change of culture" has proven a far more difficult task than anticipated and possibly warranted. Paradoxically, retaining the retention/transition culture, let alone making it thrive within higher education institutions has become a major challenge for practitioners and strategists. While underlying factors militating against it do vary from institution to institution, a number of them stand out to the point of becoming so insurmountable as to being barely mentioned. Chief among them are the increasing casualisation of academic staff, the bias towards research in preference to or in direct opposition to a scholarship of teaching, and the unsolved ambivalence between curriculum and co-curriculum. Compounding these factors are the sea-changes in public education policies, mounting reporting obligations, fluctuations in funding and quality assurance requirements, and the unrelenting pressure to remain viable in a globalised, highly competitive market. Catching up with the latest communication technologies also poses a major challenge. In this rarefied climate even the soundest of practices tend to be subjected to exacting levels of scrutiny, be miniaturised to pilot-project status, or, in the final analysis, appear as isolated initiatives.

Bearing in mind these obstacles, the cumulated experience from the Antipodes has probably lived up to the mythical "punching above its weight". Renewal of teaching and administrative practices has taken coverage under various umbrellas, but none perhaps as enduring as the "first-year experience" conferences or the deployment of graduate attributes and skills frameworks. These categories have provided a more stable ground for retention and transition initiatives than would otherwise have been practicable. And while results have been mixed, the related trilogy of retention, transition and success has become deeply engrained in the day-to-day vocabulary of tertiary education institutions in Australia. Advances in curriculum renewal and in the implementation of standards of service delivery, skills and literacies have also made it possible for retention and transition concerns to be addressed as a matter of course rather than as a mere afterthought.

Intentional vision, combined with systematic work at the theoretical and practical levels, have ensured that retention and transition concerns become regular reportable features in most institutions at various levels as a matter of good practice, thus transcending the immediate need to meet funding demands. More importantly, the emergence of a "transition(s) pedagogy" and the distillation of first-year principles stemming from some exemplary practices (and outcomes), exemplified at Queensland University of Technology, have signalled a fundamental turn towards re-conceptualising the student experience and the curriculum, which now have a clear focus on process and success (Yorke and Longden 2004). As a result, the variety of actors and institutional interventions is being more strategically harnessed through a gamut of frameworks and models. An example of this is the increasing attention being paid to outreach programs that build capacity and aspirations in secondary schools that lead more seamlessly to university (Jardine 2012).

The experience gathered at Victoria University can, in this sense, be taken as a further instance of the new paradigm just described. Reflective of its dual sector origins, and in a bid to ease the transition of students into and out of the institution, the university has established close connections and partnerships with communities and industry. Peer mentoring, student leadership and student-engagement initiatives have found powerful allies in the introduction of foundation units, the implementation of an extended orientation program and the stirrings of a fully-fledged First-Year Experience complemented by a system of monitoring learning engagement. Furthermore, efforts at embedding and scaffolding critical literacies in key units has proved a source of enrichment that transcends many of the obstacles perceived by students around support (Prebble *et al.* 2005). In line with the strategic mandate to present students with a high-quality experience, all interactions between the university and students are being streamlined and reviewed to conform to a predictable pattern of service delivery. Lines of work suggested in the previous Hobsons and Adams reports are bound to be implemented in concert with other areas within the university.

In sum, the holistic nature of the challenge posed by retention considerations is far better understood currently than two decades ago, and so are the demands and expectations placed on the panoply of strategies conceived to address them. As a result, no one retention or attrition factor is being privileged to the point of overshadowing all others and no magic solutions are proposed either. This is not a minor achievement in a field that has been prone to one-sided approaches and tokenism. Most university stakeholders realise that they have a role to play in this regard, or to put it in managerial terms, that they are also accountable for the overall levels of retention and success achieved by their students.

More importantly, this recognition has led to the increasing adoption of a transitions pedagogy as well as to the development of frameworks and a set of retention and transition principles. As a result, more systemic and holistic approaches are being implemented in Australian universities, all of which can contribute to the flourishing of a culture of true student success.

This notwithstanding, such laborious achievements can be reversed in the volatile atmospherics of higher education policies. Half-empty glass approaches can easily depict the widening of access to higher education as leading to a dumbing-down of higher education, and student success as the mirage resulting from more people meeting lower standards, a point that is often argued with little more than insider's anecdotal evidence (Van Olsen 2013; Sloan 2013) or relies only on "perceptions" (Ganobsick-Williams 2004). In such a context, it only takes a shift of focus, let us say from success to assessment, or from assessment to online solutions, for the momentum to be watered down beyond recognition.

Policy changes, moreover, may inject new meaning into the all-too-familiar terms. Reflective of the pendulum swings in the political spectrum, broad categories such as open access, democratisation of knowledge, marketisation and managerialism can dramatically change the meaning of retention and transition. Put simply, it is not the same to view retention and transition from a public-service perspective than broaching it from a user-pays standpoint.

In the current climate of ideological and financial volatility, many questions may well remain unanswered, questions such as: what are the implications of current pushes by the Australian Government towards achieving a knowledge economy well-attuned to the demands of the Asian century?; what does the goal of achieving a highly educated workforce by 2020 (40 percent of the population between 25 and 40 years old will be tertiary educated by 2020) mean in terms of job creation and entry levels of required education for most new positions?; what are the effects of the uncapping of Commonwealth-funded places, effective since 2012?; will this move create a level-playing-field market of higher education, and will this all but be a step short of authorising tertiary accredited bodies to determine the price of their own offerings?

The provisional answer to some of the above questions is that the diversification of the sector (comprising of elite, technological and dual-sector universities) may lead inevitably to the display of mutually incompatible narratives barely connected together by a ritualised vocabulary of past shared values. Each particular university, in other words, may end up becoming a discursive aspirational encapsulation of its own social makeup. Retention, transition and success will thus mean very different things among the members of an increasingly dislocated intellectual ecumene.

On a more optimistic note, the Australian experience and that of Victoria University show that retention and transition concerns, when properly managed, can have an energising effect, as they allow for a review of the university key processes (recruitment, enrolments, negotiation and navigation of expectations, curriculum design, support provision, professional development) by introducing fresh new insights across a broad range of issues (first-year experience initiatives, equity mandate, intergenerational issues, access to information, economies of scale), that call in turn for a new regulatory framework better suited to the accomplishment of its self-declared goals.

Reference List

Adams, Tony, Melissa Banks, Dorothy Davis, and Judith Dickson. 2010. *The Hobsons Retention Project: Context and Factor Analysis Report.* Hobsons Asia Pacific. [Accessed October 18, 2011]. Available from http://www.aiec.idp.com/pdf/2010_AdamsBanksDaviesDickson_Wed _1100_BGallB_Paper.pdf.

Adams, Tony, Judith Dickson, Sheila Howell, and Pauline Adams. 2011. Victoria University Retention Final Report. Melbourne, Australia.

Australian Government, Office for Learning and Teaching. 2009. *"Call for Sector-Wide FYE Standards."* Sydney, NSW. http://www.olt.gov.au/september2009-call-for-sector-wide-fye-standards

Bergquist, W. H., and K. Pawlak. 2008. *Engaging the Six Cultures of the Academy: Revised and Expanded Edition of the Four Cultures of the Academy.* Jossey-Bass Inc Pub.

Biggs, John, and Catherine Tang. 2011. *Teaching for Quality Learning at University.* Berkshire, England: Open University Press, McGraw-Hill Education .

Burnett, Lynn. 2006. "The First Year Experience Project". The University of Queensland.

Caldwell, Haley. 2011. "Strategies for Student Success: Student Experience Strategy 2009-2011". Melbourne: Victoria University, Melbourne.   http://tls.vu.edu.au/portal/site/policies/resources/student_ experience%20 strategy_Final_review.pdf.

Cuseo, Joe. 2011. *Developing a Comprehensive First-Year Experience Program: Powerful Principles & Practices.* Victoria University: Melbourne, Australia.

Dawkins, Peter. 2013. "Greatness Has New Meaning." *Campus Review*, October 14. http://www.campusreview.com.au/blog/2013/10/greatness-has-new-meaning-2/.

Deakin University. 2012. "Deakin University's Transition Framework for Commencing Students." http://www.deakin.edu.au/current-Students/ assets/resources/transition/transition-Framework.pdf.

Funston, J. Andrew. 2012. *Research Report 35: Non-traditional Students Making Their Way in Higher Education – An Australian Case Study.* Youth Research Centre. Melbourne Graduate School of Education.

Ganobsick-Williams, Lisa. 2004. "A Report on the Teaching of Academic Writing in the UK Higher Education". The Royal Literary Fund.

Hartley, Robyn, Richard James, and Craig McInnis. 2005. *The First Year Experience in Australian Universities: Findings from a Decade of*

National Studies. Melbourne: Centre for the Study of Higher Education, University of Melbourne.

Harvey, Andrew. 2012. "Student Entry Checks by Universities Carry Risks." *The Australian, Higher Education Supplement*, May 16. http://www.theaustralian.com.au/higher-education/opinion/student-entry-checks-by-universities-carry-risks/story-e6frgcko-1226356721317.

Harvey, Lee, Sue Drew, and Maria Smith. 2006. "The First-Year Experience: A Review of Literature for the Higher Education Academy." *Higher Education Research Academy* 20.

Hill, R. 2012. *Whackademia: An Insider's Account of the Troubled University*. Sydney, NSW: University of New South Wales Press.

James, James, Kerri-Lee Krause, and Claire Jennings. 2010. "The First Year Experience in Australian Universities: Findings from 1994 to 2009". Melbourne: Centre for the Study of Higher Education, The University of Melbourne and Griffith Institute for Higher Education. http://www.cshe.unimelb.edu.au/research/experience/docs/FYE_Repor t_1994_to_2009.pdf.

Jardine, Ann. 2012. "Indicators of Persistence and Their Influence on the First Year Experience of University Students from Low Socio-Economic Backgrounds". Melbourne: University of Melbourne.

Johnston, B., and R. Kochanowska. 2009. "Quality Enhancement Themes: The First Year Experience: Student Expectations, Experiences and Reflections on the First Year." http://dera.ioe.ac.uk/11601/1/student expectations D1865DFB9417.pdf.

Karimshah, Ameera, Marianne Wyder, Paul Henman, Dwight Tay, Elizabeth Capelin, and Patricia Short. 2013. "Overcoming Adversity among Low SES Students: A Study of Strategies for Retention." *Australian Universities' Review* 55 (2): 5–14.

Katkin, Wendy. 2003. "The Boyer Commission Report and Its Impact on Undergraduate Research." *New Directions for Teaching and Learning* 2003 (93) (March 1): 19–38. doi:10.1002/tl.86.

Kellogg Commission on the Future of State and Land-Grant Universities. 1997. "Returning to Our Roots: The Student Experience". Washington: National Association of State Universities and Land-Grant Universities.

Kelly, Fran. 12 July 2011. "University Rankings." *Breakfast*. Accessed from http://www.abc.net.au/radionational/programs/breakfast/2011-12-07/3716 666.

Kift, Sally M. 2008. "The Next, Great First Year Challenge: Sustaining, Coordinating and Embedding Coherent Institution–wide Approaches to

Enact the FYE as 'Everybody's Business'". Conference Paper. http://eprints.qut.edu.au/14401/.

Kift, Sally M., Karen Nelson, and John Clarke. 2010a. "Transition Pedagogy: A Third Generation Approach to FYE - A Case Study of Policy and Practice for the Higher Education Sector." *The International Journal of the First Year in Higher Education* 1 (1) (July 21): 1–20. doi:10.5204/intjfyhe. v1i1.13.

Kift, Sally M. 2010b. "Transition Pedagogy: A Third Generation Approach to FYE - A Case Study of Policy and Practice for the Higher Education Sector." *The International Journal of the First Year in Higher Education* 1 (July 21): 1–20. doi:10.5204/intjfyhe. v1i1.13.

Krause, Kerri Lee. "Which way from here? Passion, policy and practice in first year higher education." In *Seventh Pacific Rim First Year in Higher Education Conference, Centre for the Study of Higher Education, University of Melbourne.* 2003.

La Trobe University. 2012. "First Year Experience Plan." http://www.latrobe.edu.au/student-enrichment/student-enrichment-documents/First-Year-Experience-Plan.pdf.

Lawrence, Jill. 2005. "Re-Conceptualising Attrition and Retention: Integrating Theoretical, Research and Student Perspectives." *Studies in Learning Evaluation Innovation and Development* 2 (3) (December): 16–33.

McInnis, Craig, and Richard James. 2004. "Access and Retention in Australian Higher Education." In *Retention and Student Success in Higher Education*, edited by Mantz Yorke and Bernard Longden, 32–45. Maidenhead, UK: Open University Press.

McInnis, Craig, and Carmel McNaught. 1995. "First Year on Campus, Diversity in the Initial Experiences of Australian Undergraduates". Melbourne: Centre for the Study of Higher Education University of Melbourne.

Messinis, George, Peter Sheehan, and Zdenko Miholcic. 2008. "The Diversity and Performance of the Student Population at Victoria University: A Preliminary Analysis". Monograph. June. http://vuir.vu.edu.au/4815/.

Nelson, Karen J., Sally M. Kift, Tracy A. Creagh, and Carole Quinn. 2007. "Teamwork Protocol - First Year in Higher Education - Queensland." http://eprints.qut. edu.au/42084/.

Nelson, Karen J., and Sally M. Kift. 2005. "Beyond Curriculum Reform: Embedding the Transition Experience." Edited by A Brew and C. Asmar. *HERDSA* (July 3).

Nelson, Karen J., and Tracy A. Creagh. 2013. "A Good Practice Guide: Safeguarding Student Learning Engagement". Brisbane, Australia: Queensland University of Technology. http://safeguardingstudent learning.net/wp-content/uploads/2012/04/LTU_Good-practice-guide_eBook_20130320.pdf.

Nelson, Karen J., Sally M. Kift, and John A. Clarke. 2012. "A Transition Pedagogy for Student Engagement and First-Year Learning, Success and Retention." In *Engaging with Learning in Higher Education*, edited by Ian Solomonides, Anna Reid, and Peter Petocz. Libri. http://www.libripublishing.co.uk/index.php?main_age=product_book _info&cPath=&products_id=116.

Nelson, Karen J., Sally. M. Kift, Julia K. Humphreys, and Wendy. E. Harper. 2006. "A Blueprint for Enhanced Transition: Taking an Holistic Approach to Managing Student Transition into a Large University." In Proceedings ASCILITE 2005, pages pp. 509-517, QUT, Brisbane, Queensland. http://eprints.qut. edu.au/3943.

Nicol, David. 2009. "Quality Enhancement Themes: The First Year Experience: Transforming Assessment and Feedback: Enhancing Integration and Empowerment in the First Year." http://dera.ioe.ac.uk/11605/1/First_ Year_Transforming_Assess.pdf.

Pascarella, Ernest. T. 2006. "How College Affects Students: Ten Directions for Future Research." *Journal of College Student Development* 47 (5): 508–520.

Prebble, Tom, Helen Hargraves, Linda Leach, Kogi Naidoo, Gordon Suddaby and Nick Zepke. 2004. "Impact of Student Support Services and Academic Development Programmes on Student Outcomes in Undergraduate Tertiary Study: A Synthesis of the Research" Ministry of Education, New Zealand. http://www.educationcounts.govt.nz/ publications/tertiary_education/5519.

Queensland University of Technology. 2009. "QUT | Learning and Teaching Unit | Learning and Teaching Protocols and Guidelines." http://www.ltu. qut.edu.au/curriculum/protocols.jsp.

—. "Student Success Program Boosts Retention Rates." 2012. *Queensland University of Technology*. April 27. http://files.eric.ed.gov/fulltext/ EJ797562.pdf.

Seidman, A. 2005. *College Student Retention: Formula for Student Success*. Westport CT: American Council on Education, Praeger Publishers.

Sharrock, Geoff. 2013. "Students Aren't Customers…or Are They?" *The Conversation*. May 9. http://theconversation.com/students-arent-customers -or-are-they-13282.

Silburn, Jenny, and Geraldine Box. 2008. "Travelling against the Current: An Examination of Upstream and Downstream Educational Interventions across the Life Span." *Australian Journal of Adult Learning* 48 (1): 9–29.

Sloan, Judith. 2013. "Demand-Driven Uni Places Lower Quality Standards." *The Australian*, November 23. http://www.theaustralian.com.au/opinion/ columnists/demand-driven-uni-places-lower-quality-standards/story-fnbkvnk7-1226766298725.

The Boyer Commission on Educating Undergraduates in the Research University. 1998. "Reinventing Undergraduate Education: A Blueprint for America's Research Universities."

Tinto, Vincent, and Cathy Engstrom. 2008. "Access Without Support Is Not Opportunity." *Change: The Magazine of Higher Learning* 40 (1) (January 1): 46–50. doi:10.3200/CHNG.40.1.46-50.

Tinto, Vincent, and Brian Pusser. 2006. "Moving from Theory to Action: Building a Model of Institutional Action for Student Success." *National Postsecondary Education Cooperative*: 01–57.

Trounson, Andrew. 2011. "Lesson in Retention." *The Australian, Higher Education Supplement*, July 14. http://www.theaustralian.com.au/higher-education/lesson-in-retention/story-e6frgcjx-1226093338370.

Troxel, Wendy G., and Marc Cutright. 2008. *Exploring the Evidence: Initiatives in the First College Year*. National Resource Center for the First-Year Experience & Students in Transition, University of South Carolina. Accessed from http://aacu-secure.nisgroup.com/meetings /hips/docu ments/NRCCaseStudy_GeorgiaState.pdf.

Van Olsen, Peter. 2013. "Yes Minister, There Is a Crisis in Higher Education." *The Australian*, March 2. http://www.theaustralian.com.au/opinion/yes-minister-there-is-a-crisis-in-higher-education/story-e6frg6zo-122658853 2000.

Whittaker, R. 2008. "Quality Enhancement Themes: The First Year Experience: Transition to and during the First Year." http://dera.ioe.ac.uk/11595/1/transition-to-and-during-the-first-year-.pdf.

Yorke, Mantz, and Bernard Longden. 2004. *Retention & Student Success in Higher Education*. 1st ed. Maidenhead, UK: SRHE and Open University Press.

Young. 2012. "Australian Universities on the Cusp of Profound Change: Ernst & Young Report - Ernst & Young - Australia." October 24. http://www.ey.com/AU/en/Newsroom/News-releases/Australian-universities-on-the-cusp-of-profound-change---Ernst-and-Young-report.

Zipin, Lew, and Marie Brennan. 2003. "The Suppression of Ethical Dispositions through Managerial Governmentality: A Habitus Crisis in Australian Higher Education." *Int. J. Leadership in Education* 6 (4): 351–370.

Chapter Two

Getting to Know Our Students Better Through a Mixed-Methods Case Study of Their First-Year Experiences

Andrew Funston

Introduction

I was very anxious, very anxious about university, because you know finding your way around, and everything. I don't really know the area well or anything. All the information I was trying to absorb, WebCT and everything, and all the facilities. But I'm not finding it too hard now. I'm pretty settled in. [Lilly, female, age 20]

This chapter draws on my doctoral study and some ongoing investigations of the first-year experiences of humanities students at Victoria University (Funston 2011, 2012). My research connects to my role as a course coordinator in the College of Arts, and my involvement for several years in a foundation core unit as well as in a third-year graduating project unit. I get to see at close range the extraordinary progress made by most of our students over the course of their degree studies. They grow in confidence and acquire new disciplinary knowledge and advanced skills. They take satisfaction and pleasure from belonging to a learning community in which they become knowledge producers. They expand their social and professional networks. However, most students face some challenges on campus and off campus which impact on their higher- education transitions. In this chapter I want to make some of those challenges more visible. I also want to make visible some of the knowledge, experiences and insights our students bring to the university. I do this by drawing extensively on what a cohort of students had to say about some of these matters. I relate this to some current scholarship in this field and to various retention and transition strategies at Victoria University featured elsewhere in this book. I begin the chapter by introducing some concepts and useful literature.

Some Scholarly Debates

Sally Kift (2009) in her final report as an Australian Learning and Teaching Council (ALTC) senior fellow responds to an observation by American transitions expert Vincent Tinto that "substantial gains in student retention have been hard to come by" (1).[1] She argues that solutions lie in "a third generation... whole-of-institution" approach. Kift advocates "transition pedagogy" which should be guided by "intentional first-year curriculum design and support that carefully scaffolds and mediates the first-year learning experience for contemporary heterogeneous cohorts". She also emphasises the need for "cross-institutional partnerships between academic and professional staff."

Marcia Devlin *et al.* (2012) speak of the additional needs of students from low socioeconomic backgrounds. They link this to calls for more "inclusive curriculum". Devlin (2013) has expanded the conversation by asking us to unpack the sociocultural incongruities embedded in "unspoken requirements" and our institutions' untested conceptions of "the student role". Our book demonstrates how much we support the concepts and practice of intentional and inclusive curriculum, partnerships, and greater reflexivity about what we do at Victoria University.

I feel we also need to engage more with non-academic and off-campus challenges impacting on students' educational experiences, and to do that we need to know our diverse student cohorts better, especially our "non-traditional" or traditionally under-represented students, of whom Victoria University has a larger share than the still-official target of 20 percent by 2020. To do this we need to look both near and far.

Pierre Bourdieu and other scholars who build on his ideas alert us to the significance of social and cultural capital, and habitus or disposition. As Stephen Ball (2006) explains it, this is not class simply as a category of social position, but rather class as positioning, class as something that "gets done" (to quote Bourdieu). Diane Reay (2001) describes how many of the working-class students she interviewed have "deeply problematic and emotionally charged" relationships to education. Lyn Tett (2000) investigates women in Scotland who felt that university is "for other people", and that those who did attempt it were often required to make all sorts of psychological adjustments or accommodations. Wolfgang Lehmann (2009) described transitions for many working-class students as "elusive and fraught with uncertainty".

Trevor Gale and Stephen Parker (2011) argue that Australian policy makers, researchers and practitioners often fail to appreciate "students' lived reality" (36). They recommend we inform ourselves about "the extensive research literature on youth and life transitions and from education and social theory" (35). A good example for my purposes in this book is research undertaken in the United Kingdom by Diane Reay, Miriam David and Stephen Ball (2005), who expose the very circumscribed "choices" actually available to working-class men and women. They argue that traditionally under-represented students find it more difficult to access elite courses and professional training and are more likely to be channelled into vocational courses at under-resourced institutions.

Tom Woodin and Penny Jane Burke (2007) also draw on Bourdieu and Reay to remind us that non-traditional students' relationship with education is "never purely rational but involves complex psychic processes in which emotion, intuition and accident play a significant part... intertwined with wider social and institutional forces... through and against class, ethnic and gender relations and also at the micro-level, with family and peers... " (120).

Educators should be mindful of this interplay of students' capacities, dispositions, and the impacts of larger social forces and changes on our students. Youth sociologist Andy Furlong (2009) does just that when he calls on educators to consider more closely economically-driven changes in the patterns of dependency, which requires a re-think about "youth" and "adulthood":

> Young people spend a greater proportion of their lives in education, increasingly entering higher education, and entering forms of employment that are very different to those experienced by their parents. Transitions take longer to accomplish, they are less likely to involve linear movement from education to work and independent living with "backtracking" and mixing of statuses that were once distinct become even more common. (1)

In Australia similar patterns have been observed. Johanna Wyn and Dan Woodman (2007) have used the concept of "social generation" taken from Karl Mannheim (1952) to foreground social *continuities and change* when researching youth transitions in this country. Their work with the Australian Youth Research Centre Life-Patterns program at the University of Melbourne—now in its 17th year—has involved the careful tracking of young people's adjustments to difficult times. They make visible the mixed benefits of education in tight labour markets, and the pressures on young people to "make your own choices" in conditions of growing uncertainty:

> Even the highly qualified are entering into a radically restructured labour market in which greater flexibility and contingency are at play, and for whom a dilemma arises because the meaning of career has changed... a general trend towards lower-skilled jobs for both young men and women.[2]

German sociologist Andreas Walther (2006), in describing the significant differences in the way European nations intervene to provide young people with degrees of choice, flexibility and security, speaks of the "de-standardisation" of youth transitions and how they vary considerably from one country to the next. Dan Woodman (2010, 2012) identifies in Australia a particular pattern, the "*desynchronisation* of everyday life" or "life out of synch" affecting young people's relationships. He argues that in recent years many young people have suffered an erosion of sociality or capacity to sustain mutually supportive friendships because of the combination of study timetables with variable and precarious casual paid work, making it challenging for groups of friends to get together for shared time (135).

This is very relevant to the lives of our diverse students at Victoria University. Many of the study participants spoke of difficulties they encountered juggling their studies with paid work, family responsibilities and social interests. Less apparent in our students' narratives was the sort of disabling dispositions or habitus that Diane Reay and others speak about. I took that as a sign that our institution is probably doing a few things right with our intentional and inclusive transition strategies, several of them discussed in this book.

The Case Study

The 2009–11 doctoral study I report on here had several components. I analysed a large first-year cohort's academic results, and patterns of re-enrolment/retention and attrition. In 2009 I twice surveyed these commencing humanities and social science students (n. 470) who were all enrolled in a compulsory foundations subject/unit called Knowing and Knowledge, discussed elsewhere in this book by its current coordinator Brian Zammit (chapter four).

I sought information about the students' social and educational backgrounds, their career aspirations and their expectations about the course. Later in the first year I sought additional information from them about their first-year experiences. I also undertook semi-structured interviews with 33 of these students early in the academic year, and re-interviewed 20 of them later that year. Ten of these students are participating in a longitudinal study in which I am investigating non-linear life-course transitions and focusing on their employment, community engagement and any further participation in formal education and training.

My research method—informed by narrative inquiry and critical social psychology—includes collaborating with interviewees to produce highly reflexive biographical narratives about education in their lives. I attempt to link these narratives to larger social changes, including the shift from elite to mass participation in higher education in Australia and this generation of young people's less-linear life-course transitions as identified by the youth sociologist referred to earlier.

Non-traditional students, many arriving with low entrance scores

The students who participated in my case study were drawn from several different humanities and social science degrees and typically had Australian Tertiary Admission Rank scores (ATARs) in the 50–60 range which indicates comparatively low levels of preparedness for degree-level studies and heightened risk of discontinuing a course. In keeping with enrolment patterns in humanities courses in Australia, around 70 percent of the study cohort was female. Less typical of Australian university students, only 60 percent were straight from school. Around 80 percent were still living in the natal-family home. In around 35 percent of those homes, languages other than English are spoken. By the end of the first year around half of the survey cohort (n. 470) were receiving a means-tested government youth allowance, which was not surprising for Victoria University where around 22 percent of all domestic students come from the bottom quartile (based on household postcode).[3]

Full-time students with part-time jobs

Less than 10 percent of the cohort was studying part-time. Around 60 percent were doing paid work, with 40 percent working more than 10 hours per week and 20 percent working more than 20 hours per week even while attempting to study full-time. Because the surveys were anonymous it was not possible to track whether the hours of paid work during term time correlated with academic failure. In keeping with these figures the interview narratives suggest that paid work was putting considerable pressure on some of these students, which we discuss later in this chapter.

Some of the young women I interviewed described their challenging "triple shift" of study, paid work and onerous home duties which typically involved caring for younger siblings or supporting their working parents, sometimes financially.

Challenged and satisfied with their first-year experiences

Most of these first-year humanities and social science students rated their first year at Victoria University highly in the study's anonymous survey (42 percent said it was good, 25 percent said very good, 10 percent said excellent), with the course meeting expectations for 63 percent and exceeding expectations for 28 percent, and with most students performing as well or better academically than they had expected. Seventy-six percent felt they have gained significant new knowledge and skills.

These survey results align with the findings reported by Richard James, Kerri Lee Krause and Claire Jennings (2010) in *The First Year Experience in Australian Universities from 1994 to 2009*. The authors provided a fairly up-beat account of the national picture, while distinguishing different retention patterns for different population groups, regions and different types of universities. They described the 2009 students as being "more organised, pragmatic and focused than their 2004 counterparts" with school leavers reporting "an easier transition to university" (1).

Student attrition, a persistent problem with multiple causes

Attrition figures remain persistently high for some sub-cohorts (discussed later) although the situation has improved in the past two years. Around 25 percent of these first-year students had not re-enrolled in their course in the second year. The study was not able to track where departing students went, although the capacity to track student mobility has improved in Australia in the last few years. We can assume—from the Life Patterns longitudinal study and other recent reports tracking student mobility—that some of the departing students would have changed courses, or changed institutions, and others would have returned after a few year's break from study, and this was the case for several of the students interviewed for this study.

Most perplexing, a significant minority of these discontinuing students had passed all or most of their first-year subjects/units. People discontinue their courses for a range of reasons. Joan Abbott-Chapman (2011), in describing the complexity of achieving equity goals in higher education refers to the "mosaic" reality of students' experiences, and the "multiplicity of non-linear pathways" and the highly circumscribed "choices" (57) faced by many. She also argues that we need "to acknowledge and work with the complex realities of disadvantaged students' situations, starting at the school level" (57). I return to the issue of persistent attrition later in this chapter.

What becomes apparent, as I review my doctoral study and draw on some recent interviews with students, is just how hard it is for some of our students to take advantage of the full range of co-curricular supports on offer. Often students' only time spent on campus is for classes or when they are undertaking group work in the library. This makes curriculum and course design and the partnerships between academic and specialist support staff even more crucial.

Listening to Students' Stories

I turn now to my case-study interviews. I should preface this by mentioning that students helped me edit their transcripts and they were encouraged to make any changes or additions to their narratives before approving or refusing my use of their stories. They provided pseudonyms, and some additional minor changes have been made to protect privacy. Students were provided in advance of the semi-structured interviews some questions and topics. They were also provided with the name and contact details for the university counselling service in case the interview unsettled or distressed them. All the students were studying full-time, unless otherwise indicated. The students' course, their sex and age are all indicated.

Supportive families

The questions invited biographical reflexivity. I started by asking the student "How have you come to be at university? What has been your journey to university?" Most began by talking about their families, with many referring to their parents' lack of educational opportunities.

Lachlan (male, age 18) was commencing a Bachelor of Creative Arts Industries degree. He was living with his parents and a younger sister in the outer suburbs, and like several other interviewees he was travelling a long distance to attend university (most Australian university students do not live in campus halls-of-residence). Lachlan's father is a plumber and his mother, who trained as a bookkeeper, helps in the business. He explained why he decided to come to university:

So neither of them had been to university, so that kind of pushed me in a way to try and see what it would be like and get that further level of education. And they really were behind me as well to try to get into it. In regards to what I wanted to do, I didn't really know at the time, so I've kind of just gone with my interests here now. So, yeah, it was always something I wanted to do, just because my parents never really had the opportunities to go on to do it.

Lachlan had decided not to follow his father into one of the building trades, possibly carpentry, and while he felt that both of his parents were pleased he was studying, his father made it clear to Lachlan that if university doesn't work out one of his father's mates will be ready and willing to offer him an apprenticeship.

We see something similar with Tyler (male, age 18) who was commencing a Bachelor of Arts. He came from a poor rural town several hours' bus trip away from Melbourne, where his parents worked in local shops. He returned home some weekends to see the family and play in the football team his father had coached for many years:

Well, Mum was really happy when I got into the course, and she was planning everything for me like getting bags and more clothes for me, and checking stuff up and everything like that. And Dad, he didn't really care. That's just what he's like. Mum would cry every time I leave to go [to Melbourne], and run out and hug me every time I got home.

We see in several of the interviews parents who recognise the importance of their children becoming more educated than themselves. Sarah (female, age 18) who was commencing a Bachelor of Arts degree was living three days of the week with her mother and younger sisters some distance from the university and other days with her father and step-brothers closer to campus. At several points in her narrative she referred to her parents' difficult lives:

They didn't go to uni and they always wanted me to go to uni because I guess they kind of knew what happens if you don't.

For some of the older commencing students the narratives provide a window to an earlier period where higher education was much less accessible or imaginable for people from working-class backgrounds. Irene (female, age 52) who was commencing a Bachelor of Arts degree reminisces on the bewilderment she felt at the time she dropped out of school:

At the time I learnt to skip classes, but I was still totally surprised when I failed, totally surprised. You feel like you've slipped. Why didn't somebody tell my parents at that time that this was happening?

Irene's delayed journey to university reminds me of Bourdieu's concepts of cultural and social capital and, for those less privileged, a disabling habitus or disposition. Reay (2001) refers to the blocks and discouragements experienced by many working-class women in the United Kingdom. Tett (2000) similarly refers to the influence of "familial and community habitus" producing an "expectation that higher education was for other people". Irene explained it this way:

I see the class dimension as being why my parents never pushed me towards university. I have three younger brothers, so growing up in a family with three boys it was expected that the boys would do trades. It wasn't something that was expected, to go on to uni. You were expected to get out there and go to work.

Most of the younger students in this study benefitted from having parents who aspired for their children to take up the educational opportunities they did not have. In multi-cultural Australia this often connects to a family's migration story. Rajani (male, age 18) was commencing a Bachelor of Arts degree. He was living with his family several hours' train travel from the university, and was working in a factory three days a week. His parents had only limited school education in Sri Lanka, and when he was a boy the family came to Australia as refugees:

That's one of the main reasons, since I was very young, always telling me to go to university because they don't want me to suffer the way they did, like they find it hard, like they are actually labourers now, so they are working in factories and they are working very hard.

We see in some of these narratives a good deal of pressure on the students, and sometimes we see hints of family members not appreciating how difficult the educational journey might be for their children. Holly (female, age 19) referred several times to her supportive parents who had very little education before they migrated to Australia from Sardinia:

From a young age they thought I was smart, and they were kind of pressuring me, saying "you're going to be a lawyer, you're going to be a doctor", and whenever I'd say "Oh, no it's too hard" they'd say, "No, you've got to try for that, you're going to be a lawyer". My grandparents think it's amazing that I'm at university. And now like every day they say to me, "What did you do? What are you learning?"

Most of the students felt this high level of support and encouragement from their families. Madeline (female, age 18) was commencing (full-time) a Bachelor of Arts degree. Her parents were refugees from Vietnam, and their education was interrupted because of the war and fleeing their homeland by boat. She felt that contributed to their aspirations for her but she emphasised that most of all they wanted her to be happy:

> Like they said to me, if I go to uni, that's my choice, if I take up TAFE, or get a full-time job, it doesn't matter what I do as long as I'm happy. They just personally wanted me to finish Year 12. They weren't given as many opportunities as I am now. I have cousins who have taken Law and some of them hate it and they don't want me to do that, so it's whatever makes me happy.

Experienced and insightful students

Our students commence university with vast and varied experiences and knowledge, often anchored in communities and not usually visible or necessarily appreciated by university staff or fellow students. While 60 percent of the cohort was not straight from school it was not only the older students who had extraordinary experiences to share. Four weeks into his first year of a Bachelor of Creative Arts Industries Lachlan (male, age 18) spoke to me about his "gap year" after completing Year 12. He worked in a variety of jobs to save money for an overseas trip. After travelling around Europe he went to South America—a trip connected to his volunteer work in Australia—and this seems to have seeded an interest in using his degree as possibly a stepping stone to a career in education:

> Yeah, I was based in Peru for five months, in the capital city of Lima, and I did a term-and-a-half in a primary school, ranging from PE to Maths and Science at a campus up the Amazon, which was pretty crazy... I'd never contemplated becoming a teacher before but possibly at the end of this Creative Arts degree I'd go and do a Diploma of Education and get that extra qualification that I'd never considered before going over there.

Lachlan described his "constant desire to know, to keep learning" and spoke about his role on the youth committee of a major non-government organisation. He was keen to share some of his organising skills and overseas experiences with his fellow students.

Winston (male, age 18) who was a keen photographer—a source of income for him—had lived in Japan through a school exchange. That attracted him to the Bachelor of Arts course. It also seeded his love of the language and his decision to take up Japanese at university (no longer taught at Victoria University unfortunately). He hoped to spend some time on exchange to Japan during his degree and later get a teaching job there. He connected this longer-term plan to acquiring a stylish personal identity:

> In 20 years I hope to still be in Japan. Only I hope my wardrobe will be packed. I will have dyed my hair and you know eventually I want to end up like one of the teachers with skinny black jeans, dark blue shirt, hair like Andy Warhol, ageing disgracefully.

Lilly (female, age 20) another Bachelor of Arts student, spoke of the benefit of coming to Melbourne to university to escape "small town attitudes" and her social group who she saw as already stuck in early marriages and child-rearing. She described her love of basketball and anticipated a career in sports psychology:

> I was really looking for a job that was flexible, and one I was interested in obviously, and one where I could travel around the world. Because I like basketball so much I'd want to get into the professional circuit and hopefully go around the world with the professional teams.

Emmet (male, age 19) was passionate about his band (already getting gigs), which he wants to keep "non-commercial and political". He spoke of the role that music plays in bringing about social change, and referred to bands including The Clash. When I asked what he'd like to be doing in five years, he said "partying in Istanbul with the band", but went on to explain what he meant by that:

> Oh, that was just me crapping on, I don't actually think I'll be in Istanbul, it's more just symbolic. I want to be somewhere, and part of something bigger than myself, doing something with actual purpose and meaning.

This sort of idealism was apparent in several of the narratives. Madeline (female, age 18), whose parents had been refugees from Vietnam and who was studying Vietnamese at university, described her growing interest in food-security issues and was thinking about a job with UNICEF. Natasha (female, age 18) had a similar interest in international development, with a human-rights focus:

I've never been interested in just ordinary jobs. That's not me, and I prefer
something hard and difficult, and something that will make me a stronger
person. Everyone always says they want world peace and stuff, and that's
not going to happen for a while, if at all, so if I can be of benefit to some
people then that's cool. I like the difficult stuff.

Sasha (female, age 19) was commencing a Bachelor of Arts degree.
She had taken a gap year after completing her Year 12 VCE. Her family
had migrated to Australia from South Sudan. She spoke at length about her
leadership role in a Sudanese youth organisation, and her efforts to "speak
up" against the vilifications of the Melbourne's Sudanese community in
the conservative media (encouraged by several racist politicians). Through
the course of the interview it emerged that Sasha, who speaks four
languages, was also a semi-professional singer, and used her singing in her
advocacy work:

Well, through my music I just want people to recognise the world and how
things are. They should open up and see the rest of the world, and see how
some other countries in Africa aren't managing very well, and try to do
something to help. You can't just sit back and expect someone else to do
the job. Everyone has a stake in it. I will go back there and try to make a
change. I have experiences and I have ideas from being here in Australia
which I can take back home and use.

Complex aspirations

We see in these narratives some exemplary aspirations. Sam Sellar, Trevor
Gale and Stephen Parker (2011) describe aspirations as complex and
under-appreciated in this research field, especially with regard to the
arrival of students "who traditionally have not seen university as
contributing to their imagined and desired futures" (37). They describe
institutions as "failing to appreciate the aspirations of different groups,
understood as a collective cultural capacity" (37). They draw on Arjun
Appadurai's concept of global cultural economies ("ethnoscapes") with
their "large-scale, imagined life possibilities" and the power these social
imaginaries can exercise over localised or "specific life trajectories". I
think that is what we glimpse in the preceding quotes from students like
Sasha and Lachlan. Gale and Parker (2011) call for radical transformations
of curriculum directed at capacity-building not as an end in itself but as a
way of harnessing aspirations and "creating public spaces for debates
about how the imagined worlds, or desired ends, of different groups can be
resourced and realised *through* education" (48):

Where studies of students' educational and occupational aspirations have previously paid close attention to the particularities of family, peer and local community contexts... we must now account for the emergence of aspirations at the intersection of these influences <u>and</u> other influences, which are mediated through social and media networks and open up broader horizons for the formations of identities, communities and life projects.

Students were not asked in the interviews any direct questions about their political beliefs or activities on campus or off campus, but several of the narratives did convey political engagement and an interest in citizenship and participatory democracy, and it is here where we also appreciate their varied and complex aspirations. The quotes which follow were taken from interviews with students who had been at university for less than one month. These ideas were brought *to* the university. Joe (male, age 18) talked about engaging with social movements:

I am already politically engaged. I'm just a big fan of positive change, any change that's positive for the planet and humanity. You've got to sort of take on the conformism that's associated with my generation and the generation just before us. It's the media that pretty much gives that to us. You've got to hijack that [the media] and use it to change the face of the earth.

Jeff (male, age 21) reflected on his parents' harsh working lives, and his own experience working in the family's take-away food business. He used the interview to protest how "some people are really working hard, struggling, and not getting the money for their very hard work". Emmet (male, age 19) spoke of the "economic crisis" and the conservative media's coverage of unemployment issues. His father was struggling financially and Emmet expressed concern about talk of tighter eligibility tests for the dole or youth allowance. He hoped that one unintended consequence of crisis might be a wider public understanding that there simply were not enough jobs to go around:

I think this economic crisis is going to strengthen the welfare state, because with more people unemployed there will be a realisation that we just can't be treating unemployed people like crap. They sort of screw you around for a bit when you go to Work for the Dole but the fact is there aren't enough jobs for everyone to go around.

Several of the female students spoke of the need for social transformation around education opportunities for women and girls. Tess (female, age 24) who was working as a disability support person while studying full-time was supporting campaigns for improving education opportunities in developing nations:

> You educate a girl and her whole family is going to benefit. I think with education comes knowledge and power, and if you're not ignorant to something, if you're not ignorant of being taken advantage of, or having your rights taken away from you at work, then you have the ability to stand up for that. I don't think you can really function to your potential without that knowledge which comes with education.

Nada (female, age 21) also related to this issue, explaining how she was the first female in her extended family to be educated beyond primary-school level, and how in Afghanistan her mother had no access to formal education:

> Well, comparing me to my Mum, life is very different. She's told me I'm "one of the luckiest girls" right now, being able to go to university, have the freedom that I have, living in a country like Australia, not having the pressures that are on my family overseas, not have all that responsibility. She got married at a young age, by my age she had me and my brother.

Dealing with earlier school failures

I turn now to the challenges facing some of our non-traditional students, and begin by describing the legacy of unhappy schooling and earlier failures which several of the students reflected on. This should not be surprising, given that many of our students arrived with low university entrance scores, or were selected by other means into different courses (some on special pathways from further education into higher education).

Jayden (male, age 28) was commencing a Bachelor of Arts. He describes being miserable at high school, which he left after failing Year 10. I mention here that Jayden went on to get excellent academic results for every subject he studied at Victoria University and used his good results to apply successfully for his preferred course at a more prestigious university in Melbourne (this sort of mobility is quite common, and contributes to attrition). I report here on how Jayden was feeling when I interview him in the third week of his first semester at Victoria University:

> I was pretty nervous to be honest, because like I said I didn't do a Year 11 or Year 12, and I'd failed consistently through high school, and so it goes to one of the questions here. My biggest difficulty at university, my biggest fear, is academic writing. I'm really used to reading about subjects, and

used to talking to people about things, but structuring written works in a way that is acceptable at university is quite difficult for me.

Winston (male, age 18) also recalled some hard times at school, "basically through Year 7 to Year 11 I was in a coma, just following people around, not really interacting on a genuine front", and he had been traumatised by a broken-off relationship. He connected his current feelings about his parents not being sufficiently supportive with his unhappy time at school:

> Material support is important but there are times when I need emotional support, like I've just come back from a shit day [at university] and I just collapse on the couch, and they kick you off because *Underbelly* [a popular television series] is about to start, and you know, well if I say "I've had a shit day" it's very hard to get the emotional support you need.

Critical social psychologist Stephanie Taylor (2006) discusses how coherence is something worked at in our biographical narratives, and she links her notion that "trouble prompts repair" in life stories to Michael White's (2007) ideas about the power of re-storying, which is very relevant in non-traditional students' educational transitions.

Pedro (male, age 38) was commencing a combined Diploma of Liberal Arts/Bachelor of Arts degree; one of the university's pathways for non-traditional students. His schooling commenced in New Zealand and continued in Australia somewhat unhappily after migration and his parents' separation. He left school early and at the time of our first interview was working several days a week in a warehouse while helping to raise his young child. Pedro, knowing he was clever but someone who refused schooling for family reasons, was determined, now aged 38, to "finally give education a right royal go".

Loneliness on campus

Trevor Hussey and Patrick Smith (2010) talk about transition as a time of "large complex transformations" (156). For several interviewees, commencing university marked a sort of social dislocation, where old friendships were hard to sustain. Veronica (female, age 18) was commencing a Bachelor of Arts and spoke rather sadly about not keeping up with old friends from school (reminding me of Dan Woodman's thesis about fraying sociality):

> My other best friend, I haven't seen her in a long time either, because again like timetables and she's busy with her boyfriend, and I'm just, we keep

contact occasionally. We used to see each other every day, and we would just hang out, and we had all the same classes at school. And now, you know, things come in the way.

Nanette Evans Commander and Teresa Ward (2009), in their study of successful freshman learning communities at Georgia State University in the US, suggest that if people feel socially included and comfortable they are more likely to engage successfully with teaching and learning, and are more likely to become effective independent learners who also contribute to the learning of others, and they are less likely to leave university. Vincent Tinto makes a similar point about the social dimension of learning communities. For most students, commencing university marked their arrival at a physical and social environment very different from their secondary schools. Several students spoke of their initial disorientation:

> Yeah, it's very daunting because even from primary school I've always been surrounded by this group of friends, and going from primary school to high school I still had my old friends, but here I have, like, no one, so it's been sort of daunting for me, having no one here but I'm always eager to make new friends. [Jane, female, age 20]

Several students recalled in the interview their emotional state in those first few days and weeks at university, and the issue of physical disorientation in the built environment often arises. Holly (female, age 18) spoke of her initial spatial disorientation in the same breath as describing a more academic disorientation, and later links this to the topic of loneliness: "you'd not know what to do, and it seemed that everyone knows someone, so there were all these little groups, and I didn't know what to do". Holly found the breaks between classes excruciating:

> Today I have a two-hour break, and then a one-hour break, so I didn't know what to do, and then on Wednesday it was even worse, I had a three-hour gap, and a two-hour gap, and I found it really hard when I had my breaks. I didn't know what to do.

Another student who sounded quite disconsolate was Emmet (male, age 19) who was commencing a Bachelor of Arts degree. He described the difficulty of making friendships and being disappointment with himself:

> It's one thing I've found disappointing in myself, because I have this, I think I want to live by my example, when I'm hanging around and don't know people I want to go up to them and say "hey we're alive in the same place at the same time, let's connect".

Friendships on campus

Clearly, successful higher education transitions are about more than students becoming comfortable with course content, teaching modes and academic discourses. Sheila Scutter, Denise Wood and Helen Wozniak (2011) investigated first-year student experiences and described how "91 percent of students felt that having friends studying at the same university would provide support, but 25 percent did not know anyone studying at the same university" (8). In my study the importance of early connections was underscored by Joe (male, age 18) who described his commencement in quite glowing terms:

> When I first arrived I made about a fistful of friends and most of those people I still talk to, like pretty regularly, and hang around with now. I loved my first few weeks. I can sustain this, I'm very happy here.

Bernard (male, age 18) was commencing a Bachelor of Creative Arts Industries degree and found it heavy going in the first few weeks on campus until he established a social network. He had come to Melbourne to study from a rural district where he lived with his parents and sisters on the family wheat farm and was living in a student hostel. Bernard had suffered bouts of depression during his school years and expressed great relief at having found a social group at university:

> I found that it's really good if you can force yourself to introduce yourself to people you are sitting next to in the lecture. I don't know how it happened but I've got a really good group of friends now.

This sense of forcing oneself to reach out was common in several narratives. Winston (male, 18) suggested in our interview that the university could do more, including some big "gig for first years" like the "night on the town" some friends at another university had enjoyed. He described, with black humour, one approach that had worked to start up conversations with strangers on campus:

> I found that my being a smoker actually helps me to a degree because eventually you run out and you've got to ask someone for a smoke and you talk to them, and someone wants a light, and eventually you talk to them, and you find that they're in the same class as you. So in a way that helps me, but it will give me cancer.

Those students who for whatever reason made friends on campus soon after commencement seemed to benefit greatly from this, and this confirms my sense that the university should continue to invest in the social aspects of transition. Jeff (male, age 21) was commencing a Bachelor of Psychology. He described his new campus buddies as "really helpful, and I like to think that I am towards them as well":

> Like later today I'm showing my friend how to use databases and whatever because she found it a bit messy. I mean, in whatever way we can accommodate our friends and help them out, I am and a few others are more than willing to do so.

Becoming accustomed to lectures and tutorials

Marcia Devlin (2010) recognises that "achievement at university relies on sociocultural capabilities relevant to the specific context of university study" (6). She refers to Margolis's *et al.* (2001) work on the "reservoir of cultural and social resources and familiarity" enjoyed by some but not all students, making the hidden curriculum "particularly difficult for them" (5). Devlin also refers to work by Christie *et al.* (2008) who advise that "a lack of knowledge about university practice can hinder learning" (2). Rajani (male, age 18) found his first weeks particularly difficult and in part this was because of his uncertainty about the role he was expected to play in lectures:

> It was pretty hard to be honest. Like just waking up and then catching public transport here, and then you go to the lectures and then you don't know what to do. Like, you're sitting down and you're taking notes but you don't even know you're taking the right notes, and some lecturers they just go on and on and on so fast.

Lilly (female, age 20) preferred tutorials, although she found it difficult to contribute in larger groups and especially if the more confident or loquacious students were allowed to dominate:

> I wonder if I should say something now, or if I'll sound stupid... I hold back then feel annoyed and think can't you give someone else a go? I think it's up to the tutor to single out people if that's what she needs to do. Not an enforced sharing but if she already knows that someone has good opinions in the past but they don't say things that often, then why not say to them "What do you think?", and shutting those loud people out, just for five minutes.

Dina (female, age 21) described a particular problem she had with one of her tutorials where she felt there was too much unstructured conversation, allowing people to vent in ways she felt inappropriate:

> It's supposed to be about diversity, and it's supposed to be about listening, and talking, and hearing what another person says and not just saying "no, no, no", and you get a lot of people that do that. Like there's a difference between a good argument and people just having a go at each other. But that's what I don't like about tutorials when they're not structured.

Other interviewees spoke of their anxiety about the tutorial dynamic. Nicole (female, age 18) said "half of the time I find it really difficult to say something, even if I'm thinking it and it's driving me insane that I want to say it" but she continues with her reflections and rather than seeing herself as the problem, locates it more collectively:

> Even if they are trying to get everyone to talk, for example in one tutorial I'm in the tutor is great, and he always asks lots of questions, but everyone is just so intimidated, not by him, but just of each other. They just sit there and it's like a long, awkward silence.

Overcoming writing and assessment anxieties

Lectures and tutorials are not the only sources of anxiety for many commencing students. The first assessment pieces loomed large in the student narratives. As we discuss in this book, acquiring a learning identity can be very problematic for some university students. Penny Jane Burke (2008) describes how disabling for non-traditional students certain academic writing practices can be, operating as "a form of regulation over access to higher education... tied to struggles over being recognised as a legitimate student" (199). She describes the way academic writing—with its specific but contested conventions—is often exclusionary and alienating:

> Students constructed as 'non-traditional' are caught up in the politics of knowledge and identity, and the literacy practices that are privileged are often unfamiliar and intimidating. This reinforces exclusionary forces, not only at the structural level, but also at the emotional level, in which students talk about "not being good enough". (204)

Devlin (2013) describes the particular challenges facing low-SES background students seeking to bridge "sociocultural incongruity" as they attempt to understand and master "the student role" with all its implicit understandings and expectations:

> Many students from low socioeconomic backgrounds do not know that these unspoken requirements exist, never mind that they must understand and then respond appropriately to them. This lack of tacit knowledge can hinder their success and achievement at university. (941)

For Holly (female, age 18) it felt like working in the dark even though unit guides and class discussion seemed to explain quite clearly what was required. While she was successful in her first assignment, and received helpful feedback from her tutor, it was the complexity of the task which she found daunting, especially when compared to the academic writing she had been doing at school:

> I really had no idea, it was Politics, an essay plan, so you had to do a plan obviously, and the whole referencing, that's another topic, but it's all different in every subject, and we never did that at school. I mean we did a bibliography, but now it's very detailed. And it was one of those, and I didn't know how to do the referencing, so I just made it up and then with my essay plan I had no idea what I was writing, and I handed it in. And I ended up getting a good result. So I surprised myself.

Ayla (female, age 21) was commencing a Bachelor of Psychology (Interpersonal and Organisational) and like several of these non-traditional students was returning to tertiary studies after an earlier unsuccessful attempt (in a different discipline). She felt more engaged by her new course. She was also more willing to seek help from the learning-support staff: "I've seen the lady and she always frees up an extra half-hour but I think sometimes I need even more than that [laughs] because there's so much to go through". Even with that support she was anxious at the time of our first interview about a looming assignment deadline:

> Formatting, structuring essays, putting it together, and it's a bit intimidating when you are trying to do that with large essays, and you think "I've got this much time" and the time keeps getting closer and closer and you haven't done it yet. I found that very difficult.

A lot depends of course on a student's motivation and capacity to manage their time. Erin (female, 44) described how she faced the challenge of her first assignment, which involved sourcing and referencing a peer-reviewed academic article, with a Sunday in the university library:

So I went to the Footscray campus on a Sunday and spent four hours there just playing with that [online databases and search engines], and I actually found my research articles [for the assignment]. So I felt much better after that. But, you know, that's OK, I'm feeling good, I am excited, I am enjoying both the lectures and the tutes. I'm finding them stimulating and they get me thinking. You know, that's what it's about.

Perils and necessity of paid work

My survey at the start of the academic year showed that 55 percent of these Victoria University students were in some paid work (keeping in mind that 92 percent of the cohort was studying full-time) and that figure rises to 64 percent in Survey 2. By late in the academic year of those students doing paid work 24 percent were working 6–10 hours per week, 23 percent doing 11–19 hours and 14 percent doing 20 hours or more. We know from earlier studies that many students have no option but to undertake these substantial hours of paid work.

Devlin *et al.* (2008) describe students' reliance on employment to "cover basics", and how 25 percent of students who do work have to miss class because of their job. They reported on a generally worsening situation since an earlier study on student finances undertaken in 2000. A study on student finances from the Centre for the Study of Higher Education at the University of Melbourne commissioned by the sector's peak body Universities Australia reported that students in 2012 were experiencing greater levels of financial distress than in 2006.[4]

With this understanding of the *patterns* of paid work and the *necessity* of paid work for many first-year university students in Australia, and perhaps keeping in mind that only 51 percent of the cohort were in receipt of the government Youth Allowance (Survey 2), then it is not surprising that the issue of paid work and income security looms large in this study.

Clearly, some students are "doing it tougher" than others, and are more anxious about access to paid work. A few of the interviewees were without regular part-time work and were living on very low incomes. Winston (male, age 18) was making some money from his photography, although admits that was up and down and was "getting by on about $130 a fortnight allowance from the government". That meant he had to continue living at home with his parents, which was a three-hour trip from the university. He said rather ruefully, "I barely have enough money to eat and smoke, that's basically it".

Bernard (male, age 18) was living in a hostel, having come to Melbourne to study. He was financially supported by his parents but they were struggling at the time of our interview. He mentioned his mother's illness and the impact of drought on their farm. They were selling off their dairy cows and using some of the money to pay for his hostel accommodation in Melbourne.

Hayriye (female, age 18) was commencing a Bachelor of Psychology degree. She was living with her parents who are factory workers and was helping the family out financially by working "12 hours a week in a fast-food outlet". She was grateful for the work because her employers were flexible. Not all of the interviewees with paid part-time work had employers who were. Sarah (female, age 18) was working in a fashion accessories shop. When she asked about changing her hours slightly to fit her class times the employer was reluctant:

> My manager is like on and off. She'll have her good days and then she'll have her bad days. So it just depends on when I tell her. Yeah, she's supportive of it one day then when it gets in the way of work she's not happy.

Many of the interviewees described the tedium as well as the insecurity surrounding their part-time jobs. Azra (female, age 18) was looking after her siblings while studying. Her father was recovering from a back operation. She struggled to earn money to supplement her government allowance, getting irregular hours in a local florist: "Personally, I'm looking for another job all the time. I want something with more hours".

For some of the interviewees, the paid hours they had been getting since school days were drying up as they turned 18 and went on to an adult wage. Nicole (female, age 18) was working in the fast-food industry but noticed that her hours had recently been reduced from around 15 hours a week to just six since she turned 18, "I'm guessing because my pay went up so much". She had left messages with her employer, asking for an increase in hours, "but he doesn't answer".

Joe (male, age 18) described his strategy for keeping his job after turning 18: "So I thought, you know what, I'm going to work my arse off, and I'm going to go above and beyond my call so they realise that I'm actually serious about this, and that I want more hours or retain the hours I've got". Even so, there were nervous moments for him and his co-workers:

> And so we were all kind of fretting about the fact that everyone is sort of holding on to their money and don't want to buy, they're going nowhere, they are just sitting on it, so we're thinking, "Oh no, we might all lose our jobs, the company might go under, and our store will be replaced by a hair salon".

Several students spoke of their anxiety about other family members losing their job. Jane (female, age 19), who had been working in retail before Christmas was waiting to be called back, and referred to the economic downturn and the likely impact on her job prospects, doubting "there will be opportunities for me to even get a job at that point in time". Twice in our interview she expressed her worry that her Dad might lose his job, "because nothing's safe these days".

Nada (female, age 21), another interviewee with a sick parent who like Azra was helping to care for siblings, was working in a fast-food outlet, "about 16 to 20 hours a week" while studying full-time. She also expressed anxiety about her father losing his job, "because we've still got the home to pay off", and believed that if that did happen "I would just stress out watching everybody stress and not being able to do anything."

Juggling competing demands

In many of the student narratives we see evidence of people experiencing hard lives, gruelling at times, juggling competing demands placed upon them as they seek to study at university. Tess (female, age 24) seems to take this in her stride: "I've been up since six o'clock, I've already done my morning shift, I've come back from work, and I've walked the dogs'. She describes it as "a maturity thing". And a similar sense of satisfaction with managing oneself is also apparent when Jane (female, age 19) describes how "I feel more like an adult now" as she organises her time:

> Oh yeah, definitely, yeah, I can sort it out—I have a boyfriend—I can sort out uni time then homework and then going to see friends or spending time with the boyfriend, or spending time with family. I can sort of orient myself around all my commitments.

However, not all of the students felt they had the right balance in their lives as they attempted to juggle a variety of demands. Women were often expected by their families to take on additional roles. Azra (female, age 18) was studying full-time, in paid work, and helping to look after her siblings and do other housework to help her sick father recovering from an operation. When I asked whether this "triple shift" of responsibilities was having an impact on her study she describe being sleep-deprived and over-stretched:

> Yeah, it does, especially it has an impact on my sleep, because I stay up late at night trying to finish it all... and he [her father] can't do much, can't lift anything, can't drive, so I take the kids to school, take them to soccer,

take them to their friends. It is really tiring but I'm kind of getting used to
it.

Some of the students seemed to be in quite a fragile emotional state.
Jeff (male, age 21) described being in an almost constant state of alert
thinking. Even breaks from study were not relaxing, it seems:

> When I'm at home and I'm finishing studies, or I'm having a break, my break
> isn't really a break because I might be watching a movie or I might be doing
> something, but I'm thinking, "Well I need to pay for this, I need it by then, I
> haven't seen these people in a while, they're my best friends or they're my
> cousins, or whatever, and I need to see them". You know things like that
> make you think.

Discovering an inclusive Learning Community

If some of our students were stretched and stressed by external forces in
their lives most of them took pleasure from their transition into a
supportive and inclusive learning community. Winston (male, age 18)
described the stimulating conversations in his Knowing and Knowledge
tutorials, and the "rapport, for want of a better word, which makes it easy
to interact with someone based on their arguments". Veronica (female, age
18) enjoyed "meeting heaps of new people" and especially her fellow
Creative Arts students who she describes as "all a little bit wacky like me"
and able to "see things from different perspectives, which is useful in the
community where you want to be able to see things from many
perspectives". Natasha (female, age 18) described the respectfulness she
encountered in her tutorials:

> Some people are loud, some people are quiet, but everyone is really
> respectful here. There's a boy in one of my classes with a speech disability
> and people are always respectful. There's an open feel, if you have
> something to say then you are not really restricted in saying it.

This idea of respect for people regardless of background or
ability/disability is something Victoria University promotes in policy-
driven and explicit ways, and issues such as homophobia, racism, sexism,
human rights and equal opportunity are embedded in the curriculum in
many of the academic units. Australia is a postcolonial country beset by
racism and gender inequalities and for Azra (female, age 18) being a
young woman with Turkish heritage and coming from a Muslim faith
community this produced additional transitions challenges. She had
completed her Year 12 VCE the previous year at a religious non-

government school. For the most part she has enjoyed the range of views she encounters in her classes:

> Ah, it's been a big change, like as I said my school was Turkish based... so like coming to uni there's so many different cultures and background and religions especially. Like as I said my school was based more on the Islamic religion but coming here everybody's different, especially your teachers and your tutors, they have their own views as well, and [you] get to hear their views.

However, managing other people's responses to her cultural identity was difficult for her. Against her father's wishes Azra chose not to wear the veil or scarf. She commented on the rise in racist attacks on Muslim women in Melbourne after "9/11", and referred also to the scrutiny wearing a veil brings to women on campus. She felt the university was fulfilling some important cultural obligations, such as providing prayer rooms and offering halal food in the cafeteria. On the other hand, she felt "discomfort" when certain matters were raised in lectures or in tutorials and readings and felt class discussions often produced stereotypes of people of Muslim faith:

> I must say that I have felt uncomfortable in some of the lectures and one of the tutorials we were talking about extremist Muslims. Like you see how Muslims are perceived, but you can't really stereotype all Muslims like that.

Encountering difference, reflecting on one's own prejudices or that of others, understanding the historical and sociological dimensions to one's own particular experiences and world views are what you might expect to encounter throughout one's education, and especially in a humanities degree at university. And for several of the interviewees that seems to have been the case, and seems to be part of their acquisition of a learner identity which may be contributing to their successful transitions.

Tyler (male, age 18) detected a lack of understanding about the challenges faced by students (like himself) coming to the city from rural districts. He thought his fellow students who had grown up in cosmopolitan Melbourne should be open to learning from rural students about their life experiences, and he gave his own poor, drought-stricken rural town as a suitable topic for a sociology class: "I can say there's no "class", like everyone is working class, struggling, so I can have that input". In essence, Tyler's reflexivity contributes to his sense of having something important to contribute to the collective knowledge of the tutorial group.

Penelope (female, age 18) described her encounter with classroom discussions about sexuality and sexual preference. And again we see in the narrative a degree of reflexivity where "identity work" seems to be going on. She seems to be examining her own childhood prejudices born of inexperience, and conveys a sense of having travelled some distance by acknowledging and accepting sexuality different to her own:

> Yeah, when you're in school you are more sheltered, and in uni you are on your own, and meeting different people and just realising the different kind of people that are out there. I've never had, like had interaction with a gay person. So that was kind of different for me, a good experience.

Expert views on attrition

The problem of high attrition from university courses receives a lot of mainstream media attention, possibly attesting to considerable public anxiety about this. *The Australian* newspaper (14 September 2011, 23), in an article about the swelling numbers of students arriving on Australian university campuses as a result of the federal government's reforms, states that "of the 15 universities already above the 20 percent target in their recruitment of low-SES domestic undergraduates, nine also have attrition rates above 20 percent". The article suggests that these results "fly in the face of research findings that status has minimal impact on the ongoing success of students once they've secured admission to university". In another newspaper article on this topic, in *The Australian* (21 September 2011, 26) Professor Kerri-Lee Krause of Griffith University makes a similar point, that "attrition rates were also influenced by socioeconomic and family background", impacting on students choices.[5]

In a "Research Briefing" (2011) from ACER on the long-running *Australasian Survey of Student Engagement* (referred to as the AUSSE) the authors reported that in 2010 around 27 percent of first-year students "seriously considered departing an Australian university before graduating" (1). That was apparently an improvement on the 2008 ACER AUSSE survey result which indicated 35 percent were considering leaving, although the results were indicating "an upswing in early departure intentions for later-year students from 31 to 41 percent between 2008 and 2010". The figure for humanities students was a massive 57 percent nationally. The report prompted an article in *The Age* newspaper (22 June 2011) titled "Uni students struggle with degree ennui". The journalist drew on key finding that the "main reason given to stop studying was boredom, but issues including stress, workload difficulties, needing to work more and commuting problems were also high on the list". The National Union of Students president, Jesse Marshall, was quoted in the same article as putting these departure intentions down to financial and support issues:

> Stress on family relationships from inadequate income support, lack of social support through defunding of student organisations and inadequate support services to cater for increasing student numbers are starting to take their toll.

Confirming this picture, Marcia Devlin, Richard James and Gabrielle Grigg (2008) argued that student engagement is linked to financial circumstances, and pointed to the 2006 national student finances survey. They summarised the situation: "low to modest incomes, mounting debt, limited access to government assistance and reliance on gifts from family and friends... a picture of financial hardship that appears to have worsened since the 2000 study" (3). They pointed to students' heavy reliance on paid work "simply to provide for everyday needs" and the impact that has on their studies; with one quarter of undergraduates in paid work regularly missing classes, a figure that is rising because these students "literally cannot afford to go to class if there is the opportunity for work" (5).

This sense of multiple causes for attrition—including financial stress— is supported by the Michael Long's *et al.* (2006) report *Stay, Play or Give it Away?* (DEEWR), where it was argued that "it is often a combination of reasons that lead to the decision to discontinue". Vincent Tinto (1997, 2009, 2012) advocates supportive "learning communities" as a bulwark against attrition. Alf Lizzio and Keithia Wilson (2010) argue for the importance of students' "sense of purpose" underpinning academic persistence. John Hultberg (2008) refers to Rhodes and Neville's research which found that key factors for course completions included "the chance of a career, good self-confidence, and a stimulating course", while factors associated with early student departures included "debt, poor teaching, and not coping with workload". Wolfgang Lehmann (2009) found with the Canadian working-class students he studied there was evidence of high levels of reflexivity and pragmatism about whether to stay or leave a course and we see this sort of pragmatic view in the student interviews for this study.

Students' views on attrition

Many of the factors raised by the transition experts were also raised by the students I interviewed. Some of the interviewees took up this topic with degrees of biographical reflexivity. For instance, Penelope (female, age

18) described herself as "lazy" and recounted earlier problems in education because of this. She recognised that she would need to fight that, especially given the length of the course she hoped to do (completing her first degree and then studying Law):

> Well, when I think about uni and how long it's going to take me to do what I want to do, you know to be a lawyer I have to be in uni for a really long time, so I just think to myself "can I be bothered?". So I think that would be the only reason I would drop out—and I'm not planning to drop out—but if I were to drop out it is because I'm just lazy and I couldn't be bothered.

Motivation was the key issue raised by Nicole (female, age 18) who described two of her friends, at another university in their commencing year, having "no motivation", and in the case of one was "already set on dropping out because of the workload". Tess (female, age 24) offers a somewhat similar analysis of the causes for attrition in first year, when she explained that a friend of hers had discontinued her university studies for want of motivation or readiness to study hard. She was of the opinion that people should not even be allowed to attend university straight from Year 12 at school:

> I don't believe that at 17 or 18 you have any idea of what you really want to do, and I'm a perfect example of that, so are my sisters and a dozen of my girlfriends. They changed course after course after course. You don't know yourself near as well as you will when you're 20. Things become much more clear, and relevant and important, and your priorities change. Go out and get a job, budget, learn what the real world is about.

Geraldinique (female, age 22) also spoke about the length of time it would take her to finish her course, and thought that might be a reason for not completing her degree:

> Sometimes I think maybe in five years I can be working, with my degree, and sometimes I think, "I'm not going to finish". I feel really bad sometimes because I don't want to come to uni. I don't have this motivation.

Lilly (female, age 20) was convinced that some people only stayed at university because of "the social side... and stick around for that more than the actual education", and she didn't even find that quite enough for herself at one stage when she contemplated leaving in the first few weeks.

She was pleased, in hindsight, that she had stuck it out so far, and was even enjoying units she had chosen almost randomly:

> I thought, "What am I doing here? It seems so hard", because I didn't even choose, like Politics was just something I randomly chose in the last minute of deciding. So I'm like, "do I want to do Politics?" and all of the decisions I made I was kind of questioning. But I thought, "I'll give it time, I've got to give it time". I'm fine.

Dina (female, age 21) reflected on her own departure from an earlier course, when asked what she thought might be the common reasons for people discontinuing their courses, and she suggested that "a lot of people go to university because that's what they think they should do or they just don't know what they want to do". This issue of parental pressure was also raised by Winston (male, age 18) who spoke with some disdain about a fellow student who had missed most of their tutorials in the first month and was struggling with assignments. He felt she was being "pushed through by the parents" and he saw that as a common problem:

> I feel that people dropping out of university, more than anything else, there's a certain degree of them having been pushed here by their family.

What I hope is apparent here is that from these students' perspectives people leave courses for a variety of reasons, often sensible reasons, and that leaving university (possibly to return later) is not necessarily a bad thing. That is at odds with some of the scholarly literature and different from dominant institutional perspectives. However my findings generally support the less urgent or panicked view on attrition provided in the DEEWR (2006) report *Stay, Play or Give it Away?*:

> Students' comments on their reasons for dropping out highlight that it is often a combination of reasons that lead to the decision to discontinue... Many students who either discontinued or changed universities were found to gain some benefits from their year of university study and were more likely to judge their first-year experience positively than negatively. In addition, leaving university did not necessarily mean the end to study.

Conclusion

There is ample evidence of the "shock of the new" in the student narratives. Trevor Hussey and Patrick Smith (2010) describe higher-education transitions as typically entailing "large, complex transformations" (156). John Hultberg *et al.* (2008) talk about "both internal factors such as the learning environment and external factors such a student's personal life" (49). David and Alice Kolb (2005) speak about the complex processes involved in people acquiring the meta-cognitive capacities necessary to move from a "fixed self" to "learning self" and they suggest that this cannot be rushed and, again, this comment resonates with what the students said to me in interviews for my study:

> A learning identity develops over time from tentatively adopting a learning stance toward life experience, to a more confident learning orientation, to a learning self that is specific to certain contexts and ultimately to a learning self-identity that permeates deeply into all aspects of the way one lives their life. This progression is sustained and nurtured through growth-producing relationships in one's life.

Professor Kerri-Lee Krause (2008) from the University of Western Sydney and formerly from the Griffith Institute for Higher Education in Brisbane was an ALTC senior fellow. She produced a *Commentary on first year curriculum case studies: demographics and patterns of engagement perspective*. She recommends taking account of the higher-education policy context when seeking to interpret changing patterns of student engagement. I do that also in this case study. Krause also challenges her reader "to consider how these and various other strategies might be more finely differentiated to reflect the diversity of the students we teach in the first year" (6). One of my purposes with this case study is to help us know our students better, and make more visible the challenges they face on campus and off campus as well as the knowledge, skills, insights and aspirations they bring with them to the university. Other chapters in this book illustrate how we are doing this with our pathways and foundation units, and through our partnerships and research projects.

Acknowledgements

The author wishes to thank his doctoral supervisors at the University of Melbourne, Professor Julie McLeod and Professor Johanna Wyn, the chairperson of his PhD completion committee Professor Joe Lo Bianco and the external member Professor Marie Brennan. He also acknowledges the helpful feedback provided by Professor Emeritus Joe Cuseo (USA) and Professor Penny Jane Burke (UK). Andrew also thanks the students who participated in his study and especially the 33 interviewees.

Notes

[1] Vincent Tinto raises the problem of persistent student attrition in his most recent book *Completing College* (2012). He also dealt with this, and the related issue of enhancing student success, in a 2013 keynote presentation at the 16th International First Year in Higher Education (FYHE) conference in Wellington, New Zealand. He spoke of the need for institution-wide, coherently structured and proactive approaches—with a classroom focus ("one class at a time over time") with learning as the key objective and retention "simply the mechanism".

[2] The Foundation for Young Australians (2013) *How Young People are Faring 2013—The National Report on Learning and Earning of Young Australians* in "At a Glance" reports that while more young people are participating in post-school education and training, there has also been an increase in their participation in casual jobs, with fewer young people in full-time employment. Also, that "three years after completing their university course, 15 percent of Australian graduates are working in jobs for which they are over-skilled". This accords with findings given in *The Australian* newspaper (17 July 2013, 3) reporting on the 2012 Graduate Careers Australia survey which indicates that overall "the job market for graduates just out of university has yet to recover four years on from the financial crisis".

[3] Marcia Devlin (2013) in "Bridging Socio-Cultural Incongruity: Conceptualising the Success of Students from Low Status Backgrounds in Australian Higher Education" discusses moves to refine current Australian Bureau of Statistics (ABS) measures of students' status based on home-address postcode, and questions whether it is even desirable to be indentifying students as "low SES".

[4] Universities Australia (2013) *University Student Finances in 2012* includes in its key findings from a survey of nearly 12,000 students that "there was also an increase in the proportion of students indicating that they regularly go without food or other necessities because they cannot afford them: from 14.7 percent of full-time domestic undergraduates in 2006 to 18.2 percent in 2012", with this figure rising to 25 percent for low-SES students. Geoff Maslen, writing in *The Age* newspaper (22 July 2013, 14) highlighted the report's findings that "80 percent of full-time undergraduates work an average of 16 hours a week". Of particular significance for my study, he mentioned that low-SES students were more likely to say that "paid employment affected their ability to study".

[5] Questions about the correlation of students' Australian Tertiary Admission Rank (ATAR) and attrition were taken up more recently by Julie Hare in *The Australian* (10 July 2013, 25) reporting on research by Andrew Norton for the Grattan Institute which tracked students entering university in 2005 to 2011 that found that "on average, students with ATARs below 60 percent drop out at a rate of one in three... with ATARs below 50 dropping out at the rate of 50 percent" (this compares with students with scores of 90 or above having a 90 percent chance of completing their degree). Professor Richard James from the University of Melbourne, an expert on equity and student engagement, is reported in a follow-up article in *The Australian* (24 July 2013, 29) as arguing against any push by

government to create a binding national ATAR cut off, regarding the ATAR as a blunt instrument in predicting student success (for anyone with scores below 80), and suggesting that, given the correlation between ATAR and status, such a move could be expected to exclude "otherwise capable students".

Reference List

Abbott-Chapman, Joan. 2011. "Making the Most of the Mosaic: Facilitating post-School Transitions to Higher Education of Disadvantaged Students." *Australian Education Researcher* 38: 57–71.

ACER. 2011. Australasian Survey of Student Engagement (AUSSE) *Research Briefing* 11: 1–18. Alexandria, NSW: Australian Council of Education Research.

Ball, Stephen. 2006. "The Necessity and Violence of Theory." *Discourse: Studies in the Cultural Politics of Education* 27 (1): 3–10.

Ball, Stephen, Ivor Goodson and Meg Maguire (eds.) 2007. *Education, Globalisation and New Times*. London and New York: Routledge.

Bourdieu, Pierre. 1977. *Outline of a Theory of Practice*. Cambridge: Cambridge University Press.

Bourdieu, Pierre, and Jean Claude Passeron. 1977. *Reproduction in Education, Society and Culture*, London and Beverly Hills: Sage Publications.

Bourdieu, Pierre. 1990. *The Logic of Practice*. Cambridge: Cambridge University Press.

Bourdieu, Pierre, and Loic Wacquant. 1992. *An Invitation to Reflexive Sociology*. Chicago: Chicago University Press.

Bradley, Denise and Peter Noonan, Helen Nugent and Bill Scales. 2008. *Review of Australian Higher Education – Final Report*. Canberra: Commonwealth of Australia.

Burke, Penny Jane. 2005. "Accessing and Widening Participation." *British Journal of Sociology of Education* 26 (4): 555–562.

—. 2006 "Men Accessing Education: Gendered Aspirations." *British Educational Research Journal* 32 (5): 719–734.

—. 2007. "Writing, Power and Voice: Access to and Participation in Higher Education." *Changing English* 15 (2): 199–210.

Christie, Hazel. 2009 "Emotional Journeys: Young People and Transition to University." *British Journal of Sociology of Education* 30 (2): 123–136.

Coates, Hamish, and Kerri-Lee Krause. 2005. "Investigating Ten Years of Equity Policy in Australian Higher Education." *Journal of Higher Education Policy and Management* 27 (1): 35–47.

David, Miriam. 2011. "Changing Concepts of Equity in Transforming UK Higher Education: Implications for Future Pedagogies and Practices in Global Higher Education." *Australian Educational Researcher* 38: 25–42.

—. (ed.) (2010) *Improving Learning by Widening Participation in Education.* London and New York: Routledge.

Devlin, Marcia. 2010. "Non-traditional University Student Achievement: Theory, Policy and Practice in Australia." Keynote Address, 13th Pacific Rim First Year in Higher Education Conference 2010. FYHE Conference 2010. Retrieved 1/2/11
www.fyhe.com.au/past_papers.html.

—. 2013. "Bridging Socio-cultural Incongruity: Conceptualising the Success of Students from Low Status Backgrounds in Australian Higher Education." *Studies in Higher Education* 38 (6): 939–49.

Devlin, Marcia, Richard James, and Gabrielle Grigg. 2008. "Studying and Working: A National Study of Student Finances and Student Engagement." Paper presented at the 29th Annual EAIR Forum August 2007. *Journal of Tertiary Education and Management* 14 (2): 111–22.

Devlin, Marcia, and Helen O'Shea. 2012. "Effective University Teaching: Views of Australian University Students from Low Socio-economic Status Backgrounds." *Teaching in Higher Education* 17 (4): 385–97.

Evans-Commander, Nanette, and Teresa Ward. 2009. "The Strength of Mixed Methods for the Assessment of Learning Communities." *About Campus* July–August: 25–28.

Funston, J. Andrew. 2011. *Journeys to University and Arrival Experiences – A Study of Non-traditional Students' Transitions at a New Australian University.* Unpublished PhD thesis (University of Melbourne).

—. 2012. *Research Report 35: Non-traditional Students Making Their Way in Higher Education – An Australian Case Study.* Youth Research Centre. Melbourne Graduate School of Education.

Furlong, Andy (ed.). 2009. *Handbook of Youth and Young Adulthood – New Perspectives and Agendas.* Hoboken: Routledge.

Furlong, Andy, and Fred Cartmel. 1997. *Young People and Social Change: Individualization and Risk in Late Modernity.* Buckingham and Philadelphia: Open University Press.

Furlong, Andy, and Fred Cartmel. 2009. "Mass Higher Education", in Furlong, A. (2009) *Handbook of Youth and Young Adulthood: New Perspectives and Agendas* Hoboken: Routledge.

FYA. 2013. *How Young People Are Faring 2013 – The National Report on the Learning of Young Australians*. Melbourne: Foundation for Young Australians.

Gale, Trevor. 2011. "Student Equity's Starring Role in Australian Higher Education – not yet Centre Field." *Australian Educational Researcher* 38 (1): 5–23.

Gale, Trevor, and Stephen Parker. 2011. *Good Practice Report – Student Transition into Higher Education*. Surry Hills NSW: ALTC.

Gale, Trevor, and Sam Sellar. 2011: "Confronting Perceptions of Student Equity in Higher Education." *Australian Educational Researcher* 38: 1–3.

Hultberg, John, Kaety Plos, Graham Hendry and Karin Kjellgren. 2008. "Scaffolding Students' Transition to Higher Education: Parallel Introductory Courses for Students and Teachers." *Journal of Further and Higher Education* 32 (1): 47–57.

Hussey, Trevor and Patrick Smith. 2010. "Transitions in Higher Education." *Innovations in Education and Teaching International* 47(2): 155–164.

James, Richard. 2000. "Non-traditional students in Australian Higher Education: Persistent Inequalities and the New Ideology of 'Student Choice'." *Tertiary Education and Management*. 6: 105–18.

—. 2009. "Implications of the Bradley Review. Recommendations for Student Equity Groups – Will the Bradley Recommendations Improve Equity." Retrieved 1/9/10 www.unisa.edu.au/student-equity/james-bradley-recommendations.ppt.

James, Richard, Emmaline Bexley, Marcia Devlin, and Simon Marginson. 2007. *Australian University Student Finances*. Canberra: AVCC.

James, Richard, Kerri-Lee Krause, and Claire Jennings (2010). *The First Year Experience in Australian Universities: Findings from 1994 to 2009*. Melbourne: Centre for the Study of Higher Education.

Kift, Sally. 2008a. "Attending to the very Foundations: a FYE Perspective for Staff Development that Articulates a Transition Pedagogy." JUC Foundations Colloquium 2008 Enhancing Quality.

—. 2008b. "The Next Great First Year Challenge: Sustaining, Coordinating and Embedding Coherent Institution-wide Approaches to Enact the FYHE as "Everybody's Business." Hobart FYHE (First Year in Higher Education) Conference Papers.

—. 2009. *Final Report for ALTC Senior Fellowship Program – Articulating a Transition Pedagogy to Scaffold and to Enhance the*

First Year Student Learning Experience in Australian Higher Education. ALTC/DEEWR and Queensland University of Technology.

Kolb, Alice and David. 2005. "Learning Styles and Learning Spaces: Enhancing Experiential Learning in Higher Education." *Academy of Management and Learning Education* 4 (2): 193–212.

—. (2009) "The Learning Way: Meta-cognition Aspects of Experiential Learning." *Simulation Gaming* 40(3): 297–327.

Krause, Kerri-Lee. 2008. *Commentary on First Year Curriculum Case Studies: Demographics and Patterns of Engagement Perspective.* ALTC and QUT

—. 2009. "First Year Engagement: What Role Does Curriculum Play?" Keynote paper delivered to the QUT FYE Curriculum Design Symposium 5 February 2009.

Krause, Kerri-Lee, Robyn Hartley, Richard James, and Craig McInnis. 2005. *The First Year Experience in Australian Universities: Findings from a Decade of National Studies.* Canberra: AGPS.

Kuh, George. 2007. "What Matters to Student Success in First Year University." Brisbane FYHE (First Year in Higher Education). Conference http://www.fyhe.com.au/past_papers.html.

Lehmann, Wolfgang. 2009. "University as Vocational Education: Working-class Students' Expectations for University." *British Journal of Sociology of Education* 30 (2): 137–49.

Lizzio, Alf and Keithia Wilson. 2010. "Strengthening Commencing Students' Sense of Purpose: Integrating Theory and Practice." FYHE Conference 2010. Retrieved 1/2/11
www.fyhe.com.au/past_papers.html.

Long, Michael, Fran Ferrier and Margaret Heagney. 2006. *Stay, Play or Give it away? Students Continuing, Changing or Leaving University Study in Their First Year.* Australian Government DEST. Retrieved 1/6/09   http://www.dest.gov.au/NR/rdonlyres/678FF919-3AD5-46C7-9F57-739841698A85/14398/final.pdf.

Marks, Gary. 2007. *Longitudinal Surveys of Australian Youth – Research Report 51: Completing University: Characteristics and Outcomes of Completing and Non-completing Students.* ACER

—. (2008. *Longitudinal Surveys of Australian Youth – Research Report 55: The Occupations and Earnings of Youth Australians: The Role of Education and Training.* ACER   http://research.acer.edu.au/lsay_research/

McLeod, Julie and Rachel Thomson. 2009. *Researching Social Change.* London. SAGE.

McMillan, Julie. 2005. *Longitudinal Surveys of Australian Youth, Research Report 39: Course Change and Attrition from Higher Education* Melbourne: ACER (Australian Council for Educational Research). Retrieved 6/6/10
    http://tls.vu.edu.au/sls/slu/FOR_STAFF/Staff_Resources/research%20
    papers%201%20(national)/Course%20Change%20and%20Attrition%2
    0from%20Higher%20Education.pdf.

Nelson, Karen, Sally Kift and John Clarke. 2008. "Expectations and Realities For First Year Students at an Australian University." Hobart FYHE Conference http://www.fyhe.com.au/past_papers.html.

Nelson, Karen, Judith Smith and John Clarke. 2011. "Enhancing the Transition of Commencing Students into University: an Institution-wide Approach." QUT Digital Repository
    http://eprints.qut.edu.au/39690/.

Pascarella, Ernest, and Patrick Terenzini. 2005. *How College Affects Students: Volume 2*. San Francisco, CA: Jossey-Bass.

Reay, Diane. 2001. "Finding or Losing Yourself?: Working-class Relationships to Education." *Journal of Education Policy* 16 (4): 333–46.

—. 2003. "A Risky Business? Mature Working-class Women Students and Access to Higher Education." *Gender and Education*. 15 (3): 301–17.

Reay, Diane, Miriam David and Stephen Ball. 2005. *Degrees of Choice: Social class, Race and Gender in Higher Education*. Oak Hill, Sterling: Trentham Books.

Reid, Anna and Ian Solomonides. 2010. "Diverse Transitions." FYHE Conference 2010. http://www.fyhe.com.au/past_papers.html.

Scutter, Sheila and Denise Wood. 2009. "Enhancing The First-Year Student Experience Through Quality Improvements of Courses," in *Proceedings of the 32nd HERDSA Annual Conference, Darwin 6–9 July 2009*: 357–68.

Scutter, Sheila, Edward Palmer, Ann Luzeckyj, Karen Burke da Silva, and Russell. 2011 "What Do Commencing Undergraduate Students Expect from First Year University." *The International Journal of the First Year in Higher Education* 2(1): 8–12.

Sellar, Sam and Trevor Gale. "Editorial: Globalisation and Student Equity in Higher Education." *Cambridge Journal of Education* 41 (1): 1–4.

Sellar, Sam, and Trevor Gale. 2011. "Mobility, Aspiration, Voice – A New Structure of Feeling for Student Equity in Higher Education." *Critical Studies in Education* 52 (2): 115–34.

Sellar, Sam, Trevor Gale and Stephen Parker. 2011. "Appreciating aspirations in Australian Higher Education." *Cambridge Journal of Education* 41(1): 37–52.

Taylor, Samantha. 2006. "Narrative as Construction and Discursive Resource," *Narrative Inquiry* 16 (1): 94–102.

Tett, Lyn. 2000. "I'm Working Class and Proud of It" – Gendered Experiences of Non-traditional Participation in Higher Education." *Gender and Education* Vol.12 No.2: 183–194.

—. .2004. "Mature Working-class Students in an 'Elite' University: Discourses of Risk, Choice and Exclusion." *Studies in the Education of Adults* 36 (2): 252–264.

Tinto, Vincent. 1993. *Leaving College: Rethinking the Causes and Cures of Student Attrition.* Chicago: University of Chicago Press.

—. 1997. "Classrooms as Communities: Exploring the Educational Character of Student Persistence." *Journal of Higher Education.* Vol 68 No.6: 599–623.

—. 2003. *Learning Better Together: The Impact of Learning Communities on Student Success.* Syracuse University Higher Education Monograph Series, 2003–1.

—. 2008. *Access Without Support is Not Opportunity.* Presented at the 36th Annual Institute for Chief Academic Officers, the Council of Independent Colleges, November 1, 2008, Seattle, Washington

—. 2006. "Research and Practice of Student Retention: What Next?" *College Student Retention: Research, Theory and Practice* 8 (1): 1–20

—. 2009. "Taking Student Retention Seriously: Rethinking the First Year of University Study." Keynote Paper Delivered to the QUT FYE Curriculum Design Symposium, 5 February 2009.

—. 2012. *Leaving College: Rethinking the causes and cures of student attrition.* Chicago: University of Chicago Press.

Universities Australia. 2013. *University Student Finances In 2012: A Study of the Financial Circumstances of Domestic and International Students in Australia's Universities.* Report authors Emmaline Bexley, Suzanne Daroesman, Sophie Arkoudis, and Richard James, Centre for the Study of Higher Education. The University of Melbourne.

Walther, Andreas. 2006. "Regimes of Youth Transitions – Choice, Flexibility and Security in Young People's Experiences Across Different European Contexts." *Young* 14 (2): 119–39.

Wetherell, Margaret. 2006. "Formulating Selves: Social Psychology and the Study of Identity." *Social Psychology Review* 8: 62–72.

—. 2008. "Subjectivity or Psycho-discursive Practices? Investigating Complex Intersectional Identities." *Subjectivity* 22: 73–81.

White, Michael. 2007. *Maps of Narrative Practice*. New York, W.W.Norton and Co.

Wilson, Keithia. 2009. "Success in First Year – The Impact of Institutional, Programmatic and Personal Interventions on an Effective and Sustainable First-year Student Experience." FYHE Conference 2009. Retrieved 1/6/10 www.fyhe.com.au/past_papers.html.

Woodin, Tom and Penny Jane Burke (2007) "Men Accessing Education: Masculinities, Class and Choice." *The Australian Educational Researcher* 34 (3): 119–134.

Woodman, Dan. 2010. *The Post-secondary School Transition and the Desynchronisation of Everyday Life*. Unpublished PhD Thesis (University of Melbourne).

—. (2012) "Life out of Synch: How New Patterns of Further Education and the Rise of Precarious Employment Are Shaping Young People's Relationships." *Sociology* 46 (6): 1074–90.

Wyn, Johanna. 2004. "Becoming Adult in the 2000s. New Transitions and New Careers." *Family Matters* 68:6–12.

—. 2007. "Generation and Class: Young People's New, Diverse Patterns of Life and Their Implications for Recognising Participation in Civic Society." *International Journal of Children's Rights* 15: 165–179.

—. 2009. *Youth Health and Welfare – The Cultural Politics of Education and Wellbeing*. South Melbourne, Oxford, New York: Oxford University Press.

Wyn, Johanna, and Woodman, Dan (2006) "Generation, Youth and Social Change in Australia." *Journal of Youth Studies* 9 (5): 495–514.

Wyn, Johanna, and Woodman, Dan (2007) "DEBATE – Researching Youth in a Context of Social Change: A Reply to Roberts." *Journal of Youth Studies* 10 (3): 373–81.

Wyn, Johanna, and Dan. 2006. "Generation, youth and social change in Australia", *Journal of Youth Studies* 9 (5): 495–514.

Yorke, Mantz, and Liz Thomas. 2003. "Improving the Retention of Students from Lower Socio-Economic Groups." *Journal of Higher Education Policy and Management* 25 (1): 63–74. doi:10.1080/13600800305737.

CHAPTER THREE

RETHINKING ENGAGEMENT AND TRANSITION: THE CASE OF THE DIPLOMA OF LIBERAL ARTS

MICHAEL HALLPIKE

Introduction

The following chapter is addressed to all concerned with teaching and learning in the Arts. It critically reflects upon current preoccupations with "student engagement" and "transition" in higher- education policy and argues that this discussion needs to be reframed, as marketing and accounting imperatives tend increasingly to trump pedagogical concerns. The paper first of all attempts to unpack related pedagogical questions and curriculum design issues by way of a critical reflection on the case of the Diploma of Liberal Arts, which was co-designed by educators from TAFE and the Arts faculty at Victoria University in the early 1990s[1]. The course provides a scaffolded induction into the discourses of the humanities and social sciences for diverse cohorts of non-traditional students. Following Barnett and Coate (2005) and Zepke and Leach (2010), a central concern of the chapter will then be how to shift discussion from *operational* issues to an *ontological* conception of engagement—a shift that has already had a 20-year rehearsal in the design and successive revisions of the Liberal Arts curriculum.[2] I conclude by suggesting that the question of ontological engagement is ineluctably bound up with questions concerning the uncertain fate of the project of the "public university", as well as questions concerning the possibility of reconciling the inherited aims of an Arts education with a more sophisticated form of vocationalism than that which is currently on offer.

Transition Pedagogy: The Liberal Arts Approach

As universities have opened their doors more widely in recent decades, recruiting increasing numbers of non-traditional students from low socioeconomic status (SES) and culturally and linguistically diverse (CALD) backgrounds, including increasing numbers of low-achieving school leavers, there is a growing consensus across the Australian higher education sector that student engagement and retention, especially in the first year of university study, demands a whole-of-university approach to curriculum and pedagogy.[3] There is also a growing acceptance, especially across dual- and multi-sector institutions, of an idea that has a long pedigree in Academic Language and Learning (ALL) and Adult Learning research and practice, namely, that curriculum should be informed by an explicit "transition pedagogy" (Kift, Nelson and Clarke 2010; Nelson, Smith and Clarke 2012), aimed at facilitating non-traditional students' transitions from diverse, pre-university educational backgrounds, into an academic learning environment. It was precisely with these aims in mind that a group of TAFE teachers and academics at Victoria University designed the Diploma of Liberal Arts in the early 1990s. A rehearsal of some of the curriculum design and pedagogical issues encountered by the course designers, which Liberal Arts educators have in various ways attempted to address over the past 20 years, may make a useful contribution to this larger discussion.

Sally Kift *et al.* (2010) argue that universities need to "centralise the curriculum in the student experience" and develop a "transition pedagogy" that "intentionally and proactively takes account of and seeks to mediate the reality of commencing cohorts diverse in preparedness and cultural capital" (12). These aims, and the general principles that Kift *et al.* have advanced as a framework for developing a holistic transition pedagogy—attentiveness to students' diverse backgrounds, motivations, aspirations and specific transition needs, reflexive curriculum design and explicit pedagogy, strategic approaches to student engagement, best-practice approaches to assessment and evaluation—all make good sense and will not be news to teachers working with non-traditional students across a wide range of pre-tertiary courses.

At the outset designers of the Liberal Arts course asked themselves the following questions: How shall we design a course that will provide non-traditional students with a scaffolded induction into the discourses of the humanities and social sciences? How shall we do this in a way that does not presuppose that commencing students arrive at the door with ready-made scholarly orientations, prior grounding in privileged bodies of knowledge, or competence in privileged cultural and academic literacies? What kind of invitation may we extend to non-traditional students, so that they will be likely to accept the challenges involved?

The experience of the Liberal Arts course provides an exemplary instance of a sustained attempt to address these questions, both by virtue of the task that the course set for itself at the outset, namely, inducting non-traditional students into the discourses of the humanities and social sciences, and also by virtue of the unique positioning of the Further Education division of TAFE in the context of Australian postsecondary education.[4] The two-year Diploma of Liberal Arts was designed to serve both as a stand-alone course and as a credit-bearing supported pathway into a range of degree courses in the Arts.

Both the unique positioning and special focus of this course have served to open a space in which a two-sided problematic has been kept in view that otherwise would tend too easily to be concealed. On the one hand, there is the question of who our diverse cohorts of non-traditional students are: What culturally and linguistically diverse worlds, experiences, motivations, hopes and aspirations do they bring along with them? The designers of the diploma were determined to avoid a "deficit" approach and sought instead to find ways to enable non-traditional students to draw on the rich cultural resources and alternative knowledges and ways of knowing that they bring with them to the course. This seemed to the designers of the course to be the first principle of student engagement; and this commitment continues to inform the Liberal Arts curriculum and teaching practices.

On the other hand, there are questions concerning the changing nature of the discourses of the humanities and social sciences, and related questions concerning the nature of the induction process, and the changing social functions of a general education in the Arts at postsecondary level. A postsecondary curriculum that is designed to scaffold students' learning, induct students into the discourses of the humanities and social sciences, and provide credit-bearing pathways, must therefore be vitally connected to those discourses and remain open to continual revision, in close collaboration with colleagues involved in the design of undergraduate degree programs.

These two sets of issues overlap in complex ways that need to be better understood if we are to take the question of student engagement and transition seriously—that is, if we are to take this to be a serious pedagogical question, as opposed to a question about factors impacting on student retention. From a pedagogical standpoint, questions about who our students are, questions concerning the changing nature of academic discourses, questions about the nature of an induction into the discourses of the humanities and social sciences, questions about the relationship between induction into specialisations and a broad education in the Arts, questions about the rapidly changing conditions that impact on the perceived purposes and status of a broad general education in the Arts, are aporetically crossed by questions concerning the kind of *invitation* that we imagine we are extending to our students: What prior understandings do we imagine that students might have about the meaning and value of an Arts education, and what do we think they might hope to gain from an induction into the discourses of the humanities and social sciences?

Building a Halfway House for Non-Traditional Students

The designers of the Liberal Arts course paid very close attention to the question of how to provide the necessary scaffolding to ensure that students would not be disadvantaged by the distance they had to travel from their diverse cultural and linguistic backgrounds before they could somehow find themselves at home in the university—and this question has been central to Liberal Arts practitioners ever since. The course was designed as a two-year sequential study, comprising a one-year certificate that can either be completed as a stand-alone course before enrolling in a degree, or as the embedded first year of a two-year, credit-bearing diploma. This course structure made it possible to offer non-traditional students a two-year, intensive, face-to-face course that was intentionally designed as a sort of "halfway house" between the various worlds inhabited by our diverse cohorts of students and the "discourse communities" of the humanities and social sciences. For those who feel ready to move on more quickly, the one-year certificate would gain them access to a wide range of degree courses.

It was agreed at the outset that the course would not serve to screen out the already able from the unable, that students' success would not be dependent on their having already acquired the background cultural attributes privileged by academic discourses. The term "academic discourses" is used by Liberal Arts practitioners to refer to highly structured, knowledge-generating, *but also socioculturally situated*, discursive practices, in and through which academic disciplines and fields of study not only communicate but also constitute themselves (Hyland 2009). It is *within* such discursive practices that insiders achieve mutual recognition, through distinctive forms of written and oral communication. How then do outsiders become insiders? Who do they have to be in the first place to gain entry? What obstacles will they meet? What do they need to know? What do they need to be able to do?

We use the term "academic discourses", rather than speaking about disciplines or fields of inquiry, partly to emphasise the "multidisciplinary" nature of the curriculum and to be clear about the fact that the Liberal Arts course is not designed to induct students into specific disciplines; but partly also because the Liberal Arts course seeks to locate itself in a discursive space that is at once *supra-* and *infra-* disciplinary, rather than *multi-* or *inter-*disciplinary. Such a space is a *necessary* construct in an undergraduate program; there is a *necessary* mediation, and creative tension, between the task of inducting of students into strictly disciplinary discourses and the provision of general education to students who may never seek to be "insiders". Many students, perhaps most, will never aspire to "insider" status, even after completing a three-year major sequence; yet all students will nevertheless need to find their way into these discourses to some extent and to feel that they are doing something that has meaning for them.

This supra-/infra-disciplinary space is also necessarily constructed whenever academics play a role as "public intellectuals". It is also necessarily constructed when discussions and debates, dreamings and imaginings concerning a wide range of matters that concern us all, be they philosophical, moral–practical, social, cultural or political, draw academics, students and a wider public together. In saying that the course seeks to locate itself in such a space, I am suggesting that such a space is, from a pedagogical standpoint, a necessary construct, since it is clear that disciplines and fields of inquiry are not operationally closed, self-referential systems, however strong may be the tendency towards such closure.

For all that, the space we are talking about here will not necessarily come fully into view in a traditionally structured undergraduate program. Degree courses are typically structured in such a way that students are treated from day one as if they are there to commence an "apprenticeship" into specialisations. They enrol immediately into the first units of their three-year majors, they attend lectures and have minimal contact with their lecturers; and their tutors are generally postgraduate students who have no teacher training, who are immersed in their disciplines and who will therefore naturally see their students as novices and comport themselves as mentors. Some students will find themselves at home in this context whilst others will adapt; but a significant number of students will experience estrangement. Despite the best efforts of individual lecturers and tutors, the pedagogical question concerning the induction of non-traditional students into academic discourses will, for self-evident structural reasons, never come fully into view within a traditionally structured undergraduate program.

This is not to suggest that such a space cannot be opened up to view in a well-designed undergraduate program; for all that, a foundation course that maintains a degree of autonomy is well placed to stay focused on the pedagogical question and potentially to provide a corrective to a tendency of academic disciplines and fields of inquiry to become operationally closed and self-referential, despite the best efforts and intentions of lecturers who design and deliver undergraduate courses. This operational closure is often wrongly characterised as a tendency of academics to retreat into their "ivory towers". Clearly, one cannot even begin to understand this operational closure without a) taking into account the complex networks through which academics seek to establish and maintain their scholarly reputations—Shapin (1994) refers to them as global networks of intimate circles; b) grasping the fact that disciplines and fields of inquiry reproduce themselves across global networks; and c) acknowledging the complex field of tensions that connects all of this to the internal organisational dynamics of universities, on the one hand, and the external drivers to which those organisational dynamics must effectively respond, on the other. If this description is correct, then there will inevitably be tensions between the induction of students into specific disciplines and the broader educative functions of an undergraduate degree in Arts.

Whilst the Liberal Arts course is not designed to rehearse students' induction into specific disciplines, its unique positioning made it possible to open this space, bring this field of tensions into view, and stay focused on the pedagogical question. Yet it was clear to all from the start that it would not be easy to design a curriculum that would be non-threatening and "doable" and yet still fulfil the aim of inducting diverse cohorts of non-traditional students into the discourses of the humanities and social sciences. It was clear to the course designers that very specific sets of background cultural attributes are deeply inscribed into academic discourses:

> Universities were and continue to be structured for an "ideal" student: large lectures, reading lists, prescribed essays, more or less voluntary tutorials giving students an opportunity to hear, read, and participate in, the debates which constitute the humanities. The "ideal" student is taken to desire the knowledge and identity the university offers, has a background of cultural references which university training builds upon and enriches, is independent, and, of course, is highly literate. Secondary education

traditionally both produced this student and excluded from university those who had not developed this complex of attributes (Moraitis 2001).

It is easier to declare intentions than to understand what a curriculum and teaching practice that made no such assumptions would look like, let alone to carry this through in practice. Aspects of the Liberal Arts course design, and support materials produced by the designers of the course, bear the strong imprint of a shared commitment to provide the scaffolding that will enable students to build their own bridges across from their diverse cultural and educational backgrounds into the discourses of the humanities and social sciences. The course is rich in content and designed to make accessible, and to contextualise, constellations of cultural references that form shared background understandings across a range of disciplines and fields of study. This background awareness is generally taken for granted in the academic texts that students will need to make sense of and engage with; and some of this background may even be taken for granted by some of their university lecturers.

One danger here is that of defaulting to a "deficit" approach, adopting the mindset of an Eric D Hirsch Jr (1989) and cramming into our students' heads all the background knowledge that we think they need to know. Another danger is that we produce an intensive study in western traditions that further alienates our culturally diverse cohorts of students. Liberal Arts practitioners have striven to avoid both traps by, for example, developing content that builds on the stories that students bring with them to the course (Julie Fletcher's chapter also discusses a curriculum innovation that further develops this idea), emphasising cross-cultural and inter-civilisational encounters in some of the historical material, pointing up examples where students are likely to see their own stories reflected, rather than remaining invisible, and equipping students with some of the basic tools of critique, in ways that will be immediately meaningful for them. Liberal Arts practitioners have remained committed to the idea that students' induction into academic discourses should not require them to leave their own cultural backgrounds behind, nor to learn to compartmentalise and live two lives in parallel universes. We need to travel much further in this direction. We need to learn more and we need to do more.

Rather than seeking to induct students into specific disciplines, the course designers created multidisciplinary units of study that would scaffold students' induction into academic "cultures" (an inadequate but more or less serviceable term) that span several disciplines, and which overlap and replicate themselves within various disciplines. Several aspects of the course design and some of the content that has been handed down over successive iterations, bring three such cultures into focus, which may be conceived as privileging different "ways of knowing" and approaches to knowledge: namely, nomothetic approaches that emulate the natural sciences; dialogical and dialectical approaches that give centre-stage to deliberation and argument; and ideographic, semiotic and interpretative approaches. The course encompasses all three, whilst privileging the culture of argument on the one side, and the culture of interpretation on the other.

As well as thinking about ways to build a curriculum that would induct students into different ways of knowing/being in an academic world, the course designers decided to create a core group of units in the course that would focus intensively on academic writing and reading, whilst linking closely with other units in the course. Rather than building a curriculum based on a deficit model of essential knowledge acquisition, the designers of the Liberal Arts course chose rather to draw on the fact that certain problematics, themes and ongoing debates tend to cut across disciplinary boundaries and play out in various ways in different disciplines across the humanities and social sciences.

As Andrew Abbott (2002, 213) observes, the humanities and social science disciplines all overlap in terms of subject matter, theories, and methodologies: "As cultural systems the disciplines are astonishingly diverse internally, and that diversity so spreads them out into each other that to imagine that there are explicit disciplinary turfs is to make a profound mistake." Yet for all that, as Abbott concedes, whilst "economists and sociologists both write about poverty... [they] say different kinds of things". Moreover, when they say different kinds of things, they say and write them in different ways, following different conventions, speaking/writing as insiders, establishing their bona fides as insiders in ways that will not be visible to an outsider (Hyland 2009; Becher 2001, 2006).

Ergo, students need to be inducted into disciplines. As Charles Bazerman (1992) has noted, reflecting on his extensive studies of disciplinary writing, "disciplines and professions are largely constituted through networks of literate practices. As a consequence, increasing students' participation in their education through writing is precisely drawing them into the literate web that is the means by which disciplines make themselves". Overlaps in subject matter, theories and methodologies notwithstanding, there is no way of drawing students into this literate web except from within the disciplines themselves.

Yet whilst students need at some point to learn how to write for discipline-specific purposes, they also need to learn how to write their way into the discourses of the humanities and social sciences in ways that are not so narrowly specialised. Learning how to write in this way nevertheless needs to be deeply contextualised; whereas generic and genre-based approaches to the teaching of academic writing tend to occlude this dimension. So once again, it is a *supra-* and *infra-*disciplinary space that needs to be opened up in order to bring the pedagogical issues to the fore and keep them clearly in focus.

Induction into Academic Discourses

The Liberal Arts curriculum was designed at a time when the space we are talking about here had, in any case, come into view in relations between the universities and the wider society, and there were strong and visible connections between public discourses and academic discourses. Although the course was designed in the early 1990s, it was suffused with an idea that had captured the collective imagination of educators through the 1970s and 80s, namely, that there was a vital internal connection between the university and democracy as a form of life. The Habermasian view of this was that there was an internal relationship between the university's unique "bundling" of various functions—research, general education, professional training and public enlightenment—and the "lifeworld" (Habermas 1987a). This way of viewing the university was naturally in tension with conceptions of the institution as an autonomous cognitive complex, whose core functions, viz., generating new knowledge and safeguarding the transmission of privileged bodies of inherited knowledge, required careful boundary maintenance and immunisation against contamination from politics, art, religion and commerce.

The field of tensions in which participants in public and academic discourses take up identifiable positions in discussion and debate was itself thematised and incorporated into the Liberal Arts curriculum: this was achieved by introducing students to four ideologies, namely, liberalism, conservatism, socialism and feminism, which Liberal Arts teachers have tended to describe, rightly or wrongly, as "traditions", if only to point up the way they persist through time, in and through the position-takings and articulations of participants in ongoing debates. The introduction of the thematic of the four ideologies/traditions into the curriculum provided conceptually and historically rich material for scaffolding and rehearsing shifts from private-to-public-to-academic in written and spoken communication, enabling students to "try on" different discoursal identities and value-orientations, and to discuss writing conventions and model academic writing in ways that make these shifts and reorientations explicit.

The course was designed to provide an intensive induction into the discourses of the humanities and social sciences for non-traditional learners who did not bring with them the bundle of background knowledges, skills, attributes and orientations to self, other and world that tend to be taken for granted by those already "socialised" into academic discourses. A fundamental insight shared by designers of the course was that elements of this background would need to be thematised and made explicit in a curriculum designed with non-traditional learners in mind.

Given this aim, a strong connection with the Arts faculty was and remains crucial; for now as then, the pedagogical question: What kind of induction is needed to prepare non-traditional students for successful participation in the discourses of the humanities and social sciences?, cannot meaningfully be addressed in isolation from the disciplines and fields of inquiry themselves; and, in the final analysis, induction into the disciplines can only be fully accomplished within the disciplines themselves. The special task that the Liberal Arts program set for itself was to position itself as a halfway house between students' everyday lifeworlds and university study.

The original curriculum and support materials, and practices handed down by teacher-mentors, also bear the imprint of a determination to make explicit, through modelling, the "linguistic affordances"[5] by means of which participants in academic discourses establish their bona fides and communicate authoritatively in their writing and speaking, and to provide opportunities for students to rehearse these positioning moves in their own writing and speaking. Over the years, Liberal Arts practitioners have drawn upon a large and diverse body of language and learning research demonstrating that non-traditional students (and indeed, if we are to continue to move towards universal access to higher education, arguably all students) need contextualised and carefully scaffolded language and learning programs to facilitate their induction into discipline/field-specific literacies, and to give students access to the linguistic affordances that will enable them to become effective, critical readers and writers and to take up credible positions in discussion and debate across a range of academic discourses.

Entry into academic discourses can be described as involving a kind of *socialisation* process. There is a rapidly growing literature on curriculum innovations attempting to make aspects of students' "socialisation" within academic disciplines and practice-fields explicit in curriculum design and in teaching practices. Once again, Liberal Arts practitioners have continued to draw on this literature, both in reviewing and revising Liberal Arts course materials and in cross-faculty collaborative curriculum design. There is an extensive literature on pedagogical approaches that focus in various ways on the interaction between language, learning and knowledge acquisition through this academic socialisation process, employing a range of concepts and metaphors, such as "discoursal identity" (Burgess and Ivanic 2010; Ivanic 1990), "discourse communities" (Hyland 2009; McCormack 2002; Candlin and Hyland 1999; Bartholomae 1996; Swales 1990; Bazerman 1988),[6] "apprenticeship" and "induction" (Woodward-Kron 2004; Candlin and Plum 1999; Berkenkotter, Huckin and Ackerman 1991).

Drawing on these various approaches, in order to create a framework for collaborative work in a theoretically rich space, whilst remaining uncommitted to any one theoretical position (on the contrary, remaining fully engaged in the discussions and debates going on in the highly contested academic language and literacies domain), Liberal Arts practitioners have tried to elucidate, whilst at the same time attempting to understand, the dynamics of this socialisation process, and to develop an explicit practice, helping students to rehearse taking up new "subject positions" and "trying on" new "identities" in their writing and speaking, whilst also inviting them to reflect critically on these performances. The linguistic dimension of this process has been a central focus in developing the Liberal Arts curriculum. In case the notion that our task is to induct students into discourse communities should appear to be endorsing and facilitating, either consciously or unwittingly, students' unquestioning assimilation of the codes and conventions of academic discourses, suffice it to say that the explicit pedagogy developed in Liberal Arts is designed in such a way as to invite students, at each step along the way, into a space where they can take up a critical stance vis-à-vis their own "apprenticeship" (Moraitis, Carr and Daddow 2012; McCormack 2011).

Citing Mary Lea and Brian Street (1998), Roz Ivanic (2004) defines the concepts of academic socialisation and academic literacies in terms that will suffice to indicate the way these terms have been employed by Liberal Arts practitioners:

> "Academic Socialisation" is a conceptualisation of literacy based on the belief that there are different literacies in different contexts, so that students need to learn the specific characteristics of academic writing, and of the disciplinary culture into which they are entering. "Academic Literacies" is a conceptualisation of literacy based on the beliefs that literacies are heterogeneous, are shaped by interests, epistemologies and

power relations, have consequences for identity, and are open to contestation and change.

Note that Ivanic says that, from this perspective, induction into academic writing has "consequences for identity". This is because "the text and the processes of composing it are inextricable from the whole complex social interaction which makes up the communicative event in which they are situated, and meaning is bound up with social purposes for writing. Writing is purpose-driven communication in a social context". This is not to suggest that any radical shift of identity, in the strong sense of this term, is necessarily involved. Of course shifts of identity in the strong sense can and do sometimes occur, but when Liberal Arts practitioners adopt this language, the emphasis is primarily on "discoursal identity", that is, on the way participants establish their bona fides and, with varying degrees of competence, take up identifiable positions as authentic "insiders" within a discourse and speak and write with varying degrees of authority.

The Liberal Arts course was not designed to replicate what happens in the first years of an undergraduate degree; it was rather designed to create a space in which there would be "two-way traffic" between students' diverse everyday "lifeworlds" and educational backgrounds, on the one hand, and the academic discourses of the humanities and social sciences to which they were seeking access, on the other. In their initial induction into the socio-political/social-scientific regions of academic discourse, students are introduced first of all to the problematic nature of the private-public distinction-relation, and then in various ways share the experience of moving forwards and backwards between private, public-political and social-scientific discourses. Transition from public to academic discourse is rehearsed through essay writing, and the shifts in "discoursal identity" that occur in the process are made explicit. In their initial induction into literary studies/cultural studies and related regions of academic discourse, our students share their own personal and family stories and celebrate the rich diversity of ways of being in the world that they bring with them. Their introduction to semiotics begins with photographs and images through which they discover connections (and disconnections) between their own stories and the larger stories that their cultures "tell themselves".

One core aspect of the Liberal Arts course that calls for critical reflection here is the way it evokes the figure of an idealised agonistic space, within which students rehearse taking up subject positions in these competing discourses and critically engage with each other, whilst simultaneously also being encouraged to take up the role of second-order observer, as the contingent nature of these subject positions and the competing representations that they bring to these imaginary encounters is made explicit. In keeping with this constructivist rehearsal of encounters between contingent subjectivities and representations, the course also explicitly privileges critical, dialogical, deliberative and hermeneutical over positivistic approaches to knowledge, whilst leaving open and unresolved competing claims to validity of these competing approaches. Students are introduced to nomothetic approaches to knowledge when they study a unit entitled Economy and Society, and again in the second year of their studies, when they are introduced to a range of research methodologies; and the course introduces students at a very basic level to some of the epistemological and ontological problems that arise within this field of tensions.

The pedagogical intention behind this approach was, and still is, to make explicit the contingent nature of the "subject positions" and identities that students engage with, and "try on" (or not), in this two-way movement; to make visible—and available for critique—the various dimensions (sociolinguistic, political, cultural) in which (as well as the "affordances" by means of which), these shifts and self-constitutive reorientations take place in time and space; and lastly, to invite students into a space where the resulting experiences of de-familiarisation will be anticipated, and made explicit. Managed skilfully, and with care, this kind of staged induction can be liberating, rather than frightening or confusing; and it can arouse a passion for critical inquiry, as students come to see their own personal experiences mirrored in the wider society and culture and in the sociohistorical transformations through which the selves that we are have been constituted—transformations in which we are all consciously or unconsciously involved. But there are many assumptions that need to be unpacked here. It still remains an open question as to the conditions under which students will accept the invitation to participate in this kind of induction process.

The Students

The Liberal Arts course was designed to provide an intensive induction into the discourses of the humanities and social sciences for non-traditional adult learners who were returning to study; most of whom, going by anecdotal evidence, were returning to education for its perceived intrinsic value, whether or not they were also seeking a supported pathway into higher education. More recently it has served this latter purpose for growing numbers of exiting Victorian Certificate of Education (VCE) students—who by and large appear to be extrinsically rather than intrinsically motivated—whilst still continuing to attract highly motivated mature-age students, along with a significant minority of ESL students wanting a bridge between their ESL courses and higher education. There has been a steady increase in the number of low-achieving exiting VCE students seeking credit-bearing pathways into degree courses. This has occurred against the backdrop of "credential inflation" (Collins 1979) and a fierce competition among universities to attract low-SES and low-achieving students into degrees via fast-track diplomas.

Sadly, casualisation of teaching staff is occurring at precisely the moment when collaborative approaches to curriculum design and delivery by teams of experienced and committed teachers are most desperately needed.[7] One of the saddest losses that results from this casualisation process is the "inevitable loss of practitioner memory" (McCormack, unpublished chapter).

I do not wish to make any generalisations concerning the specific motivations, goals, hopes and aspirations of these new cohorts of students; suffice it to say that many appear to be very confused about where they are heading and what they hope to achieve through their studies, and that responding to the needs of these students will require a radical rethinking of the undergraduate curriculum. This rethinking is urgently required in a context where students who would previously have found their way into very low cost TAFE courses are now being recruited into degree courses and who are thereby, whether they are successful in their studies or not, accruing significant debt. The Grattan Institute (2013) reported in January 2013 that student debt had reached $26.3 billion. A media release by Universities Australia on 15 July 2013 reported, "Around two-thirds of students have reported incomes below the poverty line as student debt soars by almost 30 percent in just six years according to the findings of the University Student Finances in 2012 report". This is a global phenomenon; student debt in the US had reportedly reached $1 trillion by 2012, after surpassing the consumer debt in 2011 (Ross 2013).

Intensive recruitment of under-achieving students from low-SES backgrounds into undergraduate degree courses, on the one hand, and credential inflation across all areas of employment, on the other, have raised expectations as well as anxiety levels among students and their parents. Not surprisingly, high levels of attrition and student dissatisfaction with higher education have been reported (ACER 2010; James, Krause and Jennings 2010). This poses special challenges both for re-evaluating the Liberal Arts course and for rethinking what induction into the humanities and social sciences might entail for our diverse student cohorts.

The problem is not simply one of reconciling preparation for higher education with general education. The original course design sought to reconcile these two aims: providing an induction into academic discourses in the humanities and social sciences whilst offering a stand-alone curriculum that would be of benefit for students who did not necessarily intend to enrol in a degree. It would also be fair to say that Arts courses have historically had great success in reconciling the aims of inducting novices into academic fields of inquiry, whilst also providing general education and contributing to public enlightenment, all of which has resulted in wide recognition of the value of an Arts degree that has continued to resonate across the professions and throughout the wider society. The problem we are facing now is very different.

It may perhaps be best to bookmark this discussion by observing first of all that Arts courses have generally managed very well to reconcile the above aims on behalf of those students who were being groomed for professional and paraprofessional employment, and that undergraduate programs have progressively become more inclusive, as universities have paid greater attention to curriculum issues and to teaching. The universities, particularly, if not exclusively, in the Arts, have become increasingly reflective about cultural biases inherent in the curriculum, more reflexive in their approach to curriculum development, and more intent on going beyond the equation of social justice with access, seeking a deeper understanding of the dynamics of inclusion and exclusion.

Moreover, the special programs designed to enable non-traditional students to gain access to higher education (including preparatory programs and various forms of "embedded" academic skills development) have served to broaden access to professional and semi-professional employment as well as providing non-traditional students with an opportunity to engage in what was previously seen as the preserve of the affluent upper-middle classes, namely, pursuing higher education—whether "for its own sake", or for "self-improvement", or however else non-vocational educational aims may be described. The problem now is quite different. The question now is: how to reconcile all of these above aims with the possible need to design a "Year 13" for increasing numbers of students who are neither heading towards professional employment outcomes nor pursuing higher learning for edifying purposes—but who are nevertheless being inducted into lifelong debt.

The kind of intensive collaborative work that curriculum designers, teachers and teacher-mentors need to do, in order to find ways to respond to this situation, is deeply undermined by casualisation, on the one side, and accounting regimes that favour rigidity and an endless "reproduction of the same", on the other. At the same time, tragically, the very students who are most in need of a two-year intensive preparatory course before undertaking studies at undergraduate level are being promised fast-track pathways into degrees. In my view, precisely those features of the present context that bring the pedagogical question we are concerned with to the fore also, paradoxically, conceal it.

Two aspects of the present context stand out in this respect: first, the question of how to prepare non-traditional students for higher education is both compounded and complicated by the question of how to determine and address the educational needs of under-achieving school-leavers who are being recruited into higher education under pressure of credential inflation; second, the pedagogical question is being conflated with issues relating to competitive recruitment and retention. Whilst a high level of student attrition will obviously increase the urgency with which the pedagogical question presents itself, educators are increasingly forced to reframe this question in ways that conform to the logic of accounting: crudely, according to this logic, high student attrition and poor student satisfaction surveys mean that we have a "student engagement" problem to address, whereas low levels of attrition and positive student satisfaction surveys mean that students are "engaged".

From an accounting perspective, any other considerations will fail to show up on the radar. If, for example, retention can be increased by reducing student workloads and the amount of face-to-face contact, and by making pre-packaged resources available online, then from an accounting point of view this would be regarded as a successful "student engagement" strategy, regardless of what the implications might be for successful induction into the discourses of the humanities and social sciences. Naturally, educators will take a very different view of student engagement.

Kift *et al.* (2010, 12) appear to hold the view that there is a happy convergence between a bottom-up transition pedagogy that is grounded in a concern for social justice, and top-down, whole-of-university approaches to student engagement, being promoted under the sign of the *first-year experience*. It "seems reasonable", they think, "to assume that transition pedagogy in action would be of considerable economic benefit to an institution". In my view there are several reasons for remaining sceptical about such happy convergences, just as there are good reasons to be sceptical about the notion that we are moving towards universal access (Trow 2000).

One of the facts conveniently overlooked by the elite-mass-universal progressivist narrative, as Tony Becher and Paul R Trowler (2001) observe, is the increasingly vocational orientation of expanding areas of

HE (4–5). Putting it bluntly, the progressivist narrative covers over the fact that the apparent expansion of access to higher education, especially in its most recent phase, which is aimed at low socioeconomic status (SES) and low-achieving cohorts, who would in the past have enrolled in TAFE courses at minimal cost, actually turns out to be access to a very expensive, and, often as not, very hit-and-miss, form of vocational training, to pay for which these students must enter into a lifelong debt.

Shifting from Operational to Ontological Engagement

Zepke and Leach (2010) have identified three recurrent themes in the large body of recent research on student engagement: 1) Students "want to exercise their agency" and do best when they are intrinsically motivated; 2) Student engagement requires engagement between teachers and students; 3) Institutional support is needed to create an educational environment that is supportive, conducive to learning and responsive to the changing needs and expectations of diverse cohorts of students. From a pedagogical perspective, these three statements would appear to be axiomatic; and it is perhaps a sign of the times that they need to be stated at all. Following Barnett and Coate (2005), Zepke and Leach argue that institutions need to shift focus from *operational* engagement to *ontological* engagement, fostering active citizenship and building the social and cultural capital of non-traditional students.

From the *operational* perspective, student engagement is viewed in "mechanical" terms (Barnett and Coate 2005). The crudest example of this would be when an auditor can be satisfied that the "engagement" of a non-attending student is verified by an exchange of emails between teacher/manager and student, thus ensuring that the institution will retain its funding for this student. From this *operational* perspective then, addressing the issue of "student engagement" can be summed up as the sum of measures taken to ensure expanding market-share and maximum student retention, and to micromanage "the ordering of curriculum elements so as to produce the greatest output possible as economically as possible".

Zepke and Leach (2010) agree with Barnett and Coate that the bulk of mainstream literature on student engagement is too narrowly focused on students' attitudinal dispositions and motivations and on assessment and operational issues. Based on their review of the literature on engagement from the early 1990s to 2003, McMahon and Portelli (2004) have also observed that: "the primary focus is on procedural aspects that relate to engagement, that is, on specific procedures, strategies and skills that teachers ought to develop or implement in order to secure student engagement". I would add that this literature is often transparently allied to an institutional preoccupation with student retention that is driven by accounting rather than pedagogical concerns.

The First-Year Experience Report (James, Krause and Jennings 2010) produced by the centres for higher education research at Melbourne and Griffith Universities is a case in point. It is an impressionistic survey of student reports on their own behaviours, dispositions, aspirations and experiences of undergraduate study. Its main conclusions appear to be geared towards the kinds of strategies being promoted by managers to keep students enrolled at any cost (preferably at very low cost), which invariably means at the expense of academic rigor. For instance, after comparing 2004 and 2009 cohorts and noting that the 2009 students are "spending fewer days and less time on campus", the authors of the Report leap to the happy conclusion that: "These findings suggest students are instrumentally balancing their time commitments and are adept at regulating their academic experiences to achieve their goals" (71). After noting also that "staff-student interactions are down from the 2004 figures," the authors of the report go on to point out that there have been "dramatic rises in the use of various forms of ICTs" and leap to another happy conclusion: "Given that the 2009 students appear committed to their studies and are highly self-regulating, we suppose they manage their time effectively and use ICT and peer support strategically to supplement the apparent reduction in course contact time." (71)

Based on highly selective arrangement and tendentious interpretations of data, the report arbitrarily constructs and generalises the figure of an autonomous agent who makes rational choices and is "highly self-regulating". She is a consumer of education as a private good. She is clear about her goals. She is "strategic" in her engagement with peers and teachers, balancing her time capably and efficiently. As in so many other examples of this "tell-the-managers-what-they-want-to-hear" genre, ICT is presented as the universal medium through which this ideal-typical neo-liberal individual can effectively access all the information she needs and compartmentalise her various commitments.

Barnett and Coate (2005, 144) acknowledge that "In a marketised age students may or may not want to be stretched cognitively and personally." The question remains, however, whether educators simply accept this as a given and fall into line with management priorities, that is, whether they follow the line of least resistance and submit to the imperative of keeping students "engaged" in the merely *operational* sense, or whether they hold onto a larger conception of their role as educators, defend their autonomy on this basis, confront this situation in all of its complexity and revise their curriculum and pedagogical goals accordingly.

It would, of course, be naïve to suppose that this is a straightforward either/or question. To begin with, as Barnett and Coate observe, we cannot expect students to commit to higher education with the level of seriousness that may be expected of them by lecturers who are completely immersed in their scholarship and research. In a "marketised age," relatively few students will be likely to present with scholarly orientations and motivations; and this is especially so of school leavers (as opposed to mature-age students) from non-traditional backgrounds. It follows that they will feel immediately alienated in a learning environment that simply takes such orientations and motivations for granted. Nor will they "develop in significant ways if the atmosphere is one of indifference, disrespect, undue gravity or excessive emotional risk". Indeed, this is how it will be for them if those who design curriculum and those who teach are not able to meet these students halfway and *engage* with them, if not quite on their own terms, then at least in terms that acknowledge who they are and welcome them as they are whilst *inviting* them to enter into a new kind of space and to "try on", as it were, new ways of relating to self, other and world.

How to Conceptualise Ontological Engagement?

Against the grain of the narrow, operational focus of mainstream policy discussion about student engagement, Barnett and Coate (2005) seek to initiate a richer discussion about engagement that encompasses epistemological, moral–practical and ontological dimensions. Whilst it may well be second nature to many Arts educators to understand student engagement in something like these terms, there are two reasons for bringing this issue to the fore at this point in time: First, the policy discourse concerning student engagement is being constructed in regions of the university which are far removed from, and seemingly immunised against contamination by, the aims and concerns of particular disciplines and fields of inquiry. Second, it is doubtful in any case that Arts educators today have even a common language, let alone shared understandings, that would enable them to generate a counter-discourse about engagement and induction (or "socialisation") into the humanities and social sciences.

Engagement in what?

Arguably, Arts educators have never had such a common language. There were inherited ways of thinking—however vaguely articulated—about the nature and value of an Arts education, which centred on ideas of individual self-development, self-realisation and general edification. This "liberal-humanist" (i.e., secularised Protestant) conception underwent several mutations both in the Anglo-American pastoral tradition, which foregrounded teaching over research, and in the Germano–American (Humboldtian) tradition that privileged research over teaching; yet in both traditions the induction into higher learning is conceived as a thoroughgoing self-transformative experience. This idea was reinterpreted as the modern university transformed itself from an elite to a mass institution. Barnett and Coate's (2005, 146) account of student engagement appears to be drawn ineluctably back into that tradition. They rehearse an idea of education with a long pedigree, namely, that to enter into higher education is to embark upon a self-transformative journey that "has a time horizon", that it will involve trusting, giving over, in the anticipation that this will be a journey of self-discovery, culminating in "a new self-belief".

Through the second half of the 20th century there were also emergent ways of thinking about the role of the humanities and social sciences in both general education and public enlightenment, ideas that were closely bound up with democracy as a form of life and with the emergence of the New Social Movements. The pedagogical project that opens up in this context places emphasis on education for active citizenship, responsible autonomy and critique. The Diploma of Liberal Arts belongs squarely within this more recent tradition—yet, having said this, it also belongs as surely as any Arts program to the former tradition; indeed, it is hard to imagine that any pedagogical project could exit completely from the discourses of self-development and self-realisation. The question is whether or not these ways of thinking are still current, and, if so, whether or not they could generate the kind of counter-hegemonic projects that would be needed to rethink student engagement in *ontological* rather than *operational* terms.

Against the grain of the mainstream operational discourse, McMahon and Portelli (2004) complain that the bulk of the literature on engagement is generated from conservative or liberal perspectives that "fail to address substantive ethical and political issues relating to student engagement". They argue that this is because both conservatives and liberals, important differences between them notwithstanding, "see engagement as politically and educationally neutral, and as such serve to reinforce the status quo including the inequities embedded in it even if their aim is not consciously to do so". McMahon and Portelli argue for a politically engaged, "critical-democratic" concept of student engagement (15).

Zepke and Leach (2010, 8) also seek to promote a "democratic-critical conception of engagement that goes beyond strategies, techniques or behaviours, a conception in which engagement is participatory, dialogic and leads not only to academic achievement but to success as an active citizen." They advocate a shift of paradigm, restating Barnett and Coate's three dimensions of ontological engagement (knowing, acting and being) in terms of active citizenship:

> The first is that students learn how to make legitimate claims in a world of uncertainty and to negotiate challenges to such claims. The second is how students can learn to act constructively in the world by using ethical political processes. The third involves students becoming aware of themselves and their potential to effect change in a world that is open, fluid and contested.

Liberal Arts: a curriculum for ontological engagement?

Whilst it remains an open question as to whether or not the conditions still exist for reviving the project of a public-collegial university with an emancipatory and democratic mission, it nevertheless seems still to be a worthwhile aim to re-imagine a curriculum that would address, in various ways, the three dimensions of student engagement outlined by Barnett and Coate as revised by Zepke and Leach above: 1) students need to learn how to "make legitimate claims," and they need to know how to "negotiate challenges" to their knowledge claims—and to do this effectively within the university and within those regions of life to which higher education provides privileged access, they must not only learn the rules of the game but also develop understanding and insight through deep learning, along with the linguistic and technical competence needed to engage in critical analysis, rational deliberation and argument; 2) they need also to acquire a fine sense of judgment and a capacity for responsible autonomy in the moral–practical sphere; and 3) they need to develop self-awareness, along with a strong capacity for reflexivity and creative self-alteration—in a postmodern "risk society" that no longer provides any clear guidelines.

A cursory glance over the Liberal Arts curriculum will show that it is oriented towards a conception of active citizenship that resonates strongly with Zepke and Leach's formulations. The curriculum also reflects a conception of ontological engagement that lends itself very well to critical analysis and revision in terms of the threefold schema discussed above. Yet the question that I find most troubling here is whether or not the conditions exist at present for the realisation of such a pedagogical project. Insofar as ontological engagement in the discourses of the humanities and social sciences is realised through the Liberal Arts curriculum, it is above all achieved through the evocation of a vital and dynamic internal relation between the discourses of the humanities and social sciences within the modern university, on the one hand, and the figure of deliberative democracy as a form of life, on the other.

The Liberal Arts course was first formally accredited in 1993 but its fundamental aims, its curriculum design and the pedagogy underpinning it grew out of a context that, whilst it had roots in an educational milieu initially fostered by the Whitlam government, was also in crucial respects unique to Victoria in the 1970s and 80s, which saw a robust culture of experimentation and innovation at grass-roots level. This was also a time when there were vital connections between academia and the New Social Movements ("second-wave" feminism, the New Left, civil rights, postcolonial movements, environmentalism, gay activism), and when the idea that there was some kind of internal relationship between a robust and inclusive higher education system, a critical public sphere and participatory democracy, were still strong, even if the conditions for realising this idea had already dissolved in reality.

The Liberal Arts curriculum still bears the imprint of this historical moment, and many features of the course rest on the expectation that students can be provided with the knowledge and know-how to become active participants in this imagined space that connects the modern university to the critical public sphere and to deliberative and participatory democracy as a form of life. So if we are to seek to understand what a shift in thinking about student engagement, from operational to *ontological engagement*, might mean now, we must remain open to the possibility that this moment may well have passed. Times have indeed changed—the student cohorts have changed, the social movements have all suffered the consequences of "mainstreaming," and the social, economic, political and cultural contexts have all radically changed—so we must avoid any temptation to reassure ourselves that what appears to have "worked" in the past can continue to work in the future.

Where to From Here? Rethinking the Public University?

The court is still out on whether or not the necessary conditions exist at this historical moment for reviving the project of a public–collegial university with a democratic mission (Habermas 1987a; Calhoun 2006, 2009; Marginson 2006). It is my contention that shifting the discourse of student engagement from an operational to an ontological plane hinges directly upon this question—hinging, that is, not so much on the answer to it as the serious asking of it. This is not to say that reflection on the question of student engagement in the ontological sense must wait upon some kind of cosmic realignment of forces that will once again provide the necessary conditions for a counter-hegemonic project of this kind to resurrect itself; on the contrary, I would argue that rethinking student engagement across the humanities and social sciences ought to be the starting point for making the necessary imaginative leap—and this in turn requires a leap of faith.

It is also important, I think, that in opening this question we remain mindful of the fact that this project has had a very short and tenuous lifespan. The question concerning the possibility of reigniting the project of the public university must remain open, but under present conditions it seems clear that the often-cited special relationship between academic freedom and the various freedoms and rights celebrated in the constitutions of modern democracies has a very short recent history and has only ever been partially realised. Through the 1970s and into the early 1980s the project of the public university seemed capable of realisation. [8] By the end of the 1980s, enthusiasm for this project was already succumbing to internal critiques on the one side and powerful external forces on the other. I draw attention to this situation, neither out of nostalgia nor to give way to pessimism, but rather to suggest that any coherent discourse about student engagement in the Arts must take account of it—or, putting it slightly differently: In my view, "Whither the Arts?" and "Whither student engagement?" are one and the same question.

Reflecting on the question of whether the project of the public–collegial university with a democratic mission can be reignited under present conditions, Marginson (2006) draws attention to an underexploited potential: "Universities have neglected the evolution of two-way flows and flat dialogue. But they have the technologies and discursive resources for conversation at a previously impossible scale". This, of course, can only appear *as* an unrealised potential from within the normative horizons of the project of the public university. Viewed from the perspective of the *longue durée*, the apparent anomaly disappears. From a long-range historical perspective, the attempt to forge deep connections between the modern research university and deliberative democracy as a form of life is a very recent and very fragmentary development; and it is yet to be seen how tenuous or how durable those links are. As Calhoun (2009) observes, whilst the link between *research* as a ceaseless quest for new knowledge (the definitive idea of the modern university), free inquiry and the public good was conceptually underpinned and justified by Enlightenment ideals, its condition of possibility was an intimate connection between the elite university and the state. Leaving aside the question of how far this special connection between the elite universities and the state has remained intact through the massification of higher education, on the one hand, and the transformation of the state, from fiduciary state to client state, under pressure of economic globalisation, on the other, the deepening chasm between the elite research universities and the "intensive teaching vocational universities" is now starkly manifest (Marginson 2006).

Whilst the privileging of research over other functions has continued apace, research is increasingly driven by "pressures for short-term productivity, the organisation of research on the basis of private property rights and the pursuit of revenue, and intensified hierarchy and competition" (Calhoun 2009). This translates into a high degree of academic freedom for a very privileged few. Meanwhile, the public mission has been scaled back, a process that has been aided, ironically perhaps, by the identification of the public good with state interests, whilst the welfare state has been systematically dismantled and succeeded by the neoliberal state. As Calhoun observes, in the neoliberal state there is a residual connection with the idea of the public good in the idea that universities offer students access to careers and to social mobility. Given the doubtful prospects for fulfilling this promise, coupled with the burgeoning student debt, it is difficult to see how this illusion can be sustained.

Reconciling Vocationalism with an Arts Education?

Discussion and debate about the transformation of the university from an elite to a mass institution began in a context in which progressivist educational ideas and ideas about the public mission of universities were widely current. Questions that arose in that context present themselves today in a dramatically altered world, as the "imaginary" of a public–collegial university with a social-critical and democratic mission has given way to a world in which higher education policy is increasingly shaped by intensifying managerialism and marketisation. One aspect of this shift is the drive to position students as consumers of private goods and seekers of competitive advantage in a volatile job market where access to attractive employment options is constrained by credential inflation; another is the colonisation of the public–collegial academic system and the increasing subsumption of disciplinary structures and collegial relations by line-management.

Students are under increasing pressure on all sides to buy into the crude vocationalist, competitive marketplace narrative. Meanwhile, the concept of lifelong learning, originally the centrepiece of an adult-learning discourse about self-discovery and enrichment, has also been hijacked by neoliberal agendas. Ronald G. Sultana (2011), invokes the Althusserian concept of "interpellation" (which refers to the manner in which an individual is "called out", as it were, and invited to re-constitute herself as a Subject in terms of the dominant ideology):

> The client, customer or user is interpellated by the neo-liberal state as a free-floating, self-directed, enterprising individual, who is invited to access services to maximise individual benefit, and the devil take the hindmost: private consumer interest prevails over public interest (Rose, 1999). This is nothing but a "hollowing out" of citizenship, marking the decline of the public (Marquand, 2004).

Insofar as the student accepts this invitation and re-constitutes herself as Subject in terms of the dominant (crude-vocationalist and private-consumer) narratives, to that extent her potential for effective socialisation and for critical self-evaluation and self-alteration, within a public-collegial scholarly *habitus*, will be arrested, in some cases perhaps even permanently. Students need to be invited to take a step back, to develop the capacity for critical reflection, and to discover something of intrinsic value in the courses they are studying.

For all that, students will be more inclined to accept this invitation when their future employment aspirations and their anxieties about outcomes have been assuaged, and where transitional arrangements, and further study and vocational outcomes are clear to them. As Richard Teese (2012) puts it:

> If a university draws heavily on schools which have a high proportion of middling to low achievers, this carries implications regarding the mix of intrinsic (classroom-based) and extrinsic (economic and career) benefits that the university must work into its teaching program. It must do more than impart academic routine—how to research an issue, what resources to use, how to report learning in an academically acceptable way. The intrinsic incentive to learn represented by an inspiring teacher enlivens the classroom experience of the student. But to sustain the learning effort and continue to engage the student requires the teacher to connect learning to what the student already knows (through their personal experience), why a topic or issue is of wider importance (the social challenge and the public benefit) and where the learning leads (the economic or private benefit).

The challenge ahead for Arts faculty and, indeed, for whole-of-university approaches to a wide range of policy issues, from student engagement and transition to the discourse surrounding "graduate capabilities", may be to find new ways to recover vital elements of a broad general education centred on the Arts and reconcile these with an enriched and more sophisticated form of vocationalism. The way ahead will not be straightforward. Rising to this challenge will require somehow steering a course between the Scylla and Charybdis of the "strong state/free market paradigm" and staying well clear of an increasingly intrusive "interventionist state" (Hickox 1995). Yet despite the difficulties, at this historical moment, of heeding Dewey's call to "combine contextualisation with depth of learning" (Ryan 2003), this may yet be the surest way to meet our students halfway and offer them opportunities to expand their horizons whilst accepting their more immediate and limited concerns and their "instrumental" approach to postsecondary education.

Besides, as Ryan (2003, 3) observes, speaking in this case from a US higher education context, there are at least two pedagogically sound reasons for attempting such a reconciliation: "The first is cognitive: students may find it easier to understand an idea or a theory when it is taught in a practical context. The second is motivational: students may try harder to learn a theory or a formal technique when it is taught in a practical context." Ryan goes on to report (11) that, by contrast with the tendency of secondary "voc. ed." courses to entrench and exacerbate social inequalities, recent research indicates that postsecondary vocational education tends rather to "produce economic benefits for participants, increase average educational attainments, and reduce the inequality of educational and social outcomes".

In an effort to move beyond "the economic/vocational versus liberal/academic binary that traditionally underpins philosophical debate about the purpose of HE", Peach (2010) advocates adopting a "socially critical vocationalism (SCV)". This approach, by contrast with the crude vocationalism and "possessive individualism" that has been the subject of a variety of sociological critiques (Hickox 1995), "is about enabling individuals to act and think more autonomously, critically and responsibly in both their social and working lives" (Peach 2010). If the critical dimension were to be realised in practice, this form of vocationalism would, Peach argues,

> ... develop the student's understanding of the role of his or her profession within contemporary society and the role that it plays in shaping the social, political, economic and cultural contexts in which we live. It may also lead students to challenge the way a profession is practiced and organised, and whether the way it influences society is democratic, fair and just.

A comprehensive and holistic approach to curriculum design with such aims in view can also benefit from paying close attention to what the research is telling us about the motivations of different cohorts as well as students' changing motivations over time. Damon Anderson (2012) reports on recent research that "while young school leavers starting their careers are largely driven by instrumental and explicitly vocational motives", students aged 25 years and above, including those seeking to upgrade their qualifications for career advancement or retraining purposes, "are motivated to an increasing degree by the perceived intrinsic value of further study in VET and its role in meeting their personal growth and development objectives".

It is not clear from Anderson's account whether the liberal-humanist catch-all terms, "personal growth" and "development," adequately capture what the students interviewed would have wished to express, or rather whether, as I would suspect, a wide variety of non-vocational, or at least non-instrumentalist, aims and aspirations. Reflecting on my own experience in the Liberal Arts program, this nomenclature sadly fails to capture the rich diversity of life stories that students bring along with them, and the narratives that they construct as they progress in their studies. As students progress through their studies they do, as Anderson's study shows, tend to become less "instrumental" in their approach to learning; but they nevertheless very often become more purposive too, and tend to articulate larger goals. Their horizons expand; they become more aware of the world around them, more critical and more inclined to want to be part of something larger than themselves. Anderson's account might create the impression, whether he intends this or not, that this expansion of students' horizons, the widening of their "hermeneutical circle", and the honing of their critical skills, somehow entails a turning away from the "vocational" to the "personal". What is screened out from this account is the way these developments can deepen and enrich students' sense of vocation. The problem here I think is that the available discourse about vocation is impoverished.

If a "whole-of-institution" approach to student engagement is to take account of the diversity of life stories that students bring with them, then the conditions must first be there to foster the kind of dialogue across the university and the wider community that will make us all better able to listen attentively and respond to those stories. There are many stories to tell, but at this moment, as I write, I keep thinking about the senior postal officer who attended night classes for four years, not for career purposes or because he wanted to go on and complete a degree, but because he felt a burning need to be, as he put it in his valedictory speech, "part of the conversation"—that is, he was expressing the need to be part of what Leesa Wheelahan (2010) describes as society's conversation about itself.[9]

Yet the question remains as to whether the conditions exist to create a space for engagement of the kind we are contemplating here; it is also open to question whether the conditions exist that would make it possible to reconcile the inherited commitments of Arts educators to general education, public enlightenment and social critique, with a more enlightened form of vocational education than is currently on offer.

Postscript

An Australian Research Council (ARC)-funded project that examined emerging "organisational cultures" across 17 universities through the 1990s found that the shift to corporate models and "a new kind of strategic leadership," "partly detached from the academic units below", was "greater than expected" (Marginson 2000). Two aspects of this transformation are particularly pertinent to the issue at hand. First, an increasing distance between managers and academics (and the increasingly subordinate status of academics). Second, a disjunction between the kind of investments required to develop comprehensive, long-term, whole-of-university collaborative projects, as opposed to the radically unstable forces driving this process of change, which continually (and often intentionally and explicitly) disrupt conditions required for ongoing commitments of any kind and militate against any long-term, university-wide projects. As Marginson and Considine (2000, 234) explain, "What is in question is the capacity of the newly reformed systems to connect organically to the academic side, and to nurture a process of institutional development that is grounded, inner controlled, distinctive and long-term in character". The challenge that this situation presents to educators who would hope to take a holistic and theoretically grounded approach to curriculum design, and to engage in long-term, cross-faculty collaborative approaches to student engagement and transition issues, cannot be overstated.

Acknowledgements

I wish to thank the following colleagues for their generous support and critical feedback. First of all, special thanks to Peter Moraitis, who read several drafts very closely and provided throughout a masterly blend of rigorous critique, timely advice, and encouragement. I have learned a great deal about teaching and learning from Peter over my past eight years of teaching in the Liberal Arts program, so much so that the train of thought running through this chapter seems to me to be a distillation of that eight-year conversation. The following people have also been significant interlocutors over varying periods of time, and I wish to express my gratitude for the care they took in reading earlier drafts and providing invaluable critical feedback: Paul Ashton, Roger Averill, Steven Butcher, Amanda Carr, Andrew Funston, Miguel Gil, Dion Hallpike, Edward Lock, Robin McCormack and Jacinta Richards.

Notes

[1] The course was designed by a group of teachers from the Further Education area of the Western Melbourne Institute of TAFE (WMIT) and lecturers from a range of disciplines in the humanities and social sciences at Victoria University. It was first accredited by the Victorian Government accrediting body in 1993.

[2] The fundamental principles and practices underpinning the Liberal Arts curriculum—i.e., a scaffolded induction of non-traditional students into academic discourses; a strong emphasis on ontological engagement and critical agency across public and academic regions of the discourses of the humanities and social sciences; metacognitive approaches to language and learning and "ways of knowing"; and *writing* as the primary activity in and through which non-traditional students take up authentic "subject-positions" in academic discourses—all grew out of the curriculum of an earlier Return to Study (RTS) course developed for adult learners at WMIT. The crucial texts describing the approach in the RTS and underpinning the Liberal Arts curriculum are McCormack and Pancini (1991) and especially McCormack (2002).

[3] This policy development was precipitated by the Australian Government's decision, in response to the *Review of Australian Higher Education* by Denise Bradley *et al.* (2008), to provide special funding to support the recruitment and retention of increasing numbers of students from low-SES backgrounds. This recruitment drive has resulted in a marked increase in enrolments of students who are first in their families to study at university, as reported in *The First Year Experience in Australian Universities*, jointly published by the centres for HE research at Melbourne and Griffith universities (James, Krause and Jennings 2010, 63).

[4] In some respects the Liberal Arts course stands in a similar relation, at least in structural terms, if not in pedagogical, epistemological and ontological terms, with community colleges in the US.

[5] A widely used concept in linguistics with a long pedigree: There is no space here to illustrate the ways in which this concept has been deployed in the teaching of academic writing, but Van Lier (2004) identifies three definitive features of the concept: First, "an affordance expresses a relationship between a person and a linguistic expression (a speech act, a speech event); it is *action potential*; it is a *relation of possibility*". Second, "linguistic affordances are specified in the linguistic expression, and available to the active interlocutor (or addressee) who may pick up one or more of those affordances as they are relevant at the moment".

Third, "the affordances picked up serve the agent—depending on his or her abilities—to promote further action and lead to higher and more successful levels of interaction".

[6] For an example of a cross-faculty collaborative approach to curriculum design working within the conceptual framework of a "Discourse Community", see Moraitis, Carr and Daddow (2012).

[7] The NTEU reports that the proportion of academic teaching staff employed on a sessional or short-term contract basis is now at 60 percent (cited Dann 2012)

[8] This, I think, is why there was such intense interest in Habermas' work in the Anglo-American academic world through the 1980s, given that his whole scholarly enterprise, from his early work on the student movement in the 1960s, via *The Theory of Communicative Action* to his later work on law and democracy and "discourse ethics," places the university-based scholar-researcher in a privileged position at the centre of the projects of autonomy and democracy.

[9] Leesa Wheelahan's (2010) call to bring knowledge back into the curriculum is motivated by a concern that, without access to society's conversation about itself, non-traditional students "will always be on the outside looking in" (163).

Reference List

Abbott, Andrew. 2001. *Chaos of Disciplines,* Chicago: University of Chicago Press.

—. 2002. "The Disciplines and the Future," in Steven Brint, ed., 2002: 205–230.

Anderson, Damon. 2003. "Individual Learners, Choice and Lifelong Learning." *Strategic Directions for VET,* 7th National Conference of the Centre for the Economics of Education and Training (CEET), held at Monash University, 15 September 2003, Ascot House, Melbourne.

—. 2004. "Adult Learners and Choice in Further Education and Training Markets: Constructing the Jigsaw Puzzle." *International Journal of Training Research,* 2 (2):1–23.

—. 2008. "Productivism, Vocational and Professional Education, and the Ecological Question," *Vocations and Learning* 1:105–129. doi: 10.1007/s12186-008-9007-0.

Barnett, Ronald. 2001. "Relationships Between Teaching and Research in Higher Education in England." *Higher Education Quarterly* 55 (2): 158–174

—. 2013. *Imagining the University*, Routledge/Taylor and Francis, USA

Barnett, Ronald, & Kelly Coate. 2005. *Engaging the Curriculum in Higher Education*, Maidenhead, UK: Society for Research into Higher Education and Open University Press.

Bartholomae, David. 1986. "Inventing the University." *Journal of Basic Writing*, 5 (1): 4–23

Bartholomae, David, and John Schilb. 2011. "Reconsiderations: 'Inventing the University' at 25: an Interview with David Bartholomae." *College English* 73 (3): 260–282.

Bazerman, Charles. 1992. Review of "Contending Rhetorics: Writing in Academic Disciplines," by George Dillon, in *Society* 21 (3):501-503, Cambridge University Press, [Accessed: 16/10/2013 20:12] Available from http://www.jstor.org/stable/4168376

—. 2005. "A Response to Anthony Fleury's 'Liberal Education and Communication Against the Disciplines': A View from the World of Writing." *Communication Education* 54 (1):86–91

Becher, Tony. 1981. "Towards a Definition of Disciplinary Cultures." *Studies in Higher Education* 6 (2):109-122. doi: 10.1080/03075078112331379362

—. 1989. *Academic Tribes and Territories: Intellectual Inquiry and the Cultures of Disciplines*, Milton Keynes [England]; Bristol, PA., USA: Society for Research into Higher Education: Open University Press.

—. 1994. "The significance of Disciplinary Differences." *Studies in Higher Education* 19:2, 151–161. doi: 10.1080/03075079412331382007.

Belcher, Diane. 1994. "The Apprenticeship Approach to Advanced Academic Literacy: Graduate Students and Their Mentors." *English for Specific Purposes* 13(1):23–34.

Berkenkotter, Carol, Thomas Huckin and John Ackerman. 1991. "Social Context and Socially Constructed Texts: The Initiation of a Graduate Student into a Writing Research Community." In *Textual Dynamics of the Professions* edited by Charles Bazerman, and James Paradis, 191–215. Madison, Wisconsin: The University of Wisconsin Press.

Berkenkotter, Carol, and Thomas N. Huckin. 1993. "Rethinking Genre from a Sociocognitive Perspective." *Written Communication* 10 (4):475-509. doi: 10.1177/0741088393010004001.

—. 1995. *Genre knowledge in disciplinary communication: Cognition/culture/power*. Hillsdale, New Jersey: Lawrence Erlbaum.

Bernstein, Basil. 1999. "Vertical and Horizontal Discourse: An Essay." *British Journal of Sociology of Education* 20 (2): 157–173.

Bradley, Denise, Peter Noonan, Helen Nugent, and Bill Scales. 2008. *Review of Australian Higher Education: Final Report*. Department of Education, Employment and Workplace Relations. [Accessed August 20, 2012]. Available from www.deewr.gov.au/he_review_finalreport.

Brint, Steven, ed. 2002. *The Future of the City of Intellect: The Changing American University.* Stanford, CA: Stanford University Press.

Burgess, Amy and Roz Ivanic. 2010. "Writing and Being Written: Issues of Identity Across Timescales." *Written Communication* 27(2) 228–255. doi: 10.1177/0741088310363447.

Calhoun, Craig, ed. 1993. *Habermas and the Public Sphere*, Cambridge, Massachusetts, MIT Press.

—. 2006. "The University and the Public Good." *Thesis Eleven* 84:7–43. doi: 10.1177/0725513606060516.

—. 2009. "Free Inquiry and Public Mission in the Research University." *Social Research* 76 (3): 901–932.

Candlin, Christopher N., and Ken Hyland, eds. 1999. *Writing*: *Text, Processes and Practice*, London and New York, Longman.

Candlin, Christopher N., and Guenter A. Plum. 1999. "Engaging with Challenges of Interdiscursivity in Academic Writing: Researchers, Students and Tutors," in *Writing: Texts, Processes and Practices,* edited by Christopher Candlin and Ken Hyland, 193–218. London: Longman.

Castoriadis, Cornelius. 1997. "The Crisis of the Identification Process." *Thesis Eleven* 49: 85–9.

Collins, Randall. 1979. *The Credential Society: an Historical Sociology of Education and Stratification,* San Diego, Academic Press. Dann, Caron E. 2012. "Casual Not Smart," *Times Higher Education* 5/24/2012, Issue 2051, 19–19.

Flowerdew, John. 2001. "Discourse Community, Legitimate Peripheral Participation, and the Nonnative-English-Speaking Scholar." *TESOL Quarterly* 34 (1):127–150.

Funston, Andrew. 2012. *Non-traditional Students Making Their Way in Higher Education: An Australian Case Study.* Research Report 35. Parkville Victoria: Youth Research Centre, Graduate School of Education, University of Melbourne. Available from http://web.education.unimelb. edu.au/yrc/linked_documents/RR35.pdf.

Graff, Gerald. 2003. *Clueless in Academe*: *How Schooling Obscures the Life of the Mind.* New Haven and London: Yale University Press.

Habermas, Jürgen. 1971. *Towards a Rational Society: Student Protest, Science and Politics.* Translated by, Jeremy J. Shapiro. London: Heinemann Books,

—. 1987[a]. "The Idea of the University: Learning Processes," Translated by John R. Blazek, New German Critique, Special Issue on the Critiques of the Enlightenment, 41: 3–22.

—. 1987[b]. *The Theory of Communicative Action, Volume II*. Translated by Thomas McCarthy, Boston, USA: Beacon Press.

—. 1988. *On the Logic of the Social Sciences*. Translated by Shierry Weber Nicholson & Jerry A. Stark, Cambridge, UK: Polity Press.

—. 1991. *The Theory of Communicative Action, Volume 1*. Translated by Thomas McCarthy, Cambridge, UK: Polity Press

—. 1992. *The Structural Transformation of the Public Sphere: An Enquiry into a Category of Bourgeois Society*. Translated by T. Burger with F. Lawrence, Cambridge, UK: Polity Press

—. 1996. *Between Facts and Norms: Contributions to a Discourse Theory of Law and Democracy*. Translated by W. Rehg, Cambridge, Massachusetts: MIT Press. Hickox, Mike. 1995. "Situating Vocationalism." *British Journal of Sociology of Education* 16 (2): 153–163.

Hirsch, Eric Donald Jr. 1989. *Cultural Literacy*. Sydney Aust: Schwartz Publishing

Hyland, Ken. 2009. *Academic Discourse*: *English in a Global Context*, London: Continuum

Ivanic, Roz. 1998. *Writing and Identity*: *the Discoursal Construction of Identity in Academic Writing*, Philadelphia, PA, John Benjamins.

Jamelske, Eric. 2009. "Measuring the Impact of a University First-Year Experience Program on Student GPA and Retention." *High Education* (2009) 57:373–391. doi: 10.1007/s10734-008-9161-1

Kift, Sally. 2009. *Articulating a Transition Pedagogy to Scaffold and to Enhance the First Year Student Learning Experience in Australian Higher Education - Final Report for ALTC Senior Fellowship Program*. Australian Learning and Teaching Council. [Accessed October 1, 2013]. Available from http://www.olt.gov.au/resource-first-year-learning-experience-kift-2009.

Kift, Sally, Karen Nelson, and John Clarke. 2010. "Transition Pedagogy: A Third Generation Approach to FYE - a Case Study of Policy and Practice for the Higher Education Sector." *The International Journal of the First Year in Higher Education* 1 (1): 1–20.

Kimber, Megan. 2003. "The Tenured 'Core' and the Tenuous 'Periphery': the Casualisation of Academic Work in Australian Universities." *Journal of Higher Education Policy and Management* 25 (1):41–50. doi: 10.1080/ 1360080032000066988.

Lea, Mary R., and Brian V. Street. 1998. "Student Writing in Higher Education: An Academic Literacies Approach." *Studies in Higher Education* 23 (2): 157–172.

Lea, Mary R. 2004. "Academic Literacies: A Pedagogy for Course Design." *Studies in Higher Education* 29 (6):739-756. doi: 10.1080/03075070 42000287230.

McCormack, Robin and Geraldine Pancini. 1991. *Learning to Learn: Introducing Adults to the Culture, Context and Conventions of Knowledge : a Guide for Teachers*, Melbourne : Division of Further Education, Ministry of Education.

McCormack, Robin. 2002. *Learning to Learn*: *The Next Step*: *Teaching Adults How to Read and Write the Academic Discourse*, Melbourne, Language Australia for Victoria University.

—. 2011. "Glossing and counter-glossing." *Fine Print* 34 (3): 11–19.

—. 2013. "The Four Literacies: an Exercise in Public Memory." Unpublished Chapter.

McMahon, Brenda, and John P. Portelli. 2004. "Engagement for What? Beyond Popular Discourses of Student Engagement." *Leadership and Policy in Schools* 3 (1): 59–76.

McQuarrie, M. 2006. "Knowledge Production, Publicness, and the Structural Transformation of the University: An Interview with Craig Calhoun." *Thesis Eleven* 84:103–114. doi: 10.1177/0725513606060525.

Marginson, Simon. 1997. *Markets in Education*. St. Leonards, Australia: Allen and Unwin.

—. 2006[a]. "Putting 'Public' Back into the Public University." *Thesis Eleven* 84:44–59. doi: 10.1177/0725513606060519.

—. 2006[b]. "Engaging Democratic Education in the Neoliberal Age." *Educational Theory* 56 (2): 205–19.

—. 2007. "The Public/Private Divide in Higher Education: A Global Revision." *Higher Education* 53 (3): 307–33.

Marginson, Simon, and Mark Considine. 2000. *The Enterprise University: Power, Governance and Reinvention in Australia*. Cambridge, UK: Cambridge University Press.

Mathieson, Susan. 2012. "Disciplinary Cultures of Teaching and Learning as Socially Situated Practice: Rethinking the Space between Social Constructivism and Epistemological Essentialism from the South African Experience." *High Educ* 63:549–564. doi: 10.1007/s10734-011-9458-3.

Moraitis, Peter. 2001[a]. *Pedagogy for the Liberal Arts*, in *Liberal Arts: Course Support Materials*. TAFE Frontiers: Melbourne.

—. 2001[b]. "An Introduction to Liberal Arts" in *Liberal Arts: Course Support Materials*. TAFE Frontiers: Melbourne.

Moraitis, Peter, Amanda Carr and Angela Daddow. 2012. "Developing and Sustaining New Pedagogies: A Case for Embedding Language, Literacy and Academic Skills in Vocational Education Curriculum." *International Journal of Training Research* 10 (1): 58–72.

Moraitis, Peter, and Robin McCormack. 1995. *Public Literacy: a Curriculum for Adult Basic Education* Melbourne, Victoria: Adult, Community and Further Education Board.

Nelson, Karen, Tracy Creagh, Sally Kift, and John Clarke. 2010. "Transition Pedagogy Handbook : a Good Practice Guide for Policy and Practice in the First Year Experience." (Unpublished). [Accessed November 17, 2013]. Available from http://eprints.qut.edu.au/41745/

Nelson, Karen J., Judith E. Smith and John A. Clarke. 2012. "Enhancing the transition of commencing students into university: an institution-wide approach." *Higher Education Research & Development*, 31 (2), April 2012: 185–99

Norton, Andrew. 2013. "Mapping Australian Higher Education, 2013 version." Grattan Institute Report No 2013-1. ISBN: 978-1-925015-39-3.

Peach, Sam. 2010. "A Curriculum Philosophy for Higher Education: Socially Critical Vocationalism." *Teaching in Higher Education* 15(4): 449–60.

Percy, Alisa, and Rosemary Beaumont. 2008. "The Casualisation of Teaching and the Subject at Risk." *Studies in Continuing Education* 30 (2):145-157. doi: 10.1080/01580370802097736.

Ryan, Paul. 2001. "The School-to-Work Transition: A Cross-National Perspective." *Journal of Economic Literature* 39 (1): 34–92

—. 2003. "Vocationalism: Evidence, Evaluation and Assessment." *Des Journées d'Études Céreq – Lasmas-IdL,* Caen, 21, 22 et 23 mai 2003.

—. 2003[b]. "Evaluating Vocationalism." *European Journal of Education,* 38 (2): 147–162.

Rubin, Mark. 2012[a]. "Social Class Differences in Social Integration Among Students in Higher Education: A Meta-Analysis and Recommendations for Future Research." *Journal of Diversity in Higher Education* 5 (1): 22–38. doi: 10.1037/a0026162

—. 2012[b]. "Working-class Students Need more Friends at University: a Cautionary note for Australia's Higher Education Equity Initiative." *Higher Education Research & Development* 31 (3): 431–33.

Shapin, Steven. 1994. *A Social History of Truth: Civility and Science in Seventeenth Century England.* Chicago: The University of Chicago Press.

Smith, Erica, and Kennece Coombe. 2006. "Quality and qualms in the marking of university assignments by Sessional Staff: An Exploratory Study." *Higher Education* 51: 45–69. doi:10.1007/s10734-004-6376-7.

Sultana, Ronald G. 2011. "Lifelong Guidance, Citizen Rights and the State: Reclaiming the Social Contract." *British Journal of Guidance & Counselling* 39 (2): 179–86.

Teese, Richard. 2012. "Big Ideas for a University Curriculum and where they Lead." A paper for the Curriculum Commission, Victoria University. [accessed August 1, 2013]. Available from https://kit.vu.edu.au/engage ment/CurriculumCommission/default.aspx

Tinto, Vincent, and Brian Pusser. 2006. *Moving from Theory to Action: Building a Model of Institutional Action for Student Success*. National Postsecondary Education Cooperative. [Accessed November 17, 2013]. Available from http://nces.ed.gov/npec/papers.asp.

Trow, Martin. 1999. "From Mass Higher Education to Universal Access: The American Advantage." *Minerva* 37: 303–28.

van Lier, Leo, ed. 2004. *The Ecology and Semiotics of Language Learning: A Sociocultural Perspective*. Boston, Dordrecht: Kluwer Academic.

Wheelahan, Leesa. 2010.*Why Knowledge Matters*: *a Social Realist Argument*, Abingdon, Oxon; New York, NY: Routledge

Willcoxson, Lesley. 2009. "The Whole of University Experience Project: Lessons on Attrition From First Year and Beyond." *HERDSA News*, December 2009.

Willcoxson, Lesley, Julie Cotter and Sally Joy. 2011. "Beyond the First-year Experience: the impact on Attrition of Student Experiences throughout Undergraduate Degree Studies in Six Diverse Universities." *Studies in Higher Education*, 36 (3), May 2011, 331–52. doi: 10.1080/03075070903581533.

Woodward-Kron, Robyn. 2004. "'Discourse Communities' and 'Writing Apprenticeship': an Investigation of These Concepts in Undergraduate Education Students' Writing." *Journal of English for Academic Purposes* 3 139–161. doi:10.1016/j.jeap.2003.09.001.

Woodward-Kron, Robyn. 2009. "'This Means that': a Linguistic Perspective of Writing and Learning in a Discipline." *Journal of English for Academic Purposes* 8:165–79.

Zepke, Nick, and Linda Leach. 2010. "Improving Student Engagement: Ten Proposals for Action." *Active Learning in Higher Education* 11(3) 167–77. doi: 10.1177/1469787410379680.

Zepke, Nick, Linda Leach and Philippa Butler. 2011. "Non-institutional Influences and Student Perceptions of Success," *Studies in Higher Education* 36 (2), March 2011, 227–42. doi: 10.1080/03075070903545074.

CHAPTER FOUR

EMBEDDING A THIRD-GENERATION TRANSITION PEDAGOGY: THE ROLE OF CORE FOUNDATION UNITS

BRIAN ZAMMIT

… there is much that we have not yet done to translate our research and theory into effective practice. (Tinto 2006/2007, 2)

Introduction

Massification and the related diversification of the student body have had a significant impact on higher education (HE) in Australia over recent decades (Bradley *et al.* 2008; Putnam and Gill 2011; King and James 2013). Further change has been driven by the former federal government's adoption of key recommendations of the landmark 2008 Bradley Review (the *Review of Australian Higher Education*, to give it its full title), namely demand-driven funding, its target of increasing higher education participation rates to 40 percent of 25 to 34 year olds and setting a goal of 20 percent of all higher education enrolments for low socio-economic status (SES) students by 2020 (Bradley *et al.* 2008, xiv). The impact has been fairly immediate, with a 2.9 percent increase in domestic bachelor student commencements from 2010 to 2011, while low-SES commencing student numbers (at undergraduate as well as postgraduate level) rose by 3.3 percent over the corresponding period (Department of Industry 2011a; b).[1] This was followed by further increases of 9.3 percent and 9.1 percent respectively in 2012 (Department of Industry 2012b; c).[2]

Social inclusion, equity, the needs of a globalised knowledge economy, a democratic participatory society: all feature prominently in debates surrounding tertiary participation rates, particularly of low-SES students (Putnam and Gill 2011; Bradley *et al.* 2008). At the same time, though, rising participation rates present various challenges to the tertiary education sector, such as its capacity to absorb greater numbers of students and the related and politically sensitive issue of government funding (Putnam and Gill 2011, 181–2; King and James 2013).

Of most interest here, however, is the crucial role of institutional support for commencing students in this shifting tertiary environment. "To achieve the government's ambitious attainment targets there will... need to be an increased emphasis on improving the student learning experience in order to boost retention, progress and ultimately, completion rates" (Australian Government 2009, 15). This chapter discusses a "whole-of-institution" approach to the First-Year Experience (FYE) termed "transition pedagogy" (Kift 2009). Within this framework, I will outline ongoing curriculum development in a transdisciplinary core foundation unit (CFU) offered in the College of Arts at Victoria University (VU). If generalisable, this model, envisaged as a locus for curricular and co-curricular activities as well as for collaborative partnerships between academic, support and professional staff, can potentially play an important role in institutional efforts to enhance the FYE.

Context

Student attrition levels, which remain stubbornly high (albeit with some notable fluctuations from university to university), are especially concerning to the sector (Adams *et al.* 2010, 10). Yorke and Longden group the various factors which contribute to student attrition under four main headings: "unsatisfactory experience, inability to cope with academic demands, wrong choice of course, and a range of personal factors" (in Jansen and van der Meer 2012, 2). Attrition is linked, for example, to problems associated with commuting, to the difficulties of balancing work, study and family commitments, to financial issues, lack of academic preparedness, a failure to engage with social networks on campus, and a perceived mismatch between course and career goals (Scott, Shah, and Singh 2008, 11; Adams *et al.* 2010, 5; Jansen and van der Meer 2012; Thomas 2002; Kift 2009, 17; Brinkworth *et al.* 2009). More recently, attention has been drawn to a "[r]edefinition in the notions of 'career' and 'education' held by young people" (Milne 2008, ii) as well as the less linear life paths that are increasingly becoming the norm (Funston 2012, 8).[3] Attrition, however, is not monocausal; in other words, it is generally the case that students leave due to a combination of factors (Wilcox, Winn, and Fyvie-Gauld 2005, 711). Furthermore, the first year at university is critical, with the first few weeks, when stress and anxiety are at their height, being a particularly significant period (Adams *et al.* 2010, 3–5;

Kift and Nelson 2005, 229; Palmer, O'Kane, and Owens 2009, 37–8; Tinto 2009; Reason, Terenzini, and Domingo 2006; Kuh *et al.* 2008; James, Krause, and Jennings 2010).

Challenges tend to be more pronounced where low-SES students are concerned. [4] James, Krause and Jennings (2010) report heightened concerns and anxieties around financial pressures, work/study balance, teaching styles, the possibility of failure and difficulty in engaging with discipline content while Milne (2008, ii) highlights uncertainties over the relevance of tertiary study (Tranter 2010; Ballantyne, Madden, and Todd 2009, 306). In addition, there is a correlation between low-SES students, low university entry scores (Australian Tertiary Admission Rank or ATAR), low levels of academic preparedness and attrition (Funston 2012, 5; Scott, Shah, and Singh 2008, 10–11; Messinis, Sheehan, and Miholcic 2008, 36). In a recent study, Devlin focuses on the "notion of "sociocultural incongruence" to describe the circumstances where students from low socioeconomic backgrounds engage with the discourses, tacit expectations and norms of higher education" (Devlin 2011, 6–7). Similarly, Ryan and Gamble (2004, 7) found that non-traditional students in the United States were "less attuned to the culture of academia", while Collier and Morgan (2008) identified the difficulties that low-SES students encounter due to implicit expectations surrounding assignments, to take one example (Henderson and Hirst 2007; Collier and Morgan 2008; Devlin *et al.* 2012; Thomas 2002; Putnam and Gill 2011).

Attrition can represent a considerable cost to students in terms of forgoing the "long-term cognitive, social, and economic benefits" that are associated with tertiary qualifications (Kuh *et al.* 2008, 540; Scott, Shah, and Singh 2008, 10). There is, of course, a negative impact on tertiary institutions as well, with Adams *et al.* (2010, 16) estimating attrition costs to the Australian tertiary sector at $8500 per enrolment (Williford and Schaller 2005). [5] "[S]uccessfully reducing early attrition rates and stabilising enrolments permits a more efficient allocation of resources as well as providing improved return on the institution's investment" (Martinez, in Brinkworth *et al.* 2009, 170; Kift, Nelson, and Clarke 2010, 13). Furthermore, federal government programs such as the Higher Education Participation and Partnership Program (HEPPP) link performance-based funding to participation, retention and completion of low-SES students, further encouraging institutional action. It should be emphasised that the institutional rationale for addressing attrition is more than narrowly financial; it is reputational and also ethical (Palmer, O'Kane, and Owens 2009, 39; Williford and Schaller 2005). It is incumbent upon tertiary institutions to provide the optimal conditions to support student success: "access without a reasonable chance of success is an empty phrase" (International Association of Universities, in Devlin 2011, 1; Tinto 2008). To quote Gill, Lombardo and Short (2013, 2), "the university has an obligation to intentionally provide the necessary conditions and opportunities for student transition and success" (Devlin 2010; Kift, Nelson, and Clarke 2010, 12; Bradley *et al.* 2008; Scott, Shah, and Singh 2008; Devlin *et al.* 2012 6; Klinger and Murray 2012).[6]

Consequently, student retention, student engagement, transition and the First-Year Experience (FYE) are areas that are being prioritised by the Australian higher education sector. Thus, these have been the subject of extensive research over the past decades, mirroring developments overseas (Tinto 2006/2007). In Australia, this is reflected in dedicated conferences, an example being the *International First Year in Higher Education Conference*, journals such as the *International Journal of the First Year Experience*, longitudinal studies including the *First-Year Experience in Australian Universities* and the *Australasian Survey of Student Engagement* (AUSSE) as well as government funded national research projects including *Articulating a Transition Pedagogy to Scaffold and to Enhance the First Year Student Learning Experience in Australian Higher Education* (Kift 2009) and *Effective Teaching and Support of Students from Low Socioeconomic Backgrounds* (Devlin *et al.* 2012).

Recent years have also witnessed an exponential growth in related projects implemented in Australian universities, as a glance through papers presented at past *First Year in Higher Education* conferences attests (First Year in Higher Education n.d.). With respect to early intervention strategies, for instance, some random examples would include "track and connect" at the University of Sydney, the Student Success project at Queensland University of Technology, the Early Alert program at the University of New England, First-Assessment First-Feedback at Griffith University and the JumpSTART program at Curtin University (Marrington, Nelson, and Clarke 2010; Wilson and Lizzio 2008; Khamis and Kiernan 2013). At Victoria University, some of the more recent initiatives have included the Students Supporting Student Learning (SSSL) program, college teams of Academic Language and Learning (ALL) lecturers, an "at risk" strategy in partnership with an external organisation as well as the appointment of First Year Champions (discipline lecturers) and dedicated transition/retention support staff (see Miguel Gil's chapter one, in this volume).

Challenges

However, despite "an impressive body of research, practice and policy designed to enhance the first-year experience", outcomes have arguably been somewhat disappointing (Kift, Nelson and Clarke 2010, 2), with federal government data (2012a) showing no more than a marginal improvement in attrition rates between 2001 (19.16 percent) and 2011 (18.98 percent). Broadly speaking, as can be seen in Figure 4-1 below, attrition rates have tended to oscillate within a relatively narrow band. Some caveats are pertinent here, though. First, the picture is more encouraging when one adjusts for cross-institutional mobility (that is, where students transfer from one university to another), suggesting that fewer students are currently being lost to the sector. Second, some institutions have historically performed better than others (Department of Industry 2012a). Finally, one could speculate that there are some positive signs in the absence of a pronounced spike in attrition rates in 2010 and 2011, that is, in the post-Bradley environment with its higher enrolments of students often deemed to be under-prepared for tertiary study.

Figure 4-1: Attrition rates—Australian universities 2001–2011

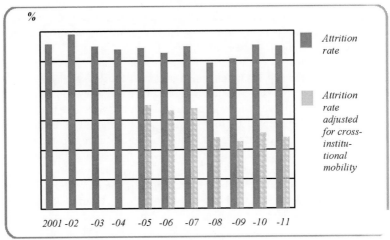

Source: Department of Industry (2012a)

A similar mismatch between research output and retention outcomes can be evidenced in the United States. Tinto has observed that while "[s]tudent retention is one of the most widely studied areas in higher education… most institutions have not yet been able to translate what we know about student retention into forms of action that have led to substantial gains in student persistence and graduation" (2006/2007, 1,5). Significantly, Tinto and Pusser draw attention to a "continuing failure to promote the persistence of low-income students" in the US (2006, 2).

Various factors contribute to these less than encouraging outcomes. To begin with, a number of the attritional factors referred to earlier, such as financial pressures and balancing work, study and family commitments, are of an "external" nature (Adams *et al.* 2010, 3–4) and consequently largely beyond "the immediate ability of institutions to effect" (Tinto and Pusser 2006, 4–5). Adams *et al.* note, for instance, that so-called "academic issues account for only the minority of withdrawals" both in the United Kingdom and Australia (2010, 4). Elsewhere, Tinto has raised the issue of universities' failure to "align their reward systems to the goal of enhanced student retention" (2006/2007, 8–10). Another major challenge is that associated with making the quantum leap from pilot project to sustainable practice, particularly in a tertiary sector increasingly struggling with funding constraints (Wilson 2009, 1; Tinto 2006/2007, 8–10; Marrington, Nelson, and Clarke 2010, 2). In this context, Palmer, O'Kane and Owens (2009, 39) caution universities against basing decisions relating to the sustainability or otherwise of individual projects on unrealistic expectations that these should identify direct causal links to a decline in attrition.[7] This, in their view, leads to institution-centred, rather than student-centred, strategies (2009, 39).

More specifically, Tinto and Pusser (2006) have looked at the difficulties experienced by tertiary institutions in the US with respect to translating research into practice. To begin with, they point to an assumption that understanding why students leave *ipso facto* equates with understanding what steps need to be taken. Second, despite a recent shift to a greater emphasis on practice, research outcomes have too frequently been limited to "theoretical insights" that do not necessarily translate into "definable courses of action". Third, research often deals with "external" attritional factors (referred to above); according to Tinto and Pusser, such research is of limited practical value to institutions. Fourth, definitional confusion surrounding key concepts such as "student persistence" tends to "muddy the waters", so to speak, at policy implementation stage. Finally, much current research has too narrow a perspective, to the detriment of sound planning and decision-making (2006, 4–5).

Here, Tinto and Pusser (2006) are principally concerned with factors that militate against the implementation of an "institutional model of action". Yet, a "whole-of-institution" approach, with a strategic focus on the FYE and targeting those attritional factors that lie within institutional control, is arguably key to the attrition puzzle (Kift, Nelson, and Clarke 2010, 2; James 2012; Adams *et al.* 2010, 3,6). A failure to adopt such an approach could, for example, explain in part why attrition rates remain stubbornly high despite the myriad projects, programs and initiatives that have characterised the Australian tertiary sector over recent years. As Krause *et al.* (2005, 89) argue,

> ... first-year support efforts have tended to be piecemeal in the main, developed and sustained by individuals or small groups who champion the cause of first-year transition. We have now reached the stage where universities must recognise the need for institution-wide approaches to enhancing the first-year experience.

An institution-wide approach is not new to the tertiary sector in Australia; for example, the First-Year Experience project was launched at La Trobe University in Melbourne in the mid-1990s (Pitkethly and Prosser 2001). In a rather bleak assessment, though, Kift observed in 2009 that "all institutions [in Australia] are struggling with whole-of-institution integration, coordination and coherency" (Kift 2009, 2).[8] As indicated above, the challenges faced by institutions should not be underestimated; take, for instance, the need to commit long-term to embedding relevant programs, tensions between centralised approaches and traditionally autonomous faculties, building stakeholder consensus as well as the pitfalls associated with tokenistic consultative processes (Kutieleh and Egege 2013; Kift, Nelson, and Clarke 2010, 2; Kift 2008). However, conceptualising and moving purposefully to a "whole-of-institution" approach has taken on added urgency in the post-Bradley Australian tertiary sector; it is, Kift (2008) argues, the "next, great first-year challenge" (Paterson Kinniburgh 2013).

Transition Pedagogy

Kift (2009) contends that, confronted with the imperative of "providing a high quality first-year experience for a diverse body of students" (Smith 2011, 3), the higher education sector in Australia should now adopt a fresh so-called third-generation approach to the FYE. Wilson (2009) identifies a first-generation approach centred around co-curricular activities (typified by, for example, orientation programs and academic skills workshops) which was generally the domain of professional and support staff. This was followed by a shift to a second-generation approach, characterised by the greater involvement of academic staff and an emphasis upon the curriculum, including course design (Wilson 2009, 10). Kift argues that a further shift is now required, to a more strategic third-generation approach where "first-generation co-curricular and second-generation curricular approaches are brought together in a comprehensive, integrated, and coordinated strategy that delivers a seamless FYE across an entire institution" (Kift 2009, 1). This "whole-of-institution" approach, termed "transition pedagogy", is premised upon "intentional first-year curriculum design", a broader understanding of "curriculum" that incorporates curricular as well as co-curricular activities[9] and, crucially, sustainable partnerships between academic, support and professional staff (Kift 2009, 1,9; Kift, Nelson, and Clarke 2010).[10]

This chapter will propose that core foundation units (CFUs)—here defined broadly as compulsory, credit-bearing units of study, whether discipline-specific or transdisciplinary, taken in commencing semesters that, through a range of strategies, intentionally support first-year students as they negotiate the transition to tertiary study—could play a pivotal role in the effective implementation of a third-generation transition pedagogy.[11] CFUs are envisaged here as a locus for (a) curricular and co-curricular activities, hence addressing "the necessity for an 'organising device' to bring the two [curricular and co-curricular activities] together for program coherence" (Kift, Nelson, and Clarke 2010, 4) and (b) collaborative efforts between academic, support and professional staff, transcending those "silos of academic, administrative and support areas" that frustrate an "integrated and holistic FYE" (Kift, Nelson, and Clarke 2010, 2,13; McInnis, in Kift 2009, 10).

CFU: A Case Study

I will now turn to a case study based on a core foundation unit offered in the College of Arts at Victoria University in Melbourne, Australia. Victoria University is a multi-campus, dual-sector university with an enrolment currently of approximately 55,000 students. Its student body is diverse, with a considerable representation of low-SES, non-English-speaking background (NESB) and first-generation or "first-in-family" students (with a significant percentage of students, it is worth pointing out, "sharing" all three criteria). As Milne notes, "Victoria University enrols the second largest proportion of low-SES students, relative to total intakes, of all Australian universities" (Milne 2008, 12; Messinis, Sheehan and Miholcic 2008, 19).[12]

Knowing and Knowledge A (K&K A) is a compulsory, credit bearing unit in the Bachelor of Arts, Bachelor of Creative Arts Industries,

Bachelor of Music, Bachelor of Laws/Arts, Bachelor of Youth Studies and Bachelor of Education (Early Childhood/Primary). Students are required to attend a weekly one-hour lecture and a two-hour tutorial. The unit is offered across two campuses, with an average enrolment in semester one of approximately 500 students. The unit is also offered in semester two, with a smaller cohort of mid-year intakes, that is, students who commence in July.

Given that this unit caters to students from a number of courses, including a generalist Bachelor of Arts program which offers 15 specialisations, its focus is necessarily transdisciplinary.[13] Broadly speaking, unit content, which is themed around notions of Australian identity, has been designed (a) to encourage students to draw on existing knowledge and experiences (to illustrate, examples drawn from Australian Rules football, the major winter sport in Melbourne, are used to introduce certain key concepts during lectures) and (b) to encourage critical thinking, with lectures following a deliberate dialogic pattern (Zimmerman, Bucher, and Hurtado 2010; Black 2005; Thomas 2002, 432–5).

This unit has been the site of ongoing curriculum development, with various strategies having been piloted and subsequently embedded over the past few years. These will be outlined below, with an emphasis upon collaborative partnerships between teaching staff and various support areas within the university, including the School of Language and Learning, the Library, the Students Supporting Student Learning (SSSL) program and the Language, Literacy and Numeracy (LLN) unit.

Academic Literacy

As a foundation unit, K&K A has a key responsibility to provide academic literacy support to students who are new to tertiary study and, in addition, to underpin the process whereby they "learn to be successful students" (Wilson 2009, 11) by, for example, supporting their transition to independent learning (Wilcox, Winn and Fyvie-Gauld 2005, 712). To contextualise, this is against a background of increasing concerns within the sector at large regarding the academic preparedness of commencing students in the post-Bradley environment.

Academic skills, ranging from critical reading to academic integrity, referencing and note-taking, are embedded in the curriculum and addressed in tutorials on a weekly basis. It is made explicit to students that the unit's role is to scaffold their development of "a repertoire of literacy practices that would facilitate their successful engagement with university studies", in other words, practices that are transferable to their disciplinary areas of study (Henderson and Hirst 2007, 35). This "repertoire" includes transferable skills associated with information literacy; tutorial time is allocated to customised sessions, led by library staff and scheduled to coincide with assignment deadlines which cover research skills demanded by specific assessment tasks (Andrews and Patil 2007).

Academic staff collaborate with Victoria University's Language and Learning staff in the design, structuring and sequencing of weekly activities. The latter's involvement, though, extends beyond curriculum development to the delivery of a set number of lectures, providing ongoing support to teaching staff and sourcing of teaching materials. Fundamental to this partnership are workshops which scaffold individual assessment tasks by focusing on assignment requirements and related academic skills. Depending on funding and staff availability, workshops have been held in class time or, alternatively, separately timetabled. Most recently, a team-teaching approach has been adopted, with academic staff supporting Language and Learning staff in their role as lead facilitators.

From late 2012, Language and Learning, library and teaching staff have collaborated in the development of a series of online academic skills modules that complement tutorial activities.[14] Material is framed around the unit's set readings, reinforcing the linkage between unit content and its academic skills component. Modules, which are accessed via the university's Learning Management System (LMS), are assessable, with students required to complete five graded, albeit low-stake, online quizzes based on this material.[15]

"At Risk": Early Identification and Intervention

Research has underscored the value of early identification of students who are deemed to be "at risk", whether on the basis of being underprepared for tertiary study, regularly missing classes or of not submitting or failing assignments; crucially, of course, identification is followed by timely interventions (Chanock *et al*. 2012; Cuseo 2011, 6; Adams *et al*. 2010, 15–16; Wilson 2009, 13). A three-pronged early intervention strategy has been embedded in K&K A, the first of which centres on a Post-Entry Language Assessment (PELA) test. All students are required to undertake a diagnostic exercise in the first week of semester that is measured by staff from the university's Language, Literacy and Numeracy unit against the Australian Core Skills Framework (ACSF) for writing skills.[16] Results for individual students, based on the ACSF's five levels of performance, are relayed to teaching staff, who are then in a position to provide targeted and ongoing support, where and as needed, throughout the semester.

Second, an "academic recovery" strategy (Wilson 2009, 11) targets students who do poorly in assignments. Tutors refer students to one of a number of options, depending on the level of support deemed necessary, starting with generic academic skills sessions run by Language and Learning staff, escalating to meetings with student writing-mentors (a peer mentoring program offering students general advice regarding assignments) and culminating in one-on-one sessions with Language and Learning staff. In such cases, re-submission of assignments is conditional on attendance at the relevant sessions (Thomas 2002, 432–5). Finally, mechanisms have been put in place to identify students who miss tutorials or assignment deadlines. Briefly, students who evince a pattern of missing tutorials from around the third week of semester (that is, to allow for late enrolments and for student traffic between tutorials to settle down) are identified and followed up by teaching staff; where warranted, matters are passed on to the unit coordinator. A similar approach is adopted with regard to students who do not submit assignments on time.[17]

Peer Mentoring

"We know from research that peer mentoring is effective in not only assisting students to connect and engage, but also to be more successful academically" (Muckert, Wilson and Lizzio, in Wilson 2009, 15; Zepke and Leach 2005, 51). Victoria University has taken important steps over recent years to embed various peer mentoring strategies, the establishment of the Student Supporting Student Learning (SSSL) unit with overarching and coordinating responsibility for mentoring programs across the university being a key development (see Gill Best's chapter eight in this volume).

There has been ongoing collaboration with SSSL with a view to incorporating peer mentoring into K&K A. For example, Learning Commons Rovers[18] and the abovementioned student writing-mentors, both critically important resources for commencing students as they transition to university life, meet students at a lecture early in semester. Details about these programs are made explicit in the relevant unit guide, with regular reminders to students in lectures, tutorials and via the LMS.

In addition, Peer Assisted Tutorial sessions (PATs) have been introduced during second semester when the student cohort is made up overwhelmingly of mid-year intakes, the rationale being to provide additional support to students who, commencing in mid-year, face particular challenges.[19] SSSL recruits and trains mentors (senior students with strong academic records) and provides ongoing support throughout the semester. Mentors, working in pairs, attend weekly classes where their role is two-fold. First, they participate fully in tutorial activities by, for instance, leading group work sessions and contributing to class discussions. Second, they mentor students in a broader sense, from de-mystifying Victoria University's bureaucratic structures to sharing their experiences about expectations around study and preparation for classes and assignments (Ballantyne, Madden, and Todd 2009, 309). In addition, mentors encourage commencing students in the process of building social networks on campus, of some considerable importance, one could argue, where this particular student cohort is concerned (Wilson and Lizzio in Adams *et al*. 2010, 6).

What Next?

"As with all things, this is a work in progress", to borrow from Wilson (2009, 2), and there is further scope to expand this model, an example being working towards developing a more seamless curricular relationship with the two mentoring programs referred to above. For instance, student writing-mentors could be embedded in workshops facilitated by Language and Learning staff, thereby introducing peer mentoring more directly to students and potentially leading to greater student patronage of this important resource. More broadly, two additional strategies could be incorporated into this model, targeting specific aspects of the FYE, namely student–staff interactions and information flows to students, that student surveys have suggested require institutional attention (Australian Council for Educational Research 2011a; 2012; 2009; James, Krause and Jennings 2010).

Student-staff interaction

Student surveys have consistently highlighted dissatisfaction with the level of interaction with academic staff (Australian Council for Educational Research 2012; Cuseo 2011, 11; Adams *et al*. 2010, 7; Zepke and Leach 2005, 50). Yet, "[s]tudents' relationship with academic staff are an important part of their integration into academic life" (Wilcox, Winn, and Fyvie-Gauld 2005, 716). Moreover, interaction with staff may be particularly important where low-SES students are concerned, Ballantyne, Madden and Todd (2009, 309) finding in a study based on an outer-suburban campus in Brisbane that "more than 20 percent of lower-SES students did not report confidence in their capacity to build rapport with lecturers" (Scott, Shah, and Singh 2008; Devlin *et al*. 2012, 33–5).[20] Thus,

Thomas argues that an important element in supporting low-SES students is staff attitudes that minimise the "social and academic distance" between staff and students (Thomas 2002, 439).

CFUs could underpin institutional strategies designed to provide students with greater accessibility to, as well as increased opportunities to experience less impersonal interactions with, teaching staff. To take an example, CFU teaching staff would be tasked with meeting informally with commencing students, individually or in groups, on perhaps two occasions during semester. In addition, they can assume a broad mentoring role, an example being some measure of responsibility for providing course advice (another area students report dissatisfaction with) as well as general advice on matters such as the university's bureaucratic processes (Milne 2008; Trewartha 2008, 36; Zepke and Leach 2005, 50; Adams *et al.* 2010). CFU teaching staff could further support students as they "navigate the unfamiliar terrain of the university" (Tinto 2009, 3) by, for instance, advocating on behalf of student clubs and societies, a key to social engagement. This would demonstrate institutional backing for such activities while also encouraging student participation in campus life (Australian Council for Educational Research 2012). It should be emphasised here, though, that this strategy would necessitate limiting class sizes in CFUs; small classes must be the norm. This would promote richer student/staff interactions but also mitigate that sense of de-personalisation experienced by many commencing students in an environment where resource-strapped institutions tend to herd students into ever-larger classes (Milne 2008; Thomas 2002; Cuseo 2011, 19–20; Kuh *et al.* 2008, 557; Kift and Nelson 2005, 230–31).

Extending orientation information flows to students

As Tinto has argued (1988, 451),

> … [m]ost orientation programs are only partially successful… for they frequently fail to provide the long-term academic and social assistance new students require during the first months of their college careers… Rather than concentrate their attention on the few days just prior to the beginning of the academic year, orientation programs should span the first six weeks of the first year, if not the first semester.

Furthermore, Cuseo suggests that institutions should actively reach out to students, especially to those "students who are unlikely to seek it [support] out on their own" (2011, 6; Trotter and Roberts 2006, 374).

An important element here is students' accessibility to just-in-time information relating, for example, to the various support services that are provided by tertiary institutions. However, maintaining information flows to students over an extended period of time can be problematic; for instance, exit surveys point to students often having been unaware of the range of support services available to them (Australian Council for Educational Research 2011a, 11–12). Generally speaking, institutions tend to rely on email while simultaneously retreating to online support, although the latter, to a large extent, demands a proactive attitude of students. Recently, there has been a move towards greater use of SMS text messaging as well as an ongoing debate about the efficacy of social media such as Facebook or Twitter. Yet, in a recent study, Lodge found that students generally "prefer not to communicate with or receive communication from the university about academic or administrative issues" via social media (Lodge 2010, 103). Students' preference is for institutions to use alternative channels, whether face-to-face interaction, the Learning Management System, or email (Lodge 2010, 103).[21] However, universities seem to fall into the trap of deluging students with emails, although Waycott *et al.* (2010) note (and this would be supported by anecdotal evidence) that students might not access their emails as regularly as assumed

As Lodge points out, "[t]he challenge for academic and professional staff alike is to manage and coordinate the communications being sent to students" (2010, 104). Institutional responses to this challenge would be strengthened by a discrete communications channel operating through CFUs. Complementing broader university strategies, this entails a collaborative arrangement between academic and professional staff, whereby the latter would be virtually embedded in CFUs (Shumaker and Tyler 2007, 21; Kuh *et al.* 2008, 556–7). This strategy would be coordinated by professional staff, including those tasked specifically with responsibilities for transition support. Just-in-time, targeted information would be delivered to students, via the LMS, at key points throughout their first semester on campus (Adams *et al.* 2010, 7–8). Examples include information relating to enrolment deadlines, advice regarding time management and work/study balance as well as routine reminders about critical dates and the various support services available to students, such as careers and counselling. Various benefits could flow from a virtually embedded partnership of this nature, including improved communications with students and, given the increased accessibility of such information to students, greater student take-up of support services (Cuseo n.d., 11).

Discussion and Concluding Remarks

The model outlined above rests upon two pillars, namely (a) a web of collaborative partnerships between academic, support and professional staff and (b) the consolidation of curricular and co-curricular activities, including academic language and learning support, early intervention strategies, opportunities for peer mentoring and student–staff interaction as well as improved information flows to students. Moreover, this model takes a holistic approach, collaborative partnerships being "essential to the successful integration and implementation of co-curricular and curricular activities and the seamlessness of the student experience" (Kift, Nelson, and Clarke 2010, 4).

It is proposed that this model, if generalisable to CFUs—whether discipline-specific or transdisciplinary—across an institution, potentially represents a key plank in effectively embedding a third-generation transition pedagogy. Some further comments, which bear upon the question of generalisability, are pertinent here. First, the phrase "retention is everybody's business" peppers literature on the FYE and yet, curriculum is where the action is. "[I]t is within the first year curriculum that commencing students must be engaged, supported, and realise their sense of belonging. In this way, the curriculum has an important role to play in first year transition and retention" (Kift and Field in Kift 2009, 8–9). This model harnesses the curriculum to impact on the totality of the student experience, in the sense of students' academic as well as social engagement (Kift, Nelson and Clarke 2010, 2).

Second, this model allows for a more resource-efficient and seamless approach to enhancing the FYE. Ideally, retention-related curricular and co-curricular activities should be coordinated as far as possible through one focal point or, to put it differently, brought under the one "roof". To use an analogy, it is now well accepted that initial responsibility for academic literacy should be assigned to dedicated units. This rationale should be extended, where feasible, to allocating principal responsibility for various retention strategies (an example being diagnostic tests) to CFUs, as distinct from dispersing such responsibilities across the first year. Implementing this model would, of course, require the commitment of additional resources to, for instance, fund peer-mentoring programs or to meet the costs associated with smaller class sizes. However, streamlining in this fashion, that is, consolidation under the one "roof", would be advantageous in the current tertiary environment characterised, as it is, by stretched resources. For one thing, it would be cost-efficient for institutions to focus attention on CFUs, rather than taking a more piecemeal approach and duplicating certain retention strategies across a number of first-year units. Second, committing additional resources to supporting CFUs is justifiable, as Trotter and Roberts (2006, 372) point out:

> … prioritising first-year resource allocation, and offsetting the extra cost of the first-year experience by savings in subsequent years, can reap dividends in improved student success. The notion of "front-loading" of institutional action is an appropriate strategy to reduce the early incidence of student departure.

Finally, as Cuseo notes (2011, 6), it would be counter-productive to locate retention strategies at the margins of university life where their impact would be limited. For instance, we have referred earlier to an at-times disappointing student take-up of support services. Krause, for example, identifies student inertia as a factor inhibiting engagement (2005, 7–8) while Cuseo cautions that universities must be proactive in "actively reaching out to students and bringing its services to them" (Cuseo 2011, 6). Focusing institutional efforts on, and embedding retention strategies in, compulsory units in commencing students' first semester on campus would bring students within reach, so to speak. "[I]f we do not harness and centralise the curriculum in the student experience, student take-up of our otherwise disparate and piecemeal efforts to support their FYE is *left to chance* [emphasis added]" (Kift, Nelson, and Clarke 2010, 12). In other words, consolidating retention strategies under a "roof" that is compulsory would maximise their impact and efficacy.

To conclude, it has been argued that Australian universities, in a post-Bradley tertiary environment characterised by widening participation including that of low-SES students, should move towards a "whole-of-institution" approach to supporting the FYE. Kift's transition pedagogy is a blueprint for universities to follow, "a guiding philosophy for intentional first-year curriculum design and support that carefully scaffolds and mediates the first-year learning experience for contemporary heterogeneous cohorts" (Kift 2009, 2).

This chapter has also suggested that the tertiary sector's attention should shift increasingly to practice if universities are to make more significant inroads into attrition rates. To quote Scott, Shah and Singh (2008, 21):

> … the key lesson for successful university renewal in the current highly volatile and competitive operating context is to focus explicitly on not only the "what" of effective change (evidence-based priorities for improving

retention) but also the "how" of effective change implementation (how to take these good ideas, secure local staff engagement with them and lead them effectively and sustainably into daily operations across the university).

The model proposed here locates CFUs at the hub of a "whole-of-institution" approach, an example perhaps of what Scott, Shah and Singh refer to as a "how". Its core features, namely a web of collaborative partnerships involving academic, support and professional staff, and the consolidation of curricular and co-curricular activities under the one compulsory "roof", align with key principles of Kift's transition pedagogy. A next step would be to trial this model in CFUs in different settings, discipline-specific or otherwise. Given its potential to "exert perennial impact on successive cohorts of students" (Cuseo 2011, 6), this model, if generalisable, could be pivotal to our efforts to support the FYE in a coordinated, seamless and systematic manner.

Notes

[1] For participation trends from 2001–09, see Australian Council for Educational Research (2011b).

[2] Edwards (2013) suggests that the growth in HE enrolments has stalled in 2013.

[3] Cross-institutional mobility is generally included in attrition data but it could be argued that it should not be interpreted as attrition *per se*, given that such students are not lost to the sector (Adams *et al.* 2010, 3 and 15). For more on "university-changers", see Long, Ferrier and Heagney (2006) and Scott, Shah and Singh (2008, 12–13).

[4] See Devlin (2011, 2) and Putnam and Gill (2011) for a critique of SES indicators.

[5] This figure is based on average tuition fees for a whole year of study per student plus factored on-costs (Adams *et al.* 2010, 16). Marrington, Nelson and Clarke (2010, 1–2) propose a figure of $30,600 on the basis of annual averaged revenue of $15,300 per full-time equivalent student load and lost revenue over a two-year period where students leave after first year.

[6] Kift puts it more bluntly: it is "essentially about doing the right thing by the students we have accepted into our programs of study" (2008, 4).

[7] The author experienced such expectations at first hand during the 2013 *International First Year in Higher Education* conference in Wellington, New Zealand. Questions along the lines of: "Was there an improvement in retention?" cropped up repeatedly during Q&A sessions at successive presentations discussing various pilot projects.

[8] Adams *et al.* similarly concluded, in a 2010 study of Australian universities, that "across various performance measures relatively few institutions can demonstrate [a] consistent and significant commitment to retention" (2010, 29).

[9] This chapter follows Kift in its understanding of "curriculum" which is "conceptualised very broadly to encompass the totality of the undergraduate student experience of, and engagement with, their new program of tertiary study. "Curriculum" in this sense includes all of the academic, social and support aspects of the student experience... and includes the co-curricular opportunities offered with which students are encouraged to engage" (2009, 9). Furthermore, "[c]o-curricular activities are non-compulsory opportunities closely aligned to curriculum and offered by the institution/faculty/discipline to support, enhance, build on or expand the learning opportunities of the formal curriculum e.g. peer mentoring; as opposed to extra-curricular activities which are non-compulsory opportunities offered more broadly across the institution which are not closely associated with the curriculum e.g. clubs and societies" (Kift, Nelson, and Clarke 2010, 8 and 4 footnote 2).

[10] Transition pedagogy is operationalised through six first-year curriculum principles (FYCPs): transition, diversity, design, engagement, assessment, evaluation and monitoring (Kift 2009). This blueprint has gained traction in the tertiary sector in Australia, arguably pioneered by Queensland University of Technology (QUT). See, for instance, Egea and McKenzie (2012), Kinniburgh (2013), Smith (2011), Kutieleh and Egege (2013), and Gill, Lombardo, and Short (2013).

[11] Examples of CFUs include, for instance, foundation units offered by Murdoch University in Western Australia: see Murdoch University (n.d.) and McGill, Fowler and Allen (2002). Elsewhere, such units have been referred to as "transition units of study" (Milne 2008), "core" and "common first-year subjects" (Chanock *et al*. 2012, 3) or "units of study with embedded language and literacy development" (Adams *et al*. 2011, 20). In the US, such units, which have a long history, fall under the rubric of "first-year seminars" and have "mainly served as a means to transition students from high school to college" (Self Trand and Eberly 2009, 7). There are two major models: academic socialisation and learning strategies; see Self Trand and Eberly (2009), Porter and Swing (2006), Ryan and Glenn (2004) and Cuseo (n.d.).

[12] "[A]bout 75 percent of Victoria University Australian students come from backgrounds in the lower half of the socio-economic distribution in Melbourne" (Messinis, Sheehan, and Miholcic 2008, 19).

[13] "[M]any university learning-support units are moving from de-contextualised, generic courses to discipline-specific, contextualised teaching" (Jansen and van der Meer 2012, 12). The CFU discussed here falls under the first category, due to historical factors and resourcing restraints. Note, however, that Brinkworth *et al*. recommend units that are "customisable and deliverable to non-subject specific academic cohorts" (2009, 170–71). In a similar vein, Flinders University in South Australia introduced a generic literacy unit in 2013, considered "more appropriate for more generalist [as distinct from professionally-oriented] courses" (Brady 2013, 3).

[14] See http://guides.library.vu.edu.au/KandKASemesterTwo2013.

[15] Curriculum development has been supported by the author's participation as project partner in an Office of Learning and Teaching-funded project, *Working from the Centre: Supporting Unit/Course Co-ordinators to Implement Academic Integrity Policies, Resources and Scholarship.*

[16] The ACSF measures levels of performance in learning, reading, writing, oral communication and numeracy; see http://www.innovation.gov.au/skills/Literacy AndNumeracy/AustralianCoreSkillsFramework/Pages/default.aspx.

[17] In 2013, Victoria University has engaged an external organisation to take the lead in identifying and monitoring students who are deemed to be at risk (see Miguel Gil's comments in chapter one in this volume).

[18] Rovers are senior students who support students in Victoria University libraries and Learning Commons. Their role is dual: they assist with specific problems such as logging in, IT issues, printing and locating resources but they also draw on their own experiences in helping commencing students become better learners (see chapter eight by Gill Best in this volume).

[19] To date, there has been very limited research in Australia into the challenges confronting mid-year intakes.

[20] Ballantyne, Madden and Todd note that this finding is "of considerable relevance to the provision of accessible and equitable tertiary education" (2009, 310).

[21] Lodge (2010, 3) also found that less than 20 percent of students regularly accessed the LMS. However, as in the case of the CFU discussed here, steady student traffic would be encouraged where students are required to access the LMS to complete online assessment tasks or to submit assignments.

Reference List

Adams, Tony, Melissa Banks, Dorothy Davis, and Judith Dickson. 2010. *The Hobsons Retention Project: Context and Factor Analysis Report.* Hobsons Asia Pacific. [Accessed October 18, 2011]. Available from http://www.aiec.idp.com/pdf/2010_AdamsBanksDaviesDickson_Wed _1100_BGallB_Paper.pdf.

Adams, Tony, Judith Dickson, Sheila Howell, and Pauline Adams. 2011. Victoria University Retention Final Report. Melbourne, Australia.

Andrews, Tara, and R. Patil. 2007. "Information Literacy for First-Year Students: An Embedded Curriculum Approach." *European Journal of Engineering Education* 32 (3): 253–59.

Australian Council for Educational Research. 2009. *Engaging Students for Success.* Camberwell, Melbourne, Australia: Australian Council for Educational Research Ltd.

—. 2011a. "Dropout DNA, and the Genetics of Effective Support." *Australasian Survey of Student Engagement, Research Briefing* 11.

—. 2011b. "Student Demand – Trends, Key Markets and the Movement Towards Demand-Driven Enrolment." *Joining the Dots - Research Briefing* 1 (1):1–11.

—. 2012. *Australasian Survey of Student Engagement - 2012 Institution Report*. [Accessed September 20, 2013]. Available from http://www.acer.edu.au/documents/aussereports/AUSSE_2012_Institut ion_Report.pdf.

Australian Government. 2009. *Transforming Australia's Higher Education System*. Commonwealth of Australia. [Accessed February 20, 2013]. Available fromhttp://www.innovation.gov.au/highereducation/Documents/Transf orm ingAusHigherED.pdf.

Ballantyne, Julie, Tammie Madden, and Nick Todd. 2009. "Gauging the Attitudes of Non-Traditional Students at a New Campus: An Australian Case Study." *Journal of Higher Education Policy and Management* 31 (4):301-313. doi: 10.1080/13600800903191948.

Black, Laura W. 2005. "Dialogue in the Lecture Hall: Teacher-Student Communication and Students' Perceptions of Their Learning." *Qualitative Research Reports in Communication* 6 (1): 31–40. doi: 10.1080/1745 9430500262125.

Bradley, Denise, Peter Noonan, Helen Nugent, and Bill Scales. 2008. *Review of Australian Higher Education: Final Report*. Department of Education, Employment and Workplace Relations. [Accessed August 20, 2012]. Available from www.deewr.gov.au/he_review_finalreport.

Brady, Kathy. 2013. "Towards a University-Wide Approach to Developing First-Year Students' Academic Literacy and Professional Communication Skills." Paper presented at 16th International First Year in Higher Education Conference, Wellington, New Zealand, July 7-10.

Brinkworth, Russell, Ben McCann, Carol Matthews, and Karin Nordstrom. 2009. "First Year Expectations and Experiences: Student and Teacher Perspectives." *Higher Education: The International Journal of Higher Education and Educational Planning* 58 (2): 157–173. doi: 10.1007/s1073 4-008-9188-3.

Chanock, Kate, Craig Horton, Mark Reedman, and Bret Stephenson. 2012. "Collaborating to Embed Academic Literacies and Personal Support in First Year Discipline Subjects." *Journal of University Teaching & Learning Practice* 9 (3):1–13.

Collier, Peter J., and David L. Morgan. 2008. "'Is That Paper Really Due Today?': Differences in First-Generation and Traditional College

Students' Understandings of Faculty Expectations." *Higher Education: The International Journal of Higher Education and Educational Planning* 55 (4): 425–446. doi: 10.1007/s10734-007-9065-5.

Cuseo, Joe. 2011. *Developing a Comprehensive First-Year Experience Program: Powerful Principles & Practices.* Victoria University: Melbourne, Australia.

—. n.d. *The Empirical Case for the Positive Impact of the First-Year Seminar Research on Student Outcomes.* University of Wisconsin Colleges, 2 October 2012. [Accessed November 11, 2012]. Available from http://www.uwc.edu/administration/academic-affairs/esfy/cuseo/.

Department of Industry. 2011a. *Summary of the 2011 Full Year Higher Education Student Statistics (Attachment B).* Commonwealth of Australia, Department of Industry. [Accessed June 15, 2013]. Available from
http://www.innovation.gov.au/highereducation/HigherEducationStatist ics/StatisticsPublications/Pages/2011StudentFullYear.aspx.

—. 2011b. *Table 1.2: Commencing Domestic Students by Age Group and Broad Level of Course, Full Year 2011.* Commonwealth of Australia, Department of Industry. [Accessed October 10, 2013]. Available from http://www.innovation.gov.au/highereducation/HigherEducationStatist ics/StatisticsPublications/Pages/2011StudentFullYear.aspx.

—. 2012a. Appendix 4.1: Attrition Rate(a) for Domestic Commencing Bachelor Students by State and Higher Education Provider(B), 2001 to 2011(C). Commonwealth of Australia, Department of Industry. [Accessed October 20, 2013]. Available from
http://www.innovation.gov.au/highereducation/HigherEducationStatist ics/StatisticsPublications/Pages/Students12FullYear.aspx.

—. 2012b. *Summary of the 2012 Full Year Higher Education Student Statistics.* Commonwealth of Australia, Department of Industry. [Accessed September 1, 2013]. Available from
http://www.innovation.gov.au/highereducation/HigherEducationStatist ics/StatisticsPublications/Documents/2012/2012%20full%20year%20s ummary.pdf.

—. 2012c. *Table 1.2: Commencing Domestic Students by Age Group and Broad Level of Course, Full Year 2012.* Commonwealth of Australia, Department of Industry. [Accessed October 10, 2013]. Available from http://www.innovation.gov.au/highereducation/HigherEducationStatist ics/StatisticsPublications/Pages/Students12FullYear.aspx.

Devlin, Marcia. 2010. "Improved Access Needs On-campus Support." *The Australian*, September 29.

—. 2011. "Bridging Socio-Cultural Incongruity: Conceptualising the Success of Students from Low Socio-Economic Status Backgrounds in Australian Higher Education." *Studies in Higher Education* 38 (6): 1–11. doi: 10.1080/03075079.2011.613991.

Devlin, Marcia, Sally Kift, Karen Nelson, Liz Smith, and Jade McKay. 2012. Effective Teaching and Support of Students from Low Socioeconomic Status Backgrounds: Resources for Australian Higher Education. Final Report. [Accessed February 15, 2013]. Available from www.lowses.edu.au/ files/overview.htm.

Edwards, Daniel. 2013. *Growing Attainment in Higher Education.* Australian Council for Educational Research. [Accessed October 2, 2013]. Available from http://rd.acer.edu.au/article/growing-attainment-in-higher-education.

Egea, Kathy, and Jo McKenzie. 2012. "Developing a Systematic Institutional FYE Approach from Top Down to Grassroots Up." Paper presented at 15th International First Year in Higher Education Conference, Brisbane, Australia, June 26–29.

First Year in Higher Education. n.d. *Past Papers.* First Year in Higher Education. [Accessed August 22, 2013]. Available from http://fyhe.com.au/ conference/past-papers/.

Funston, Andrew. 2012. *Non-Traditional Students Making Their Way in Higher Education: An Australian Case Study, Research Report 35.* Parkville Victoria: Youth Research Centre, Graduate School of Education, University of Melbourne.

Gill, Betty , Lien Lombardo, and Sharon Short. 2013. "Unscrambling the Egg: A Muddled Path to a Holistic, Coherent and Integrated Institution Wide Approach to First Year Student Transition." Paper presented at 16th International First Year in Higher Education Conference, Wellington, New Zealand, July 7–10.

Henderson, Robyn, and Elizabeth Hirst. 2007. "Reframing Academic Literacy: Re-Examining a Short-Course for 'Disadvantaged' Tertiary Students." *English Teaching: Practice and Critique* 6 (2): 25–38.

James, H. 2012. "How Can a Strategic Approach Improve Institutional Level Student Retention Performance?" Paper presented at What Works? Student Retention and Success Conference, The University of York, England, March 28–29.

James, Richard, Kerri-Lee Krause, and Claire Jennings. 2010. *The First Year Experience in Australian Universities: Findings from 1994 to 2009.* Centre for the Study of Higher Education, University of Melbourne. [Accessed March 12, 2012]. Available from http://www.griffith.edu.au/__data/assets/pdf_file/0016/211147/FYE_R eport_1994_to_2009-opt.pdf.

Jansen, Ellen P. W. A., and Jacques van der Meer. 2012. "Ready for University? A Cross-National Study of Students' Perceived Preparedness for University." *The Australian Educational Researcher* 39:1-16. doi: 10.1007/s13384-011-0044-6.

Khamis, Cassie, and Felicity Kiernan. 2013. "Track and Connect: A Tailored Individual Support Program for at-Risk Students at the University of Sydney." Paper presented at 16th International First Year in Higher Education Conference, Wellington, New Zealand, July 7-10.

Kift, Sally. 2008. "The Next, Great First Year Challenge: Sustaining, Coordinating and Embedding Coherent Institution–Wide Approaches to Enact the FYE as 'Everybody's Business'." Paper presented at 11th First Year in Higher Education Conference, Hobart, Australia, June 30 - July 2.

—. 2009. Articulating a Transition Pedagogy to Scaffold and to Enhance the First Year Student Learning Experience in Australian Higher Education - Final Report for ALTC Senior Fellowship Program. Australian Learning and Teaching Council. [Accessed October 1, 2013]. Available from http://www.olt.gov.au/resource-first-year-learning-experience-kift-2009.

Kift, Sally, and Karen Nelson. 2005. "Beyond Curriculum Reform: Embedding the Transition Experience." Paper presented at 28th HERDSA Annual Conference, Sydney, Australia, July 3-6.

Kift, Sally, Karen Nelson, and John Clarke. 2010. "Transition Pedagogy: A Third Generation Approach to FYE - a Case Study of Policy and Practice for the Higher Education Sector." *The International Journal of the First Year in Higher Education* 1 (1): 1–20.

King, Conor, and Richard James. 2013. "Creating a Demand-Driven System." In *Tertiary Education Policy in Australia*, edited by Simon Marginson, 11-20. Melbourne, Australia: Centre for the Study of Higher Education, University of Melbourne.

Klinger, Christopher M., and Neil Murray. 2012. "Tensions in Higher Education: Widening Participation, Student Diversity and the Challenge of Academic Language/Literacy." *Widening Participation & Lifelong Learning* 14 (2): 27–44.

Krause, Kerri-Lee. 2005. "Engaged, Inert or Otherwise Occupied?: Deconstructing the 21st Century Undergraduate Student (Understanding and Promoting Student Engagement in University Learning Communities)." Paper presented at James Cook University Symposium

2005 - Sharing Scholarhip in Learning and Teaching: Engaging Students, James Cook University, Townsville/Cairns, Queensland September 21-22.

Krause, Kerri-Lee, Richard James, Robyn Hartley, and Craig McInnes. 2005. *The First Year Experience in Australian Universities: Findings from a Decade of National Studies - Final Report*. Australian Government, Department of Education, Science and Training [Accessed February 20, 2013]. Available from http://www.griffith. edu.au/__data/assets/pdf_file/0006/37491/FYEReport05.pdf.

Kuh, George D. , Ty M. Cruce, Rick Shoup, Jillian Kinzie, and Robert M. Gonyea. 2008. "Unmasking the Effects of Student Engagement on First-Year College Grades and Persistence." *The Journal of Higher Education* 79 (5):540-563. doi: 10.1353/jhe.0.0019.

Kutieleh, Salah, and Sandra Egege. 2013. "Up, Down, Turning Around: The Challenges of Implementing a Whole-of-University Approach to Transition." Paper presented at 16th International First Year in Higher Education Conference, Wellington, New Zealand, July 7–10.

Lodge, Jason 2010. "Communicating with First Year Students; So Many Channels but Is Anyone Listening? A Practice Report." *The International Journal of the First Year in Higher Education* 1 (1):100–105.

Long, Michael, Fran Ferrier, and Margaret Heagney. 2006. *Stay, Play or Give It Away? Students Continuing, Changing or Leaving University Study in First Year*. Monash University – ACER Centre for the Economics of Education and Training. [Accessed June 7, 2013]. Available from
http://www.edu.monash.edu.au/centres/ceet/docs/2006stayplayorgiveit away.pdf.

Marrington, Andrew D., Karen J. Nelson, and John A. Clarke. 2010. "An Economic Case for Systematic Student Monitoring and Intervention in the First Year in Higher Education." Paper presented at 13th Pacific Rim First Year in Higher Education Conference, Adelaide, June 27-30.

McGill, Daniel , Lynne Fowler, and Maurice Allen. 2002. "A Foundation Unit in Society and Technology for First Year Engineering Students." Paper presented at First Year in Higher Education Conference - Changing Agendas "Te Ao Hurihuri", Christchurch, New Zealand, July 8–10.

Messinis, George, Peter Sheehan, and Zdenko Miholcic. 2008. *The Diversity and Performance of the Student Population at Victoria*

University: A Preliminary Analysis. Victoria University. [Accessed August 7, 2012]. Available from http://vuir.vu.edu.au/id/eprint/4815.

Milne, Lisa. 2008. *Transition Units of Study.* Victoria University, Postcompulsory Education Centre. [Accessed October 15, 2010]. Available from http://tls.vu.edu.au/portal/site/research/resources/transition_units_of_st udy.pdf.

Murdoch University. n.d. *Bachelor Studies: A General Guide.* [Accessed October 2, 2013]. Available from http://print.handbook.murdoch.edu.au/study/index.php?section=2b_bac helor#foundation.

Palmer, Mark, Paula O'Kane, and Martin Owens. 2009. "Betwixt Spaces: Student Accounts of Turning Point Experiences in the First-Year Transition." *Studies in Higher Education* 34 (1): 37–54. doi: 10.1080/0307 5070802601929.

Paterson Kinniburgh, Joanne. 2013. "A Culture of Success: Building Depth into Institution-Wide Approaches to First Year Transition." Paper presented at 16th International First Year in Higher Education Conference, Hobart, July 7–10.

Pitkethly, Anne, and Michael Prosser. 2001. "The First Year Experience Project: A Model for University-Wide Change." *Higher Education Research & Development* 20 (2): 185–98.

Porter, Stephen R., and Randy L. Swing. 2006. "Understanding How First-Year Seminars Affect Persistence." *Research in Higher Education* 47 (1): 89–109. doi: 10.1007/s11162-005-8153-6.

Putnam, Thomas, and Judith Gill. 2011. "The Bradley Challenge: A Sea Change for Australian Universities?" *Issues in Educational Research* 21 (2): 176–91.

Reason, Robert. D., Patrick T. Terenzini, and Robert J. Domingo. 2006. "First Things First: Developing Academic Competence in the First Year of College." *Research in Higher Education* 47: 149–75. doi: 10.1007/s11162-005-8884-4.

Ryan, Michael P., and Patricia A. Glenn. 2004. "What Do First-Year Students Need Most: Learning Strategies Instruction or Academic Socialization?" *Journal of College Reading and Learning* 34 (2): 4–28.

Scott, Geoff, Masood Shah, and Harmanpreet Singh. 2008. "Improving Student Retention: A University of Western Sydney Case Study." *Journal of Institutional Research* 14 (1): 9–23.

Self Trand, Patsy A., and Charlene Eberly. 2009. "Teaching Students to 'Cook': Reading in the First Year Experience Course." *The Learning Assistance Review* 14 (2): 7–20.

Shumaker, David, and Laura Ann Tyler. 2007. "Embedded Library Services: An Initial Inquiry into Practices for Their Development, Management, and Delivery." Paper presented at Special Libraries Association Annual Conference, Denver, Colorado, June 6.

Smith, Liz. 2011. "Towards a Transition Pedagogy: A Case Study of a Regional Australian University's Approach to Enhancing the First Year Experience." Paper presented at 14th Pacific Rim First Year in Higher Education Conference, Fremantle, Australia, June 28 - July 1.

Thomas, Liz. 2002. "Student Retention in Higher Education: The Role of Institutional Habitus." *Journal of Education Policy* 17 (4): 423–42. doi: 10.1080/02680930210140257.

Tinto, Vincent. 1988. "Stages of Student Departure: Reflections on the Longitudinal Character of Student Leaving." *The Journal of Higher Education* 59 (4): 438–55.

—. 2006/2007. "Research and Practice of Student Retention: What Next?" *Journal of College Student Retention: Research, Theory & Practice* 8 (1): 1–19.

—. 2008. *Access without Support Is not Opportunity*. Inside Higher Ed, June 9. [Accessed September 10, 2013]. Available from http://www.inside highered.com/views/2008/06/09/tinto.

—. 2009. "Taking Student Retention Seriously: Rethinking the First Year of University." Paper presented at FYE Curriculum Design Symposium, Brisbane, Australia, February 5-6.

Tinto, Vincent, and Brian Pusser. 2006. *Moving from Theory to Action: Building a Model of Institutional Action for Student Success*. National Postsecondary Education Cooperative. [Accessed 26 September, 2012]. Available from http://web.ewu.edu/groups/academicaffairs/IR/NPEC_5_Tinto_Pusser _Report.pdf.

Tranter, Deborah Rita. 2010. *Why Not University? School Culture and Higher Education Aspirations in Disadvantaged Schools*, School of Education, University of South Australia, South Australia.

Trewartha, Rae. 2008. "Innovations in Bridging and Foundation Education in a Tertiary Institution." *Australian Journal of Adult Learning* 48 (1): 30–49.

Trotter, Eileen, and Carole A. Roberts. 2006. "Enhancing the Early Student Experience." *Higher Education Research and Development* 25 (4): 371–86. doi: 10.1080/07294360600947368.

Waycott, Jenny, Sue Bennett, Gregor Kennedy, Barney Dalgarno, and Kathleen Gray. 2010. "Digital Divides? Student and Staff Perceptions of Information and Communication Technologies." *Computers & Education* 54 (4): 1202–1211. doi: 10.1016/j.compedu.2009.11.006.

Wilcox, Paula, Sandra Winn, and Marylynn Fyvie-Gauld. 2005. "'It Was Nothing to Do with the University, It Was Just the People': The Role of Social Support in the First-Year Experience of Higher Education." *Studies in Higher Education* 30 (6):707-722. doi: 10.1080/03075070500340036.

Williford, A. Michael, and Joni Y. Schaller. 2005. "All Retention All the Time: How Institutional Research Can Synthesize Information and Influence Retention Practices." Paper presented at 45th Annual Forum of the Association for Institutional Research, San Diego, California, May 29–June 1.

Wilson, Keithia. 2009. "Success in First Year: The Impact of Institutional, Programmatic and Personal Interventions on an Effective and Sustainable First-Year Student Experience." Paper presented at 12th Pacific Rim First Year in Higher Education Conference: Preparing for Tomorrow Today: The First Year Experience as Foundation, Townsville, Australia, June 29–July 1.

Wilson, Keithia, and Alf Lizzio. 2008. "A 'Just in Time Intervention' to Support the Academic Efficacy of at-Risk First-Year Students." Paper presented at 11th Pacific Rim First Year in Higher Education Conference, "An Apple for the Learner: Celebrating the First Year Experience", Hobart, Australia, June 30–July 2.

Zepke, Nick, and Linda Leach. 2005. "Integration and Adaptation: Approaches to the Student Retention and Achievement Puzzle." *Active Learning in Higher Education* 6 (1): 46–59. doi: 10.1177/1469787405049946.

Zimmerman, Tobias, Karen-Lynn Bucher, and Daniel Hurtado. 2010. "Hybrid Dialog: Dialogic Learning in Large Lecture Theatres." In *Learning Management System Technologies and Software Solutions for Online Teaching: Tools and Applications*, edited by Yefim Kats, 314-331. Hershey, New York: Information Science Reference.

CHAPTER FIVE

"COME AS YOU ARE":
INCLUSIVE, TRANSITIONAL
AND MULTICULTURAL PEDAGOGY
IN A FIRST-YEAR FOUNDATION UNIT

JULIE FLETCHER

For many first-generation, low-income students, college is an unknown
land at which they dream of arriving one distant day. Many of them,
through no small effort, arrive at our doorsteps to find college to be far less
magical and much more confusing than they ever imagined. Not only must
they quietly discover the unwritten rules and expectations implicit to
academia, but often they must shed parts of themselves in order to do so.
(Jehangir 2009, 33)

Introduction

Higher education in the Australian context has been characterised by
successive waves of democratisation and widening participation. In recent
decades, federal government policies have provided the conditions for
further increasing tertiary participation by "non-traditional" students,
including first in family, low socioeconomic status, mature-aged, non-
English-speaking background, recent migrants and refugees. In this
context, the issue of successful transition to university learning has
become increasingly important. Research has shown that first-year
students in particular must be supported to develop a sense of belonging
and engagement within the university, and to develop the academic and
personal skills that will enable successful transition into university
learning culture. Frequently however, such transition into the "unknown
land" of university life and learning has required that aspects of students'
differences, identities, backgrounds, knowledges and experiences must be
left at the university gate. This chapter outlines the ways in which

inclusive and transitional pedagogies and an interdisciplinary, multicultural curriculum have been incorporated into first-year foundation teaching, with the aim of fostering inclusion, engagement, and successful transition to university learning for an increasingly diverse student cohort. Within a first-year foundation unit currently being taught at Victoria University, students are encouraged to "come as they are" and bring their rich diversity of backgrounds, stories and lives into dialogue with university teaching and learning.

Widening Participation in Higher Education

Since its inception, university education in the Australian context has been characterised by successive waves of democratisation and widening participation. Trevor Gale (2009) describes this democratisation as occurring in four key stages. From the initial establishment of the sandstone universities as a democratising moment in itself, enabling Australians to receive a university education at home rather than travel abroad, he describes the next wave as occurring post World War 2, when Colleges of Advanced Education (CAEs) were established by the Menzies government, in part to provide educational repatriation for returned servicemen. The Whitlam federal government funded a further substantial expansion during the 1970s, and following this, the Dawkins reforms of the late 1980s and early 1990s saw university participation effectively widened by the creation of new universities from former Colleges of Advanced Education (CAEs) and Institutes of Technology, and the Higher Education Commonwealth Scheme (HECS) funded increases in university places. In the most recent developments, federal government policies in response to the Bradley Review have seen the establishment of equity and participation targets that, if retained, will likely constitute a fifth wave of expansion of the sector.

The latest developments in this progression from an elite to a democratised higher education sector, particularly in the decades since the turn of the 21st century, have seen ever increasing numbers of "non-traditional" students finding their way into the "unknown land" of university. These students, whether low socioeconomic status, disabled, first in family, mature-aged, rural and regional, migrant, Indigenous, international or refugee background, or a combination of these categories, arrive at the threshold of the university with richly diverse social, cultural, educational and experiential backgrounds as well as varied levels of preparedness for university.

Embedding and Integrating Transition Strategies

The need to respond to these varying levels of university preparedness among non-traditional students has produced a significant literature in the First-Year Experience (FYE) and equity fields, and a widespread transformation of practice in university teaching and support services. It has become well established in the fields of transition and foundation pedagogy that non-traditional and equity category students can achieve at a level comparable to their peers if they are effectively supported, particularly in their first year of studies (Devlin *et al.* 2012; James, Krause and Jennings 2010, Kift 2009, Gale 2009).

In the face of widening participation and increasing student diversity, issues of effective student integration, engagement, retention and transition to university learning have become increasingly important (Devlin and McKay 2011). Research into student retention and successful transition has highlighted the crucial importance of the early weeks of university experience, first semester, and the whole first-year experience as laying the foundation for successful transition into university learning, persistence and completion of studies (Kinnear 2008; Kift 2009). While "first-generation" responses to transition and retention were based upon co-curricular (add-on) programs such as mentor programs and add-on skills development courses, "second-generation" strategies focus on transforming the entire first-year experience through integrated approaches to curriculum, pedagogy, and teaching and learning practice. These work to embed transition strategies deeply within the way the university experience is organised. Finally, "third-generation" approaches require a further expansion, to undertake a whole-of-institution transformation in a comprehensive, coordinated and integrated strategy (Kift 2009).

In direct response to increasing diversity in enrolling students, Sally Kift's (2009) work argues for the importance of issues of transition becoming central to the first-year curriculum, rather than being dealt with in peripheral and "bolt-on" transition-focused programs (Kift 2009, see also Devlin *et al.*2012). She suggests that in the present mass higher education system, diversity in the academic preparedness and cultural capital of incoming university students means that transition and retention concerns must be brought to the centre of teaching and curriculum design (Kift 2009). Kift proposes a transition pedagogy framed around six first-year curriculum principles: transition, diversity, design, engagement, assessment and evaluation. First, for Kift, first-year curriculum must be consistent and explicit in assisting transition from the style of previous learning to the style of learning in higher education. Second, curriculum must be inclusive and responsive to student diversity. In this, it must be able to respond to and accommodate the needs of a range of equity and non-traditional cohorts, aware of the diversity of skills and knowledge, and also of variance in students' educational backgrounds and patterns of entry. Third, curriculum design must be explicit and relevant, learning-focused, foundational to future study, and such that it will support the development of skills, knowledge and attitudes. Fourth, curriculum and pedagogy must be engaging and involving in order to foster active and collaborative learning. The fifth principle, regarding assessment, advocates assessment that is regular and formative early in first-year studies, and becoming more complex at higher-year levels. The sixth principle suggests that evaluation and monitoring strategies should be embedded within teaching practice, to allow for regular evaluation of curriculum design, monitoring of student engagement with learning, and allow early identification of at risk students (Kift 2009).

Vincent Tinto (2009) has similarly suggested that what is central to establishing the conditions for successful transition is not the provision of add-on programs, but a focus on the character of the first year of study itself. Tinto advocates deeply integrated strategies such as learning communities and collaborative pedagogy to transform the first-year educational experience, and proposes "four conditions" for successful transition: Expectations, Support, Feedback and Involvement. In order to engage students in learning, he suggests expectations must be sufficiently high and clearly stated. Support systems must be effective to support students to meet these expectations, and feedback on student performance should be early and frequent. Finally, active involvement of students should be encouraged through engaging curriculum. Tinto argues that high levels of challenge, the perceived relevance of course content to student's lives and goals, and relationships with staff and peers can foster effective student engagement in university learning (Tinto 2009).

Engagement of students in university learning is widely acknowledged as a key component of student success. Recent research suggests that supporting first-year students, in particular to develop a sense of belonging and engagement within the university learning environment, will result in improved retention, progression, and learning (Devlin and McKay 2011; Kift 2009; Kinnear 2008; Leach 2013). A failure to engage can produce instrumental responses to course content, and "academic boredom" resulting in poor attendance and poor use of academic free time, while conversely, effective engagement is characterised by active involvement, and active collaborative learning. If first-year students are inspired and encouraged to develop a sense of engagement within the learning environment, this can result in improved performance, retention and progression, and beyond this, the establishment of patterns for lifelong learning (Kift 2009).

The formation of strong relationships with academic staff and fellow students has also been linked with engagement and persistence. The literature highlights the importance of students establishing key relationships with staff early in their student experience. Quality day-to-day interaction with approachable and enthusiastic teaching staff is conducive to both engagement and student success (Devlin and McKay 2011; Kinnear 2008; Leach 2013). In a longitudinal study of student resilience and progression within a new-generation Australian university, it was found that the development of peer-support networks among students was a key factor in promoting integration and interaction within the learning environment and a sense of belonging among students (Devlin *et al.* 2012; James, Krause and Jennings 2010; Kinnear 2008). The development of peer-support networks among students was also found to promote engagement with learning (Kinnear 2008). Furthermore, the establishment of relationships and networks with staff and fellow students was found to promote the development of help-seeking behaviours that enabled students to effectively manage the challenges and difficulties of university life (Kinnear 2008). While it was found that all students particularly valued peer-support networks, the study suggests that non-traditional, low socioeconomic status, non-English-speaking background and first-generation students may be especially likely to benefit from the integration, belonging, and support provided by peer networks (Kinnear 2008).

Deep Inclusion: From Supporting Diversity to Embracing Difference

It is now well accepted that broad-based and integrated approaches that draw together a range of complementary strategies and are embedded within the first-year learning environment, are effective means to enhance first-year student experience, engagement and transition to university study (Devlin *et al.* 2012; James, Krause, and Jennings 2010; Wilson 2010). Effective supports to enable students to develop skills, strategies to increase engagement, belonging and integration, providing academic challenge and clear expectations, formative assessment and early feedback mechanisms, fostering relationships with staff and fellow students, and flexibility in response to student employment and family demands are all means by which first-year experience can be improved for non-traditional students. Beyond this, however, it is becoming increasingly clear that for non-traditional and equity-group students, a deep recognition of, and response to, student difference is required. Differences matter, particularly for those students whose English language skill levels or social or cultural background may position them as potentially marginalised (Kinnear 2008). In order to provide an improved educational experience for non-traditional students, the learning environment needs not only to be characterised by recognition and responsiveness to a diversity of needs, circumstances, and backgrounds, but also, the positive embrace of student difference.

Marcia Devlin and Jade McKay argue for the importance of "teaching for inclusion" and draw upon the work of Griffiths (2010) to define this as an approach that:

> … extends beyond technique, respecting students as individuals who have diverse backgrounds, different learning needs, and a variety of valuable prior experiences. By facilitating learning for inclusion, individual strengths and differences are acknowledged, fostered and maximised to enrich the student's own potential, knowledge, skills, and understanding as well as that of others within the learning community. (Griffiths 2010 in Devlin and McKay 2011)

Rashne Jehangir argues that, once accepted into university, many non-traditional students encounter marginalisation and isolation, and this contributes to difficulties transitioning, persisting and succeeding (Jehangir 2009). She suggests that the gulf between the "home worlds" of these students, and the cultural world of the university means that frequently students must "shed part of themselves" in order to effectively transition (Jehangir 2009, 34). These students come to university with knowledge, life experiences and backgrounds that are not able to be heard or valued within the learning environment. Students may thus not feel they have "permission to *engage in their learning authentically as their full selves*" (Jehangir 2009, 34, my emphasis). The result of this inability to fully engage as authentic selves means that students must either leave parts of themselves at the university gate in order to transition into the (superior) cultural world of the university, or remain marginalised within it.

Trevor Gale argues that in order for non-traditional students to be fully included within the universities, a radical shift is required in how we view knowledge. Drawing on Raewyn Connell's (2007) *Southern Theory*, Gale argues that for equity strategies to move beyond targets and numbers toward a full embrace of non-traditional students, a "southern theory of higher education" (Gale 2009) is needed to "unsettle" the "centre–

periphery relations in the realm of knowledge" (Connell 2007, viii, cited in Gale 2009). Gale suggests that student supports and strategies, while vital, should not be seen as encompassing equity responses. Beyond providing supports to non-traditional students, in order to be fully inclusive universities must begin to engage with student difference at the centre of the student experience, in teaching and learning, with students being fully appreciated for their differences in background, knowledges and perspectives. Gale (2009) writes:

> Vincent Tinto's phrase "access without support is not opportunity", is now well-known (Tinto 2008). I would add that "opportunity confined to support is not equity". This is because "support", by definition, is not designed to challenge what a higher education is. Rather, its purpose is to reinforce what it currently means.

This shift in terminology, from diversity to difference, points toward a radical realignment of how we view non-traditional students, who they are, and what they bring to university life.

Gale's embrace of student difference and advocacy of a southern theory of higher education signals a way forward to a more deeply inclusive and equitable higher education system. Drawing on Connell, Gale's invocation of a southern theory calls attention to power relations and positioning, marginality and centrality within higher education. Connell's use of the term "southern" does not refer to a geographical region as such but is used to "emphasise relations—authority, exclusion and inclusion, hegemony, partnership, sponsorship, appropriation— between intellectuals and institutions in the metropole and those in the world periphery" (Connell 2007, viii–ix in Gale 2009, 2).

Elaborating a centre–periphery framework, Gale describes how the university has been constructed and positioned as the centre of a knowledge system, as the bearer and repository of knowledge, and students are positioned as peripheral to this knowledge system. Knowledge, he writes, "has been assumed to reside in the cloisters of the university, in the hands and heads of the dons. Indeed, universities and their scholars have positioned themselves as the legitimate, almost exclusive producers of knowledge" (Gale 2009). In this framework, the cultural world of the university is both centre and "inside" while students are peripheral and "outsiders". Further, non-traditional students are seen as in deficit, as lacking the requisite academic and cultural capital, and support mechanisms are provided to correct the deficit so that students may cross the border into the insider status of established patterns of participation:

> The mainstream activity of university life—the legitimation and
> dissemination of knowledge—is taken as a given, as normative. It is
> students who must adjust to it in order to be successful. Support services
> provide the mechanisms for students to achieve this, if they do not come to
> university with the capacities and resources to achieve this on their own
> (Gale 2009, 5).

In order to access this knowledge system, to cross into this cultural
world, non-traditional students are positioned as requiring "change,
adjustment, upskilling, additional resources, and so on, in order to fit in to
established patterns of participation" (Gale 2009, 6).

Very often, it can seem that the unwritten expectation of these students,
(and those involved in supporting their transition) is that they will make
the transition from being (cultural) outsiders in this "unknown land", to
insiders who have acquired the skills, language, practices, and cultural
capital, to become "one of us". Frequently also, for non-traditional
students, crossing the threshold into university learning has required that
aspects of self—such as identity, culture, background, experience—are
"shed", silenced or shelved, in order for them to effect a transition and
become accepted insiders within this culture and knowledge system. While
a great deal of work has been done on the ways in which supports can be
provided to enable non-traditional students to cross the threshold of
transition, far less attention has been given to deeper questions of student
difference, and the ways in which universities can support a fuller
inclusion.

Narrative, Voice, and Full Academic Citizenship

For Gale, non-traditional students are primarily "southerners" (Gale 2009,
3), and he argues that, in general, universities have had insufficient regard
for what these students can bring into the learning environment. For Gale,
equity groups need to be recognised as bringing with them "knowledges
about the world, of how to engage with the world, and of what the world
is, that are potentially different from and valuable to others" (Gale 2009,
9). He suggests that in an internationalised and diversified higher
education sector, rather than position teaching as "translating" knowledge
to students, teaching and curriculum should embrace the diversity of
epistemologies and ontologies that such students are themselves able to
contribute to the teaching and creation of knowledge. In the new
diversified sector, Gale suggests that full inclusion of student difference
requires that curriculum not only teach about difference, but also provide

room for different ways of thinking, knowing and engaging, to shape teaching and learning.

Gale is tentative rather than prescriptive about how such inclusion can be effected in the learning environment, but he does raise a number of possibilities. One of these is through the use of narrative approaches to draw out and draw on student experiences and knowledges. A further approach he suggests is to utilise a hybrid framework drawing from "funds of knowledge" and "funds of pedagogy" approaches (Gale 2009). This kind of approach provides the opportunity for students to share their backgrounds, knowledge and experience with others, and acknowledges the contribution this makes to the education of others. In this, students become re-positioned as experts and active participants in shaping learning and curriculum.

In a similar vein, Jehangir has overcome student marginalisation through the creation of a learning-community approach, based on narrative practices and the fostering of student voice. In this, rather than "shed" parts of themselves, students are encouraged to bring their diverse experiences, backgrounds, knowledges and social and cultural differences into the classroom, in a "learning community specifically designed to cultivate a space that allows them to practise full citizenship in the academy" and "build bridges between the academy and the life-worlds of these historically marginalised students" (Jehangir 2009, 34).

In the work of Jehangir, the concept of full academic citizenship—as a pluralistic, multicultural model of diverse "citizens" of the learning community—poses a rich alternative to an exclusionary and/or assimilationist model of insiders and outsiders (Hage 2012, cited in Beilharz), where there are those who belong, those who don't belong, and those who must shed aspects of their culture and self in order to belong. In this, as with Gale's model, Jehangir advocates for the potential of the telling of stories and exchange of experiences; to encourage peer networks, support and interaction, to support increased understanding and active collaboration and to foster deep learning and engagement amongst students. Like Gale, Jehangir's work draws upon a critical pedagogy to provide a theoretical frame through which to tackle student marginalisation. With a similar concern for ways in which relationships of power, authority, voice and silencing are created within academic settings, Jehangir's learning community seeks to empower historically marginalised students through encouraging them to voice, write about, share and reflect upon their own subject positions, identities, communities and knowledges, at the same time as these are linked to issues of the dynamics of power in relation to issues of race, class, gender, and social hierarchies (Jehangir 2009, 36–7).

The final section of this chapter will outline and discuss a unit of study developed within the College of Arts at Victoria University. This unit, like the work of Jehangir and in the spirit of Gale's southern theory of higher education, aims to foster full academic inclusion of non-traditional students at the same time as it works to support effective transition. In this unit, in order to counter implicit pressures within the university for students to shed aspects of self or background, students are encouraged to "come as they are", to bring their own voices, stories and experiences into their university classrooms and learning. At the same time, to further create a bridge between university life and learning and their own lives and experiences, students are encouraged to reflect back on these lives and experiences through the academic conceptual frames explored in the unit. For those involved in the unit, the experience of full academic citizenship and the embrace of difference within a multicultural learning environment confirms that full inclusion of non-traditional students allows for an enriched, rather than diluted or impoverished, educational experience.

The Foundation Unit: Critical Literacies in the Social Sciences

Critical Literacies in the Social Sciences is a comparatively new first-year, first-semester unit of study developed within the College of Arts at Victoria University. Critical Literacies is a credit-bearing, core unit for students enrolled in the Bachelor of International Studies, Bachelor of Community Development, and Bachelor of Social Work. It is offered to first-semester commencing students as well as a smaller cohort of mid-year commencers. This unit draws upon critical and transition pedagogies to support the effective transition and full inclusion of a very diverse student cohort, characterised by a high percentage of non-traditional students, including first-in-family, non-English-speaking background (NESB), low socioeconomic status (LSES), international, and refugee-background students. The unit has been designed to foster a sense of group identity and sense of belonging for students at the same time as it develops foundational academic skills and introduces students to broad-based, interdisciplinary social sciences concepts. While the unit itself fully embodies "second-generation" transition principles in embedding transition pedagogy and retention strategies within a content-based foundation unit, it is also part of a broader "third-generation" strategy to link first-year foundation teaching into larger university-wide initiatives and supports.

The design and delivery of Critical Literacies draws together embedded skill-building, integrated university support services, and staged and scaffolded formative assessment, with learning community principles and a themed multicultural curriculum designed to foster voice, experience-based learning, inclusion, participation, and peer interactions, relationships and support networks. Critical Literacies introduces students to the modes and methods of university learning, and makes explicit the often implicit expectations of higher education. As such, the unit is intended to be, and introduced to students as, a "travel guide" for the journey into the "unknown land" of university. But more than this, in utilising a teaching approach similar to Gale's (2009) proposed "hybrid of funds" and Jehangir's (2009) multicultural learning community. It also aims to challenge and render more porous some of the barriers to full inclusion for the students involved.

The brief for the unit design was to develop a unit of study that would support transition, retention and engagement, foster group identity, introduce social science concepts, and provide a foundation for further work in a range of academic disciplines, for students in the three target courses: International Studies, Social Work and Community Development. While Victoria University attracts a diverse student population overall, these courses attract a high proportion of non-traditional students, and both the courses and the students drawn to enrol in them reflect a strong commitment to social justice, diversity and inclusion, and international issues.

One key challenge when developing a first-year foundation unit is the need to embed skill-building and foundational principles and strategies within a meaningful, coherent, challenging and engaging content. A second significant challenge is to design such content so that it will be meaningful and workable within classes characterised by considerable differences in students' academic background and preparedness. To address these challenges, the decision was made to base the unit on the case-study theme "Internationalisation and Social Identity" in order to encompass a focus on social justice, inclusion, and international issues, and most importantly, bring the key theme of diversity to the centre of the unit. The unit design has been structured around this case-study theme, and teaching delivered in such a manner that difference and diversity in the classroom are viewed, not as deficit, but as the unit's greatest strength and resource.

As a first-year first-semester unit, Critical Literacies is intended to provide the students with an introduction to university study. In the early weeks of semester, the students are encouraged to consider the idea of coming to university as like that experience of travelling in a foreign land. The unit is introduced to them as akin to a "travel guide" for their university journey, introducing (and translating) the language of tertiary education, making explicit the (often implicit) expectations of university learning, and building the requisite skills. The unit utilises weekly lectures, tutorials and workshops, and the nature and expectations of these modes of teaching are explained to students. Lectures focus on the themed conceptual content, while tutorials and workshops provide space for the development of learning-community-style peer supports and interactions. In early workshops, students are encouraged to discuss their own experiences of displacement in the foreign land of university, and strategies that are helping them find their way.

In keeping with current thinking on first-year experience and transition, the unit aims to both support and challenge students as it provides a foundation for further study in a range of academic disciplines. Proceeding from the standpoint of student difference, no assumptions are made regarding students' prior academic background and skill levels. The themed content is challenging and engaging, but rendered more accessible by linking to everyday life and experiences. Similarly, academic concepts and terms are introduced and used, but routinely explained and translated into everyday language. Skill-building is embedded within the themed content, and integrated with assessment, rather than presented as an add-on. Weekly workshops—a number of which are provided by the College of Arts' embedded literacy and learning specialist, Pauline O'Maley, and also the College Senior Librarian, Mark Armstrong-Roper—are directly linked to the themed content and formative and staged assessment tasks, and provide space for the development of essential skills. Staff are accessible to and supportive of student needs, and allow time—and re-submission of work—for students to develop the appropriate level of skill. Adjunct workshops provided by the College literacy specialist are also offered outside class time to provide additional drop-in support for students who wish to attend. This staff member also provides a number of the in-class workshop sessions, allowing students to form a relationship with her, which supports and normalises the seeking of academic help.

The themed case-study approach is premised on the idea of "begin where you are". The early weeks provide an introduction to the theme of their own experiences of colonialism, post-colonial dispossession or displacement, or the ongoing legacies of colonialism, and begin with a consideration of self, identity and belonging. Students begin by reading a personal narrative by Tim Winton on the theme of place and belonging, at the same time as workshops discuss the experience of university through ideas of foreignness and displacement. The Tim Winton piece is examined through ideas of cultural specificity as a means of highlighting difference and diversity in the classroom. The first assessment task asks students to write a personal narrative on their own experiences, broadly linked to the case-study theme or more specifically to their experiences of home, place, belonging and or displacement.

As the semester proceeds, the students examine progressively larger realms of experience and action, moving from the self, to family, community, place, nation, and the international arena. Each of these is examined through the prism of modernity and late/post modernity, through an over-arching narrative of an increasingly internationalised world, experience and social identity. This theme allows students to be introduced, within a coherent trajectory, to a range of academic disciplines and concepts. The concepts include modernity, agrarianism, community, industrialisation, tradition, colonialism, nation, state, human rights, environmentalism, citizenship and global citizenship. Throughout the unit, the content and concepts are introduced in a narrative-based way, and the dominant or established narrative is reflected upon and challenged through students' own experiences.

The over-arching narrative presented in the lecture is one of a largely "northern" Eurocentric body of knowledge, but this is challenged and interrogated in tutorials by the drawing out and sharing of students' own experiences. To provide one example of this, in the early weeks of the unit the established notion of modernity (and late/post modernity), as characterised by a shift from an agrarian to an industrial and then post-industrial (globalised) way of life, is discussed through the example of food. The conceptual framework is introduced in lectures through a discussion of Frank Lechner's three waves of globalisation, which examines changing food production and trade from 18th-century colonial trade, through to the present globalised production (Lechner 2009). In tutorials, discussion begins with a consideration of how our grandparents ate: what kinds of food they ate, how it was produced, and what foods were purchased. Against the backdrop of the grand narrative, students' accounts tell very different small stories, frequently of rural or village lives, and localised production and consumption of very culturally- and locality-specific foods.

However, these narratives of difference and specificity tend to uncover a surprising commonality within the very multicultural classroom. I open this discussion with an account of the way my grandparents ate on a small acreage in rural Victoria, growing vegetables, raising chickens and ducks, milking a house cow, and hunting rabbits for meat. The first time I told this story, one East African refugee student stood up and very proudly told of how his grandparents were the same as Dr Julie's, hunting food, growing vegetables, raising chickens and milking cows—except that his family had many cows. Other students have surprisingly similar stories to tell. Second-generation European migrant students, Asian, African, Middle-Eastern or Pacific Islander international students, migrants or refugees almost all speak of similar village-based localised production and consumption, sometimes confined to their grandparents' generation, sometimes extending to the present day and their own life experiences. We then bring the discussion to the present, to how we eat now in multicultural, globalised Melbourne. Across the whole discussion, student experiences, backgrounds, knowledges and reflections on everyday life are linked to concepts such as modernity, tradition, globalisation, production and consumption. Bringing students' own diverse experiences, knowledge and understandings into dialogue with academic concepts and established narratives of knowledge creates a dialectic that illuminates both the academic concepts being considered and the real world examples the students relate. By creating a link between the two, students move from surface learning of unfamiliar concepts to deep learning and understanding of their significance.

The locus and starting point of the themed case study is Australia, where we all now are. After moving beyond consideration of self, family and community, the unit traces the history of Australia through European colonialism, patterns of settlement, the displacement and dispossession of Indigenous peoples, waves of migration, through to multicultural Australia. Finally the unit considers internationalisation and forms of global citizenship in human-rights-based and environmental activism. The Australian examples are used only as a starting point, however, for discussion of concepts and students' own experiences. Again, students are encouraged to link their own experiences with the academic concepts being considered. For example, students are encouraged to share their own experiences of colonialism, or the legacies of colonialism in post-colonial settings. Similarly, in discussions of place and place-making students are encouraged to reflect on the ways that migrant or refugee place-making can be seen in the world around them; for example, the ways that histories of migration are inscribed—and can be read—in the streetscapes of Footscray, or the ways that Aboriginal histories have been erased by European place-making in Victorian landscapes.

In participating in this open discussion and collaborative learning, students are empowered to share their own insights, experiences and knowledges, and by linking these to academic concepts they are given value and significance. Students are empowered to share their own insights and knowledges, for example, of the impact of modernity on rural villages in India, or the traditional way of life in a Burmese jungle village, dependent upon slash-and-burn agriculture. The students begin to recognise the expertise that they bring to the class, as well as that of their peers. They grow in confidence in sharing their experience and knowledges, at the same time as they become more confident to seek the expertise of others. This has served to support the informal formation of peer-support relationships, with students helping one another during and beyond class time, and spontaneous groups forming to workshop assessment challenges.

The pedagogical benefits to students of such interaction, and open discussion of diverse backgrounds, experiences, world views, are significant. Across the semester, students can be seen to grow in respect for and understanding of each other, and visibly deepen in their enthusiasm for and appreciation of difference. In one class, I witnessed a lively and respectful discussion on marriage and equality in marriage amongst a group of students that included a young openly gay man, a number of young women with clear views on marriage equality, and a young, already married, Muslim man from a traditional family in the Middle East. The young Muslim man was explaining gender roles and marriage in his community, detailing his grandfather's and father's social roles and attitudes to marriage, as well as his own options of having more than one wife. The group of students listening were captivated; they were challenged, attentive, respectful, and deeply engaged. The young man speaking was clearly proud to be sharing his cultural knowledge with his peers, and both empowered and significantly included by the way in which it was received. Such discussion and interaction is an important means to bridge the gulf between the cultural world of the university and the cultural and life worlds of non-traditional students.

Conclusion

One of the ways that cultures are maintained is through the creation of borders. These borders may be visible or invisible, written or unwritten, spoken or unspoken, explicit or implicit, but they nonetheless work to establish inclusion and exclusion, insiders and outsiders, us and them. Within universities, explicit borders (and points of border-crossing, gateways) include tertiary-entry rankings and scores, processes and policies. While formal gateways and borders have become more permeable to diverse and non-traditional students, implicit borders remain around cultural attitudes and practices of who does and who should "belong", what is expected, how things should be done, and what students must be or become in order to be "one of us", and most importantly, what kinds of knowledge and ways of knowing are recognised, valued, and able to be spoken (Gale 2009). As the formal aspects of university entry have been opened up to a wide range of non-traditional students, to effectively transition or "cross the border" into university learning, these students must learn to negotiate a new social environment, language and culture, as well as acquire the academic knowledge, skills and practices that are expected of them. Too frequently, these students encounter an implicit sense that in order to belong, to effectively transition into university life and culture, there are aspects of their selves, cultural backgrounds, experiences and knowledge that must be left at the university gate.

At a time when the higher education sector is characterised by increasingly democratised and diversified patterns of participation, the need for universities to go beyond access and support to enable deep inclusion for non-traditional students is becoming increasingly apparent. This chapter has outlined an example of how student difference can be re-imagined as strength rather than deficit, and a diversity of epistemologies and ontologies given voice within a first-year foundation unit. By encouraging students to draw upon their own backgrounds, experiences and knowledges and bring them into dialogue with university learning, non-traditional students are supported to "come as they are" and participate as whole, authentic selves in full academic citizenship.

Reference List

Devlin, Marcia and Jade McKay. 2011. *Inclusive Teaching and Support of Students from low Socioeconomic Status Backgrounds: A brief Discussion Paper*. Higher Education Research Group, Deakin University, Australia.

Devlin, Marcia, Kift, Sally, Nelson, Karen, Smith, Liz, and Jade McKay. 2012. *Effective Teaching and Support of Students from Low Socioeconomic Status Backgrounds: Resources for Australian Higher Education, Final Report*. Office for Learning and Teaching, Commonwealth of Australia.

Gale, Trevor. 2009. "Towards a Southern Theory of higher Education". In *Proceedings of the 12th Pacific Rim First Year in Higher Education*

Conference: 'Preparing for Tomorrow Today; The First Year Experience as Foundation', edited by J. Thomas, Brisbane, Australia: QUT Publications.
http://www.fyhe.com.au/past_papers/papers09/ppts/Trevor_Gale_pape r.pdf

Ghassan Hage. 2012, "Insiders and Outsiders." In *Sociology: Antipodean Perspectives,* edited by Peter Beilharz, Trevor Hogan, 409–13. Oxford: Oxford University Press,

Griffiths, Sandra. 2010. *Teaching for Inclusion in Higher Education: A guide to practice.* Higher Education Academy, United Kingdom and All Ireland Society for Higher Education.

James, Richard, Kerri-Lee Krause, and Claire Jennings. 2010. *The First Year Experience in Australian Universities: Findings from 1994 to 2009,* Canberra, Australia: Department of Education, Employment and Workplace Relations.

Jehangir, Rashne. 2009. "Cultivating Voice: First-Generation Students Seek Full Academic Citizenship in Multicultural Learning Communities." *Innovative Higher Education,* 34: 33-49. doi 10:1007/s10755-008-9089-5.

Kift, Sally. 2009. "Articulating a Transition Pedagogy to Scaffold and to Enhance the First Year stu1dent lear1ing Experience in Australian Higher Education: Final Report for ALTC Senior Fellowship Program". Retrieved November14, 2012.
http://www.fyhe.qut.edu.au/transitionpedagogy.

Kinnear, Adrianne, Mary Boyce, Heather Sparrow, Sharon Middleton., and Marguerite Cullity. 2008. "Diversity: A Longitudinal Study of how Student Diversity relates to Resilience and Successful Progression in a New Generation University". Perth, Australia: Edith Cowan University. Retrieved November 14, 2012.
http://www.altc.edu.au/resource-diversity-longitudinal-studyecu-2009

Leach, Linda. 2013 "Engaging Ethnically Diverse First Year Students: A practice Report." *The International Journal of the First Year in Higher Education* 4 (2): 117–24.

Lechner, Frank. 2009. *The Making of World Society.* Oxford UK: Blackwells.

Tinto, Vincent. "Taking Student Success Seriously: Rethinking the First Year of College." Paper presented at the *Ninth Annual Intersession Academic Affairs Forum, California State University, Fullerton,* 05–01, 2005.
http://www.purdue.edu/foundationsofexcellence/documents/FOE%20 Documents/ Taking%20Success%20Seriously.pdf.

CHAPTER SIX

EXPLORING FIRST-YEAR TRANSITION PEDAGOGY: INDICATORS OF ENHANCED TRANSITION AND RETENTION IN AN EXPERIENTIAL EARLY-YEARS TEACHER-EDUCATION SETTING

GWEN GILMORE

Understanding how students continue to study in the presence of such risk factors, or have some level of resilience that allows them to quickly recover from a setback, is the critical next step enhancing student retention and equity (Karimshah *et al.* 2013, 6).

Introduction

This chapter examines an experiential, work-based, partnership placement program with first-year pre-service teachers, arguing that the program, *KindaKinder*, embodies a transition pedagogy that provides an opportunity for students and their teachers to reflect on and identify their strengths and work towards forming the identity of the latter as a teacher. A number of questions are considered in this connection: Is the transition pedagogy about who pre-service teachers are or how staff respond as part of an institution? Are the students' transitions into their first year an "either–or" proposition: simply about what students bring to university, or about how professionals and the institution respond?

Binary propositions, student–institution pairs, can easily lead to false dualisms of the kind interrogated by John Dewey (1991, 52) and further exposed by Richard Pring (2000, 127; 2002, 259) when stating "no practice stands outside a theoretical framework, that is, a framework of interconnected beliefs about the world, human beings and the values worth pursuing". False dualisms pursue an either–or position in a debate. In this case study I reject that a transition experience is primarily about the student characteristics or about institutional factors. As Trevor Gale and Steven Parker (2012, 1) state, transition values worth pursing are those that develop the "lived experiences" of students' "developing" and "becoming".

For Sally Kift (2011) transition includes developing belonging but is also a process of design and delivery that is

> ... consistent and explicit in assisting students' transition *from* their previous educational experience *to* the nature of learning in higher education and learning in their discipline as part of their lifelong learning. (1)

Pedagogy, as part of that transition, part of the design and delivery, encompasses the knowledge processes and practices of learning and teaching—pedagogy—for both students and teachers as they intersect in the institutional context (Seely-Flint *et al*, 2014). Practical teaching and learning is more closely aligned with traditional schooling practices than with the institutional responses and interventions found in universities, which by and large tend to be far more formalistic and reactive. In this sense then, transition pedagogy can be defined as the process of enculturation into new ways of learning that are consciously fostered inside the traditional institutional environment.

In the following sections I will consider, rather broadly, two concepts —that of relational agency following Anne Edwards (2005, 168) and of human mediation after Alex Kozulin (2003, 18)—by using a cultural–historical activity theoretical (CHAT) approach to the research analysis. Both concepts of relational agency and human mediation are explored in the new territory of transition pedagogy and in the context of the KindaKinder teacher-education program described in a following section. I consider the interactions; cultural, situational and community aspects of learning that build on student strengths and existing knowledge forms that support transition (thinking and actions) into new forms of academic inquiry. I also seek to shed light on how building on these strengths in the context of an experiential pedagogy and curriculum relates to and influences the successful engagement of pre-service students. Similarly, Glenda Crosling and co-writers (2009) indicate institutions can use less traditional approaches to curriculum design to facilitate social interactions.

Original sources on the CHAT model (Leontiev 1978; Engeström 1987; Engeström, Miettinen and Punamaki 1999) will provide more detail on CHAT as a theoretical approach to examining research situations. I set out to provide research-informed examples of how curriculum and pedagogy comprise deliberate elements of institutional action that constructively support transition concepts. Like Vladimir Ageyev (2003, 433), I intend to make more explicit how this experiential model of early years' pre-service teacher development supports social interactions and student retention in university settings. As Andrew Funston (2011), and also in this volume, indicates, institutions need to make visible the factors that support students' agency and self-worth. By so doing, the present study contributes to the still scant Australian research illuminating the extent to which such experiential models of delivery influence student transition and retention.

This case study then, constitutes an attempt at conceptualising, through a narrative of events, university transition pedagogies and a retention initiative that has developed over the course of a number of years (Hammersley and Gromm 2000, 7). It seeks to explain the links between and amongst the various players in the teacher-education and KindaKinder settings. As Robert Stake (1994) argues, a methodological case-study process is identified as a "naturalistic generalisation"; it is possible to take the findings from one study and apply them to other similar situations. Similarly, Janet Schofield (2000, 75) strongly argues that the concept of "fittingness" is an apt approach to viewing a research site as it applies to the generalisability in case studies. In other words, it is by examining this case of experiential curriculum and pedagogy, and reflecting on one's own situation, that we discern some useful and realistic principles applicable to other sites.

The chapter starts with an elaboration of transition pedagogies in experiential settings, pre-service teacher identity, diversity in the context of transition pedagogies and the CHAT methodological approach to viewing this transition activity. I then clarify the KindaKinder research setting, the methods and the data arising from this research, offer a CHAT model for viewing this transition pedagogy and propose some conclusions.

Transition Pedagogies in an Experiential Setting

George Kuh *et al.* (2005, 11) and, more recently, Vincent Tinto (2012) indicate that student engagement, and with it transitions and graduation rates, are all enhanced by paying careful attention to the provision of institutional and academic challenges, active and collaborative learning, ongoing student interaction with university staff, enriched educational experiences and supportive campus environments. In particular, the combined concepts of challenge and support serve as an antidote to purely deficit-based notions of support (for instance, applying Australian Tertiary Admission Rank (ATAR[1]) scores or postcodes to learning support) and implied notions of limited student agency, and therefore limited student capacity to navigate institutional cultures and claims (Upcraft, Gardner and Barefoot 2005). The above key premises—institutional challenge and support, collaborative learning and interaction with university staff—are integral to the implementation of a successful transition pedagogy and curriculum.

Retention (the proportion of students re-enrolling each year) data can been taken as a broad proxy for student engagement (Adams *et al.* 2010). In a summary way, a student's decision to stay the course can be taken to indicate their engagement with their studies. Less crude formalisations of the retention concept have sought to represent it as a set of specific behaviours on the part of the student that would signal both the individual's personal professional commitment and, by implication, the institution's success in fostering such behaviours (institutional commitment) (Smith *et al.* 2012). For our purposes here, engagement is construed as being represented by factors related to academic commitments such as attendance, engagement with classmates, tutors and their other community (Crosling, Thomas, and Heagney 2008).

In terms of its approach to transition and retention, this chapter aligns with the list of guiding principles outlined by Miguel Gil in Table 1-1 (see chapter one), and in particular with the overall psycho-pedagogical principles of personal validation, active involvement, social integration, personal meaning, personal reflection and self-awareness. This extends often to the very way in which transition and retention program are conceptualised from the outset. Brian Findsen (2011, 231) elaborates on some useful principles of a transformative pedagogy and academic challenge that seem relevant here. Particular emphasis should be placed on the notions that:

- teachers and learners co-construct the learning in a forum of mutual respect
- learning is a process and a result of what learners do for themselves
- Teachers encourage students to make choices for themselves
- Responsibility and freedom are in the hands of learners. Teachers however, have a role and responsibility to intervene and share knowledge.

Having clarified some points on transition pedagogy I now consider some aspects of pre-service teacher identity.

Pre-service Teacher Identity

Issues of diversity and identity in higher education transition research are usually explored through student characteristics such as gender, postcode demographics, languages spoken at home and employment status, some characteristics of which would suggest, invite, or be amenable to various forms of institutional action. A component of identity often identified as a problem or risk factor for university transition and retention is the "diversity" of the student cohort (Billingham 2009). Whilst the concept of "diversity" is often reduced to, for example, an ethnic identity (i.e. a non-English-speaking identity), coming from a lower socioeconomic community, being the first in a family to attend university, or the like, it does not necessarily follow that subsequent attrition is related to such simplified factors (Crosling, Thomas, and Heagney 2008).

More recently, Marcia Devlin (2013) has questioned the appropriateness of assumptions linking status, as measured by postcode data, with success at university. Furthermore, the literature is unclear as to how these individual characteristics are then to be mediated, or not, in the university context. Indeed, Ameera Karimshah's *et al.* (2013, 13) recent research on low-SES students strongly reflect that retention of these students is indicated by social integration into the university, strong family networks, the fortitude to want to complete the course and a desire for financial security. Yet, as Tony Adams *et al.* (2010) note, the application of such broad-level data to specific contexts should be approached with caution as experiences between and within institutions can vary considerably. A common response to diversity in this sense has been to assume the provision of generic remedial skills programs (Stuart Billingham 2009) will suffice in bridging student histories and university experiences. But, by virtue of this subtle transfer of responsibility to the student, the institutional response is declared to be "sufficient", or "equivalent to offerings by comparable universities", with the "problem" then largely conceptualised as one of defective dissemination of information, lack of "administrative literacy", or, worse, apathy about these programs on the part of potential beneficiaries.

In chapter one of this book, Miguel Gil, following Joe Cuseo (2011), clarifies the notion that student success may be measured by who our students are when they finish their course compared with who they were when they commenced higher education. This perspective is far less deterministic than that afforded by an input model, where learning and teaching outcomes are virtually a function of the initial social characteristics; for example, ATAR scores, social and cultural capital, commuting distance and other attrition factors. Therefore, assuming pre-service teacher identity shapes, and is shaped by, strengths in conjunction with the institution, I examine next how diversity might be considered as a construct in relation to a transition pedagogy and curriculum for these first-year to higher education students.

Diversity: Transition Pedagogy and Curriculum

The previous observation regarding viewing student strengths and university outcomes as the measure of success brings to the fore a further aspect relevant to my discussion of transition pedagogy: How does diversity fare in relation to the cultural context in which this research is undertaken? The reason for elaborating this point is that the relevant strategic and policy documents issued periodically by Victoria University have consistently and repeatedly made reference to the concept of diversity with amendments to course documentation. "Diversity" is thus referred to as a valuable asset. Embracing diversity allows education to be made available to students who would otherwise not come into university.

By contrast, I espouse an expansive and wider view of culture in the context of a diverse pedagogy. Following John Fiske (1989, 23), I would define culture as the transmitted and transmissible patterns of behaviours and beliefs that characterise the operation of an individual, group or community. Culture is an active living process: it can be developed only from within; it cannot be imposed from without or from above. Similarly, the uniqueness of people is that social contexts are created through language and meaning, through relationships that are created, recreated and reciprocated in particular environments. In this connection, I propose that cohort diversity should be turned inwards when examining retention and transition matters, so as to consider how existing student cultural forms of social, historical, and personal diversity offer new possibilities for further engagement. In other words, by asking: What forms of meaning do these students, as a diverse group, make as they interact with staff, other students, the schools, and children in experiential communities? For example, what forms of socialisation does the diverse nature of the KindaKinder setting suggest to these students? In essence, what cultural and diverse forms of pre-service teacher identity are formed in these settings?

Tertiary institutions may approach their existing diversity as a given that requires no further explanation, action or redirection other than to prove a degree of conformity with social expectations (typically embedded in marketing representations of diversity, political correctness, etiquette, for example). We need to be far more explicit about how forms of diversity offer an opportunity for a wider conversation about student strengths. John Clarke *et al.* (1981, 54) argue that the starting points for students coming into a university course are not fixed and unchangeable either in and for themselves, or in relation to the starting points of these groups. Rather, it is the university's responsibility to seek to develop pedagogies and curriculum in ways that expand the range of meanings the students make and contribute to these experiential learning settings. Students coming into this early years' teacher education course will both bring and create their diverse cultural community and it is this aspect of diversity that concerns us in this study.

The next part of this case study elaborates on the research methodology, a cultural–historical activity approach.

Methodological Approach to Transition: Cultural–Historical Activity Theory (CHAT)

Thomas Kuhn (1970, 210) reminds us that "knowledge is intrinsically the common property of a group or else nothing at all". Social constructionism considers that the authority of knowledge ultimately derives from a "knowledge community" of people who agree about the truth (Warmoth 2000, 1). A social constructivist position would propose that students' ideas are eventually given meaning by their interaction and participation within their social context. It is the social context of meanings, including the historical meanings and understandings developed over time, that is epistemologically fundamental. The nature of knowledge generated by first-year pre-service teachers in relation to their emerging teacher identity is primarily informed by their individual historical backgrounds, the university contexts, their classrooms, their learning collaborators, teachers, and mentors within the practice settings.

Peter Van Huizen, Bert Van Oers and Theo Wubbels (2005, 285) suggest that using a sociocultural framework acknowledges both the individual explorations and functioning of the practice of teaching as well as the social participation in the meanings relevant to the context. Accordingly, I examine how the early years' pre-service teachers talk about and engage in their experiential community of practice. I discuss how the intersection between this first-year teacher education program facilitates, supports and enables transition into new dialogues and forms of learning. Kuh (2008, 301–2) puts it more simply: "To what extent do these students engage in meaningful learning situations and thus become more deeply engaged with the institution?"

Relational agency, a key concept in CHAT theory, is the capacity to offer support on a reciprocal basis; that is not one of fixed dependency but that is fluid and involves both a receiving and a giving process. It is the active ability to seek out others to take action and make a response with support and guidance. However, in teacher education these relationships are increasingly characterised by adherence to formal curriculum documents, with students rarely engaging with each other in developing their teaching expertise, and feedback being based on the delivery of a lesson plan handed to students by the mentor teacher. Unsurprisingly students become less responsive to children (Edwards 2005, 176). The distancing of teacher-education students from the needs of children and adherence to technical teaching matters can be questioned on pedagogical grounds and also in terms of the quality of student professional learning experience. How engaging is a course that does not then enable students to create learning environments that link to the children's needs? How do these early years' students use this experiential education course to successfully engage and transition into and with the university?

In the same sociocultural tradition, Kozulin (2003, 19) offers the concept of "human mediation"; in this case, student learning transitions in a university setting and the teacher-education placement experiences. Barbara Rogoff (1995, 146–7) indicates that there are different forms of human mediation—apprenticeship (novice guidance), guided participation (interpersonal joint activity) and appropriation (changes to individuals as a result of involvement in mediated activities)—that are useful for general orientation in researching settings while being limited to *perspectives* on interpersonal engagement. However, human mediation perspectives—in this case a KindaKinder group and mentors—may enable us to clarify what kinds of actions by the students and the university enhance transition in this context.

Participation supports the understanding of a professional identity through a dialectical relationship between the practical activity—in this case the KindaKinder literacy, play activities—and existing student sociocultural meanings of that activity (Van Huizen, Van Oers, and Wubbels 2005). Students explore their identity as embedded within their experiential community rather than necessarily coming to teacher education from specifically acquired and static forms of knowledge. The research under consideration in this chapter considers how this experiential pedagogical approach then supports, or otherwise, transition of these first-year pre-service teachers.

Anna Sfard (1998) distinguishes two dimensions of learning as a metaphor in relation to forms of knowledge, namely acquisition and participation. Her analysis of the acquisition metaphor (AM) reminds us of the dominant approach to transition into university settings (the emphasis here is on particular forms of domain-specific knowledge transmission), and strengthens our understanding of how we might more carefully consider curriculum and pedagogy in pre-service teacher education courses. This model also aligns with Paulo Freire's (1973) familiar notion of education as a form of knowledge "banking". The acquisition metaphor privileges the notion of an individual mind that takes possession of particular forms of knowledge, be they in the form of academic skills, knowledge of university systems, and so forth. The unit of analysis is individuals, and the university transition pedagogical focus is on the building of subject knowledge. An acquisition framework, in relation to this chapter, is exemplified in the perspective of Kuh (2008, 14) when he discusses programs and activities as such as academic seminars, mentoring, and developing learning communities that influence student persistence.

Sfard then elaborates on the possibilities of considering a participation metaphor (PM) in constructing the mutual, social and cultural, identities of participants in the learning situation. She notes that these two metaphors are reciprocally related in that "whilst the AM emphasises the inward movement of the object known as knowledge, PM gives prominence to the aspect of mutuality characteristic of the part–whole relation" (1998, 6). A participation metaphor, which would thus focus on enhancing the engagement strategies above, providing opportunities for academic challenge, fostering active and collaborative learning, and supportive campus environments, might then be useful in thinking about the KindaKinder norms, values and pre-service teacher identity.

Sami Paavola, Lasse Lipponen, and Kai Hakkarainen (2004, 11) propose a third metaphor for learning that could be also be considered in building theory about transitioning into an innovative community of pre-service teacher educators. Their "knowledge-creation metaphor", which "addresses processes of deliberate transformation of knowledge and corresponding collective social practices", seems an apt approach to considering this experiential project.

A crucial point here, then, is that learning activity, and in this case pre-service teacher learning in an experiential setting, cannot be reduced to the "acquisition of knowledge" metaphor or simply to a "participation metaphor", that is, knowledge of or participation in either the university or in knowledge required to become an early-years' teacher. If anything, the KindaKinder and transition pedagogy is a special kind of appreciation and appropriation by these students of their previous learning and tools: books, play materials, computers and course materials that are mediated by the new learning task in hand. The knowledge-creation metaphor is an appropriate metaphor for viewing the transition pedagogy and examining the university's roles and responsibilities. The students are participants, certainly, but participants in a process of creating a play event that makes sense for them and the children in the specific setting. Learning activities, then, are constructed that enable the pre-service student teachers to engage in a process of new learning for them, a process that allows them to become increasingly competent pre-service teachers.

As a way of illustrating the CHAT model proposed for this chapter, I provide the following figure for elaboration.

Figure 6-1: A collectively mediated experiential pedagogy

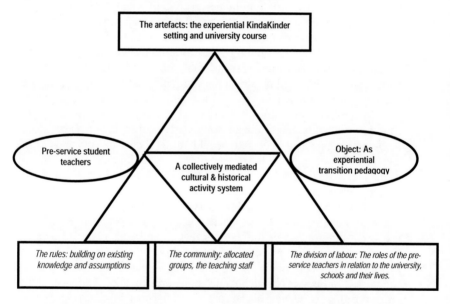

Adapted from Engeström

Figure 6-1, above, illustrates the interconnected elements of the program and participants. Starting at the top of the diagram the artefacts include all the elements of the setting and the course, including course information, unit guides, mentors, and the setting materials. The object here is an experiential transition pedagogy; with students travelling from a position of capabilities drawn from previous histories and experiences to these interactive, reciprocal events. Their working base for this experience is collectively mediated through rules, a division of labour in the context and their community.

As indicated, transition, pedagogy and curriculum concepts in this early-years' setting are theorised in social and cultural terms (Vygotsky 1978). I will argue that a sociocultural lens offers new explanatory perspectives on viewing the development of transition identities, as do Johnson and Golombek (2003).

I expand on the KindaKinder program below, locating the context for this experiential pedagogy.

The *KindaKinder* Program: Experiential Pedagogy and University Context

Victoria University is a social justice tertiary institution in the Australian city of Melbourne. The social justice elements of the university are the result of geographical location and historical connections with the technical education system. As other authors in this volume indicate, the university is mainly located in the western region of Melbourne; the most ethnically diverse community in Melbourne, with the lowest indicators, inviting opportunities for these groups of students to engage in our university site[2]. The university prides itself in offering diverse education pathways for students, some of which are apt to be of particular benefit to ethnic groups. Less obviously, literature in a similar vein can appear to distil a notion of diversity in a narrower and technical sense of the word: cultural "diversity" that bears implicitly the stigmas of a divide, a categorisation into those who have and have not, a notion that portrays culture as "otherness" (Lankshear 1997, 11).

The KindaKinder provides a unique opportunity for the development of Early Childhood pre-service teachers in the form of an experiential learning opportunity, called KindaKinder (a play on the words "kinder kindergarten"). Pre-service teachers complete a mixture of first-year theoretical input and a practical playgroup within the community, facilitated by a number of first- and second-year students.

KindaKinder was established in 2005 as an innovative program to support a local community of pre-school children and their families. This partnership model, which frames the student-learning experience so that students link ideas in such a way that practices and values are foregrounded within the play-based experience, is well described elsewhere (McLaren and Arnold 2008b, 2008a).

Enrolments in the first year of the Bachelor of Education (Early Childhood/Primary), and therefore this KindaKinder setting, have remained relatively steady over time, with 100 students in 2010, 108 in 2011, 85 in 2012, and 89 in 2013[3]. The Graduation Destination survey[4] shows of the eight graduates (61 percent response rate) in 2011, seven had full-time work. The 19 who responded to the survey (49 percent response rate) in 2012 showed 42 percent (8) had full-time work and 53 percent (10) had part-time work. This latter trend, increasing casualisation of work, is reflected in other graduate outcomes in Australia. The independent course experience survey between 2011 and 2012 shows a 50 percent (17 students in 2012) response rate and above-average satisfaction on all measures (Graduate Careers Australia 2013)[5].

The principles governing and the expectations underlying the KindaKinder pre-service teacher education curriculum and pedagogy can be summarised as follows:

- students expect and are expected to play an active role in their placement in that they develop the curriculum from their own experiences, backgrounds and history
- students will be responsible for organising the attendance of parents and children in conjunction with the placement school, and
- students develop their professional practice assisted by a mentor teacher in conjunction with their university classes

The role of the partnership—between the students, the teaching space and the school—is intended to be mutually beneficial. Students are expected to be active in the setting rather than merely experiencing the placement passively as observers or simply harvesting knowledge for the university course. Students complete all of the planning, resourcing, and facilitating necessary to conduct an hour-long play session with parents and their children from their first day in the program, rather than be provided with all the materials as in more traditional models of teacher training. In other words they are expected to *be* teachers.

Small groups of between three and eight pre-service teachers are allocated a pre-school learning site for the experiential learning, between 9 and 10 am, once a week. They are allocated a half-hour set-up and half an hour debrief and pack-up sessions. A session is made up of an hour of set-up time, an hour of delivery with children and families, and an hour of cleaning and reflection time for a total of about three hours. Each group always includes a mix of year levels, with First Year and accelerated students on a pathway from a Diploma of Children Services[6] into the Bachelor of Education Early Childhood/Primary (ABEC).

The experiential elements of the project require that students design and develop their literacy and play elements without a prescribed curriculum. They do this collectively, in groups, with the support of a mentor teacher assigned to each group. The ostensible purpose of the program in the school setting is to provide literacy and play experiences for the children and families. The school and or community element of the project is supported by a mentor teacher role. A full description of this role has also been reported elsewhere (McLaren and Arnold 2008b). The KindaKinder model emphasises the integration of academic inquiry with student literacy and numeracy within the type of play practice experience advocated by (Wagner 1986).

Indeed, the KindaKinder program sits comfortably with the wider Victoria University Praxis Inquiry protocol for site-based, school-based experiences, which comprise four questioning frameworks: practice described, practice explained, practice theorised and practice changed (Burridge *et al.* 2010; Cherednichenko and Kruger 2009; Eckersley *et al.* 2011; Kruger *et al.* 2009). The goal of KindaKinder is to use an experiential paradigm as the framework for pre-service teacher learning in the first year. The aims of the program, its philosophy, the improvement of learning and teaching that takes place through, for example, the use of reflection time, are made explicit in course documentation.

The rules of the experiential setting, both implicit and explicit, are created in conjunction with and informed by the pre-service teacher school or community settings, lectures, course unit guides and the students themselves. Students are expected to develop the play activities within the settings before they have had received substantial theoretical input about literacy. So, how do they know what "curriculum" to develop in their KindaKinder settings? As the data below clearly illustrates, students draw on their own experiences of play as children or with their own or others' children beyond their work experiences. Their mentor teachers offer suggestions on how to build on each play session, but the conversations are not prescriptive (no "you must do this or that in the next session"). The "rules" of this experiential program are understood to mean just that: there is a giving and receiving within this community where experiential rules are understood not as a fixed reliance on the individual. In this way community experience enhances the students' transition and pedagogical experiences.

In KindaKinder settings, pre-service teachers have to recruit parents and children to the program. They do not necessarily know who is going to attend a particular session (the KindaKinder sessions are not compulsory) nor are the ages of the children known in advance. Since there is a large difference in the capacity of a toddler to engage in play when compared to that of a three- or four-year-old, pre-service teachers, either individually or collectively, must be able to cope with layers of uncertainty and a need for reflexivity well beyond those usually experienced by students. Once in the experiential placement setting, the relationships between students develop as each group has by its side two practicum-experienced colleagues coming into the bachelor course from a children's service diploma course.

The KindaKinder project has matured into a secure and confident program of delivery for early years' pre-service teacher education in the western suburbs of Melbourne, with results capable of being reliably replicated and adjusted to other learning environments. Whilst many institutions have developed experiential community-learning spaces, an elementary literature review makes it clear that few occur in university settings associated with teacher education. And when they are in evidence in university settings, they are largely associated with outdoor education courses (Itin 1999).

The following sections elaborate on a mixed-methods research approach using quantitative and qualitative methods conducted amongst the 2013 early-years' teacher education cohort. The quantitative survey offered to the whole cohort is complemented by qualitative focus group interviews carried out with six students from one setting and six two-hour observations from a total of three out of 28 KindaKinder settings.

Research Methods

The research data for this case study reflects a mixed quantitative and qualitative method. The rationale for using a mixed method—relying on a quantitative survey and semi-structured focus group interviews, and drawing on a series of six observations in these KindaKinder settings—resides with the recognition of the complex nature of these individuals and their institutional settings. As Kimberley Griffin and Samuel Museus (2011, 15) argue, multiple ways of viewing the data and analysing situations are required to capture what happens at the intersection of multiple social settings.

The survey questions broadly replicated an earlier transition and retention survey conducted by Andrew Funston (2011) and also reported in this book. This kind of replication provides an opportunity for colleges to tailor specific courses or else offer generic approaches in the area of transition and retention. The survey was conducted online in April–May 2013, during the first semester of these students' course. The 144 survey participants were all students completing their first-year units: 89 enrolled as first-year students and 55 in the first-year accelerated program from the Diploma of Children's Services. In other words, these students had successfully completed an 18-month course that gave them credits into the second year of this bachelor program and were transitioning as first-year students into a bachelor course.

The 44 survey questions included some general student descriptive data: languages spoken and languages at home, employment status including nature of employment, paid/unpaid and hours and perceptions of impact on study, technology and internet access and sources, reasons for application to this university, ATAR score, perceptions of study, previous study, what they wanted out of university, skills they offered and the outcomes they wanted to achieve for their year. I personalised the Andrew Funston survey to the College of Education by asking some general questions relating to their assumptions about literacy, play and diversity that are reported and presented elsewhere by myself and Marcelle Cacciattolo (2013).

There are some limitations to the quantitative data in this research. The 25 percent response to questionnaires such as this, although limited, are regarded as relatively common as observed by Richard James, Kerri-Lee Krause and Claire Jennings (2010).

Six students from one KindaKinder group setting were interviewed as a focus group, using a digital recording, with a semi-structured interview schedule. Interviews were transcribed and data reduced with the students then having further input into the themes and key ideas emerging from the data. Interview questions were developed to extend and complement the survey questions.[7] I also conducted six observational visits to two other KindaKinder settings that I draw on for research findings in this chapter.

In the next sections I discuss the general identity factors that arise from the initial survey and then consider the more subtle transition pedagogy matters that arise from the student perspectives of their experiential pedagogy.

First-Year Early Childhood Students' Identity

Some five percent of the students in this community (3/27) were male, a proportion that replicates a traditional gender imbalance in the early childhood sector. This gender mix, with far fewer males than females, is slightly lower than that at other Education degree courses at VU. In his study, Funston (2011, 90) indicates that 25 percent of males participated in the Arts course and that this percentage was itself proportionate to general enrolments data in Education and, as is noted in other Australian research, replicates traditional over-representation of females in higher education (Krause *et al.* 2005).

Around 55 percent (15/27) of the cohort, with ages between 18 and 19, could be classed as school leavers, with the balance, 44 percent (12/27), coming mostly from age groups that included other university, life and work experiences. This figure is also broadly similar to the proportions in the study by Funston (2011, 90). Age at entry can be a factor in retention. Younger students may need more course support in understanding the increased expectations of higher education. The mature course participants may have more autonomous study habits and be more focused, however they may be less likely to collaborate with fellow students (Krause *et al.* 2005).

Surprisingly, only 26 percent of this early childhood cohort were the first in the family to go to university. This was somewhat lower than those who were enrolled in the P-12 Bachelor of Education course, where nearly 50 percent identified as "first in family"; and again lower than in the Funston (2011, Appendix one, 2) survey, where 37 percent of the students were first in the family to attend university. No apparent reason for this proportion is evident from the data and it is a point that may be worthy of further research

"First in family", it should be noted, is often indicated as a potential "risk" factor in transition and retention[8]. Commenting on several other research projects related to academic integration, and by implication retention, Tinto (1993, 73) suggests that the non-cognitive aspects of academic self-concept, realistic self-actualisation and familiarity with academic requirements and demands make important demands on students in their transition year. On the basis of this factor we might expect this group of students to have fewer problems relating to transition into the university. However, Tinto (2012) notes there are dangers in attributing a factor—like first in family or languages spoken—to some absolute risk. Better to take the perspective of this chapter in examining student success and pedagogic factors that enhance retention.

Around 17 percent of students who completed the survey identified themselves as speakers of a language other than English at home. This was similar to the proportion obtained in the Bachelor of Education P-12 (18 percent), but appreciably lower than the findings by Funston (2011, Appendix one, 2) where 33 percent of his survey participants spoke a language other than English at home. This was a surprising and perhaps concerning factor for teacher educators in these communities, given the location of the university in one of the most diverse linguistic communities in Melbourne[9]. For example, in 2011, about half of overall Victoria University students were from homes where English is not the primary language. This could perhaps reflect a self-selecting process whereby potential teacher education students from diverse communities are either not selecting to come to Victoria University or not selecting to come into teaching.

Excessive work hours are often regarded as a "risk" indicator for students in pursuing a university course (Krause *et al.* 2005). Although only 24 of the 27 answered the question, of those who did, 63 percent (15) indicated they did not work or worked between 6 and 10 hours. Seventeen percent (9) indicated they worked more than 10 hours, and one student indicated more than 20 hours. In traditional terms of examining "risk factors of students", these results might mean that the students are more likely to be retained as a result of fewer financial stressors or more stable financial affairs.

Students were asked then about unpaid work hours and 77 percent (20) indicated less than 10 hours of unpaid work. Three of the remainder who answered this question indicated that they worked, in an unpaid capacity, for more than 20 hours. Most students were working well below the conventional limit of 15 hours considered safe, if not actually positive, for retention and transition purposes. The complexity of paid and unpaid work is relatively untested in this transition and retention project and warrants further research and investigation.

The quantitative data from this survey point to an overwhelmingly female cohort, largely dominated by younger or school leavers, with a strong English-speaking background and with considerable social and cultural capital to engage in a university experience. The relatively low numbers of the cohort and the methodology used in the program—heavily participatory—would normally place this course in a privileged position to do well in terms of retention and transition. Wider university research by Krause *et al.* (2005) on first-year experiences suggest these are likely indicators for successful transition.

In the next section I discuss the students' previous experiences and their histories and communities that enabled them to successfully transition into the KindaKinder communities of learning.

Previous Experiences and Forming a Teacher Identity: Active "Being" and Collaborative Learning

This section clarifies how the experiential pedagogy promoted active, interpersonal, and collaborative learning. The pre-service students discussed how this KindaKinder experience enabled them to build on their strengths and develop new talents. Karen said[10] "I was able to use my creative experiences and apply them to this setting". Matthew, who had a sports background, indicated how the group supported him in boosting his self-confidence. Somewhat reflexively, the focus group reminded him how his sporting skills had boosted their understanding of possibilities for integrating more physical activity within their play experiences.

Students described how they were able to draw on further education, a Diploma of Children's Services in Childcare, to navigate the experiential elements of the program. For example,

- Chantelle said, "my work in children's centres has helped me in this course"
- Caroline noted, "I have brought a sense of fun, authority and ability to keep the children interested and wanting to be there"
- Jackie pointed out, "I was familiar with the (early childhood) frameworks"

We can infer from these comments, and similar ones about drawing on past experiences, the benefits students feel from the familiarity and sense of belonging and support provided by the KindaKinder program in these new educational settings.

Karen, completing the course part-time, explained that "having my own child has enabled me to see the developmental side [of the course]". Whilst she was not suggesting that all students had to have children to get the best out of the KindaKinder and a teacher education course, she was strongly suggesting how she was able to bridge the two experiences—that at home and that at university—as an element supporting the successful transition experience.

There was a very real sense during these interviews of this group working as a *Kindacommunity*. For example, when discussing how their strengths intersected with their placement experiences, Matthew felt encouraged by his colleagues to reflect closely on the contributions he was able to make: "The interactions with the others (in the group) enabled me to see the possibilities for myself."

These students conveyed a coherent set of images for how this experiential approach enabled them to engage in their KindaKinder placement: how they built on previous life experiences and understandings; the Kindacommunity they developed as a group in the school; and how they transitioned between the theoretical world of the classroom and the school (community) site. Students illustrate how the "acquisition", "participation" and "knowledge creation" metaphors play a role through the experiential pedagogy and curriculum and eased their shared transition experiences. So what elements and forms of the pedagogical relationship further supported transitions?

Pedagogy, Curriculum, and Relationships in Transition

The students considered the importance of both formal and informal relationship-building within the course; this provided a level of continuity and change that appeared achievable in this transition phase. For example, Caroline reflected on the nature of the formal course elements that supported her transition. It was, in her words, "the hands-on experiences" that enabled her to build on her strengths and feelings of confidence and belonging. Another student valued as a great strength of the program the fact that its informal elements brought them together, furnishing them with opportunities to talk about how to "establish group relationships". The community and group effects were very evident in both the focus group interview and during my observations in other KindaKinder settings.

As for the curriculum, Jackie noted: "I have understood the concept of a curriculum and the classes have given me an understanding of a KindaKinder design". These students discuss and make explicit how the experiential component (the "hands-on", the practical side, of the course) draws on their own knowledge, and how this very outcome has given them confidence in their initial transition phase as university students. In other words, how these students use their time at university, within the pedagogy and curriculum hours, becomes a marker for how well their transition is brokered. Kuh (2008, 3) notes that effective transition for all students is about how to improve the intentionality and use high impact practices that aid and ease student transition into the new settings that count. Cuseo (2011) makes similar points about the connectedness of a curriculum design in his address.

These students, in their first year of the course, are able to relate to the family elements of developing a play and literacy experience, and this despite the in-principle inhibitory presence of the parents in the sessions. Chantelle said, "The interactions with the children, families and teachers have really improved my confidence". Observations of other KindaKinder students by the researcher verified this statement. In one setting observation, a student spent 15 minutes talking to a mother about a child in order to improve understanding of the chid. Being able to relate to families gave the students some insight into how to relate to both parents and teachers in an actual teaching and learning setting. This realisation marked a significant point in the development of at least some of these pre-service teachers' identities.

Some students also described how their KindaKinder experiences enhanced and "made easier" their theoretical learning during university lectures and tutorials. For Karen this was despite being "Four years out of school and I've forgotten a lot of things and I could see the theory in action". Kuh (2008, 323) refers to the links between formal and informal relationship-building, in this case the relationship between the KindaKinder and university experiences as a successful "pervasive" approach. By this he was referring to the density of theory as it applied to the contexts.

Any university course that is new for students is likely to create points of tension between negotiating new learning spaces and home lives. Some of these students did talk about how they had hit difficult points when they had thought of leaving. So what supported them in staying? "Extensions, helpfulness and understanding have kept me here." The theme of staff understanding their role in the transition and retention process was a common topic expressed in other interviews I conducted[11].

Another more subtle but equally important dimension of the KindaKinder experience was how a student linked the previous diploma course with the bachelor course. Chantelle noted "The diploma puts theory into practice and I learn better through practice". Thus Chantelle noted how theory-building applied across the courses as students transitioned from the further education courses, the Diploma of Children's Services, to the higher education setting. Thus the similarity between the two experiences, one in diploma, and this one in the bachelor degree course enhanced their transition experience.

Orientation and Initial Connections to the University Setting

These focus-group students spoke positively about the support received from academic and other staff; for instance in getting them enrolled and inducted into the university system. They shared positive and optimistic stories of how the orientation welcome/information event run by staff provided them not just with technical information about the course, but also set a tone for their engagement with the university. Even simple mundane references like the one related by a staff member singing the praises of the best coffee shop on campus left their mark on a student who valued this comment as making him/her feel that staff were approachable. This is perhaps a good reminder of how important it is to ensure that simple opportunities for affiliation and belonging are built into the bonding experience of "orientation".

Students discussed how the layout, signage and spaces of the campus site made them feel welcomed and that the campus was "easy to navigate". Caroline recounted how in the previous year she had enrolled at another campus, in another course at the same university, and how she had felt overwhelmed by the campus, the amount of information, and the lack of personal approaches. She immediately unenrolled, rethought her career plans and enrolled the following year in a course that she was more interested in and where the campus site seemed more manageable.

Peer mentors, student volunteers and a friendly, welcoming atmosphere were also mentioned by these KindaKinder students as part of the more familiar terrain in their university transition. These students had become familiar with the peer-mentor writing support roles through their participation in Knowing and Knowledge, a unit (see Brian Zammit's chapter four in this volume), specifically designed to reinforce and develop their academic identity. As they talked during the focus group interview, they encouraged and reminded each other how helpful the process of working through academic referencing was in "becoming" part of this new academic world. Gill Best addresses this point more fully in this volume (see Coda).

The highlight of the discussion on course orientation and engagement was doubtless how myths about staff aloofness were busted. Chantelle, who had moved into this experiential course from the diploma course, recounted how they, the diploma group the previous year, were "warned" that once you move into higher education, staff were less accessible and not as available as in further-education settings. "They won't be helpful or supportive", so said the conventional wisdom. And yet, not only did these kind of predictions fail to materialise, but they were thoroughly disproven by the very nature of the experiential course, which demands of both students and staff high levels of interaction on a regular basis. The very nature of expectations—how they are formed through formal and informal conversations with peers—tells you something about how perceptions are formed.

The themes of flexibility, collegiality and a supportive campus environment were factors mentioned throughout the interviews, and have also being brought up in other Victoria University settings as important contributors to a student experience with a difference. Marketing research by Victoria University in keeping with Kuh (2008, 2005), confirm that high-quality staff interaction with students and supportive campus environments positively reinforced these students' identity and sense of belonging.

Students' KindaKinder communities (colleagues, teaching staff) were there to navigate enrolment issues and learn new ways of thinking with each other to solve inevitable confusions about expectations and placement matters in their transition year. The students' pre-service teacher identities are formed through an appreciation and appropriation of new and old learning experiences in new contexts that value their expertise.

So what does a strong orientation, staff flexibility, interpersonal interactions that intersected with their experiential KindaKinder mean in relation to academic challenge? This next section explores the student perceptions of institutional and academic challenge.

Institutional and Academic Challenge

As indicated previously, most students come into a university setting expecting to have some form of higher-level engagement with the experiential curriculum, and a commensurate yet undefined degree of challenge (Tinto 2012; Kuh 2008; Kuh *et al.* 2005). A key element of challenge for these students consists in achieving a sense of relevance from the experiential nature of the course, one that leads to new learning opportunities endowed with their own meanings and experiences. For example, Matthew talks about how he developed new creative skills and talents that surprised him. Collaboration between and amongst group members in navigating the academic clearly enabled these new forms of learning to occur.

These final sections elaborate on my earlier sociocultural propositions suggesting that a cultural–historical activity model offers a new way of viewing transition activities in this teacher-education and higher education setting

A Cultural–Historical Activity Theory Model for an Experiential Pedagogy and Transition

The conceptual model selected to support the analysis in this research is cultural–historical activity theory (CHAT), illustrated above in figure 6-1. The human mediation and relational agency concepts elaborated in the discussion above suggest the manner in this KindaKinder community of students interacting with each other and bringing stories of experience into these settings to enable a richer positioning of pre-service teachers' identity in the dynamic field of mutually constructed transitions. Students build on their existing knowledge and assumptions about the university in relation to their experiential setting. And because their actions are reciprocal and reciprocated rather than uni-directional, transition experiences are not simply an outcome of university or student communities, but in fact a dynamic and mediated intersection within the activity system and world of social and cultural constructs.

Student diversity, as an active process of meaning creation in context, also appears to be mediated by the experiential setting to both build on previous student experience and develop new ways of viewing this partnership experience. Hence, both the concepts of relational agency and human mediation become relevant to viewing the Kindacommunity. Pre-service teacher identity is shaped and shapes their being (acquiring), becoming (participation) and knowledge creation.

The way these KindaKinder students interact with, and bring stories of their experience to, these settings enables a richer positioning of pre-service teachers' identity in the dynamic field of mutually constructed transitions. Students build on their existing knowledge and assumptions about the university in relation to their experiential setting. And because their actions are reciprocal and reciprocated rather than uni-directional, "transition experiences" are not simply an outcome of university or student communities, but are in fact a dynamic and mediated intersection between the two systems. The student roles, creating play spaces for children and families extending and developing their own meanings in context, are developed in relation to their university partnership in the KindaKinder setting, which are then mediated by student colleagues.

Students' KindaKinder communities (colleagues, teaching staff) were there to navigate enrolment issues and learn new ways of thinking to solve inevitable confusions about expectations and placement matters in their transition year. The students' pre-service teacher identities are formed through an appreciation and appropriation of new and old learning experiences in new contexts that value their expertise.

Conclusion

This chapter explored an experiential transition program during the first year of an early years' pre-service teacher education KindaKinder. Two key concepts, "relational agency" and "mediation", were used to formulate and demonstrate how an experiential transition pedagogy can develop a sense of belonging and engagement that supports this university in its goals for acceptance and recognition for the academic learning potential for students. The experiential pedagogy, students creating new play spaces with colleagues, children, and families facilitated and enabled the students to develop their identity drawing reciprocally on collective strengths.

The students in this case study contribute and indicate new and successful ways of viewing a pedagogical transition. I argue that the sociocultural lens in the chapter, the *knowledge-creation* metaphor offers rich and unexplored terrain illustrating new veins to harvest in developing successful transition for all students into higher education settings.

As noted in the introduction it is possible to describe some of the actual data around student characteristics for retention, university, and institutional level factors that enhance students' persistence (such as a welcoming environment, administrative approaches, orientation). However, in this chapter I argue a mere consideration of those factors would fail to highlight the more subtle pedagogical and curriculum-led effects of a transition experience (Kuh 2008) .

Student diversity, as an active process of meaning creation in context also appears to be mediated in the KindaKinder to enable an element of persistence, resilience, and transition into their teacher identities. The academic challenge comprised generating new forms of learning in a somewhat supported environment; student learning communities integral to the pedagogy and curriculum and supportive tutors and mentor teachers.

This chapter proposes that there are purposeful actions by these pre-service teacher students and their institutional community through the transition activity of becoming a pre-service teacher within this experiential pedagogy. Actions are mediated in relation to previous experiences (thereby providing a link between the rules, the community, and roles in relation to their university experience) by the KindaKinder experience.

Acknowledgments

Firstly, I want to thank the students for their contributions. Our discussions were most valuable and have added depth and richness to the world of transition and experiential pedagogy. The project team comprised Kristy Davidson, a research officer with the College of Education who supported the development of the initial online questionnaire and analysis of the data. Dan Loton, now a research officer with the Centre for Collaborative learning and teaching has supported the project when Kristy was promoted to another university. Marcelle Cacciattolo, a Senior Lecturer in the College of Education, with a strong interest in retention matters, provided mentorship, encouragement, and expertise with the focus group interviews and writing feedback. Professor Andrea Nolan, and the Early Childhood team in the College of Education have also played a supportive, reflective and encouraging role. This project was made possible by small seeding research grant from the College of Education in 2012.

Notes

[1] An Australian measure for ranking student school achievement. http://www.uac.edu.au/undergraduate/atar/ This "score" is used for ranking and selecting students into universities.

[2] *The Good Universities Guide* rates Victoria University four stars (four is the most) for undergraduate cultural diversity and five stars for graduate outcomes (Hobsons 2013)

[3] Data from INFOVU, 5 October 2013. The change in numbers was a deliberate recruiting strategy for first-year students in order to accommodate more students coming from the Pathway Diploma in Children's Services. The overall number of students in the course remains at about 100 per year.

[4] An annual report on Australian graduate destinations (AGS) which collects immediate and post-study activities of new graduates (Graduate Careers Australia 2013).

[5] An independent survey, as in 4 above. Overall satisfaction with the course in 2012 increased significantly from 33 percent to 65 percent, illustrating how well the staff respond to student feedback and information.

[6] Semi-structured questions and survey available from the author

[7] "First in family" is also a complex and contested area of measurement, as how this phrase is interpreted varies among students, academics and the research community. It is beyond the scope of this chapter to address this, but a report by Katie Hughes, forthcoming, unpacks some of these factors in more recent detail.

[8] 2011, ABS. 2013. *Census Quick Facts* 2011 [cited 6th October 2013]. Available from http://www.abs.gov.au/websitedbs/censushome.nsf/home/quickstats.

[9] All names are pseudonyms

[10] The author conducted her research with first-year Bachelor of Education students (P-12) and a Diploma of Education course using a similar framework. These outcomes are presented elsewhere (Gilmore and Cacciattolo 2013)

Reference List

Adams, Tony, Melissa Banks, Dorothy Davis, and Judith Dickson. 2010. *The Hobsons Retention Project Context and Factor Analysis Report* 2010 [Accessed 2nd August 2013]. Available from http://www.aiec.idp.com/pdf/2010_AdamsBanksDaviesDickson_Wed _1100_BGallB_Paper.pdf.

Ageyev, Vladimir. 2003. "Vygotsky in the Mirror of Cultural Interpretations." In *Vygotsky's Educational Theory in Cultural Context*, edited by Alex Kozulin, Boris Gindis, Vladimir Ageyev and Suzanne Miller. Cambridge: Cambridge University Press.

Billingham, Stuart. 2009. Diversity, Inclusion, and the Transforming Student Experience. In *18th EAN Annual International Conference*. York: York St John University.

Burridge, Peter, Catherine Carpenter, Brenda Cherednichenko, and Tony
  Kruger. 2010. "Investigating Praxis Inquiry within Teacher Education
  Using Giddens's Structuration Theory." *Association for Experiential
  Education* no. 33 (1): 19–37.
Cherednichenko, Brenda, and Tony Kruger. 2009. "Restructuring
  Teaching for Learning: A Praxis Inquiry Approach to Teacher
  Education." In *Digital Portfolios: Reconceptualising Inquiry in Pre-
  Service Teacher Education*, edited by Fida Sanjakdar. Frenchs Forest,
  New South Wales, Australia: Pearson Education
Clarke, John, Stuart Hall, Tony Jefferson, and Brian Roberts. 1981.
  "Subcultures, Cultures and Class." In *Culture, Ideology and Social
  Process*, edited by Tony Bennett, Graham Martin, Colin Mercer and
  Janet Wooollacott, 53–79. London: Oxford University Press.
Crosling, Glenda, Margaret Hegney, and Liz Thomas. 2009. "Improving
  Student Retention in Higher Education." *Australian Universities'
  Review* 51 (2): 9–18.
Crosling, Glenda, Liz Thomas, and Margaret Heagney. 2008. "Improving
  Student Retention." London: Routledge and Taylor Francis Group.
Cuseo, Joe. 2011. Developing a Comprehensive First Year Experience
  Programme: Powerful Principles and Practices. Melbourne, Vic.
Devlin, Marcia. 2013. "Bridging Socio-Cultural Incongruity:
  Conceptualising the Success of Students from Low Socio-Economic
  Status Backgrounds in Australian Higher Education." *Studies in
  Higher Education* 38 (6): 939–49. doi:
  10.1080/03075079.2011.613991.
Dewey, John. 1991. *How We Think*. New York: Prometheus Books.
Eckersley, Bill, Merryn Davies, Julie Arnold, Tony Edwards, Neil Hooley,
  Jo Williams, and Simon Taylor. 2011. *Vision Unlimited: Inspiring
  Participant Knowldege in Schools. Researching Site-Based Pre-
  Service Teacher Education*. Melbourne: Victoria University.
Edwards, Anne. 2005. "Relational Agency: Learning to Be a Resourceful
  Practitioner." *International Journal of Educational Research* 43:168-
  182. doi:10.1016/j.ijer.2006.06.010.
Engeström, Yrjo. 1987. *Learning by Expanding*. Helsinki: Orienta
  Konsultit.
Engeström, Yrjo, Reijo Miettinen, and Raija-Leena Punamaki. 1999.
  Perspectives on Activity Theory. Cambridge: Cambridge University
  Press.
Findsen, Brian. 2011. "Making Sense of Our Contexts." In *Reflection to
  Transformation*, edited by Nick Zepke, Dean Nugent and Linda Leach.
  Wellington: Dunmore Publishing.

Fiske, John. 1989. *Understanding Popular Culture*. London: Routledge.
Freire, Paulo. 1973. *Cultural Action for Freedom*. Harmondsworth: Penguin.
Funston, Andrew. 2011. "Journeys to University and Arrival Experiences." PhD diss., Graduate School of Education, University of Melbourne Melbourne.
Gale, Trevor, and Stephen Parker. 2012. "Navigating Change: A Typology of Student Transition in Higher Education." *Studies in Higher Education* (ahead-of-print): 1–20.
http://dx.doi.org/10.1080/03075079.2012.721351.
Gilmore, Gwen, and Marcelle Cacciattolo. 2013. *Navigation and Exploration in a Pre-Service Teacher Education Course: Stories of Student Retention*, 3rd to 5th November 2013 [Accessed 4th November 2013].
Graduate Careers Australia. 2013. *Graduate Destination Survey* 2013 [Accessed 1st November 2013]. Available from
http://www.graduatecareers.com.au/.
Griffin, Kimberly, and Samuel Museus. 2011. "Using Mixed Methods to Study Intersectionality in Higher Education". In *Single issue intitutional research: Using mixed methods to study intersectionality in Higher Education*, edited by Kimberly Griffin and Samuel Museus. Hoboken, NJ, USA Wiley.
Hakkarainen, Kai, Tuire Palonen, Sami Paavola, and Erno Lehtinen. 2004. *Communities of Networked Expertise: Professional and Educational Perspectives*. Amsterdam: Elsevier.
Hammersley, Martyn, and Roger Gromm. 2000. "Introduction." In *Case Study Method*, edited by Roger Gromm, Martyn Hammersley and Peter Foster. London: Sage Publications Ltd.
Hobsons. 2013. *Hobsons Course Finder*. Hobsons 2013 [Accessed 18th October 2013]. Available from
http://www.hobsonscoursefinder.com.au/ratings/compare/VU?studyType=UG&institutionName=Victoria
Itin, Christian. 1999. *Reasserting the Philosophy of Experiential Education as a Vehicle for Change in the 21st Century* 1999 [Accessed 18th October 2013]. Available from
http://www.hmc.edu/files/institutionalresearch/Experiential%20Learning/Itin_JEE_1999.pdf.
James, Richard, Kerri-Lee Krause, and Claire Jennings. 2010. *The First Year Experience in Australian Universities: Findings from 1994 to 2009*. Melbourne: Centre for the Study of Higher Education, University of Melbourne.

Johnson, Karen, and Paula Golombek. 2003. "Seeing Teacher Learning." *TESOL Quarterly* 37 (4 Winter): 729–737.

Karimshah, Ameera, Marianned Wyder, Paul Henman, Dwight Tay, Elizabeth Capelin, and Particia Short. 2013. "Overcoming Adversity among Low Ses: A Study of Strategies for Retention." *Australian Universities' Review* 55 (2):72-79.

Kift, Sally. 2011. *First Year Curriculum Principles: First Year Teacher Making a Difference*. Australian Learning and Teaching Council 2011 [Accessed 2013 10th October]. Available from http://fyhe.com.au/wp-content/uploads/2012/11/4FYCPrinciplesFirstYearTeacher_2Nov09.pdf.

Kozulin, Alex. 2003. "Psychological Tools and Mediated Learning." In *Vygotsky's Educational Theory in Cultural Context*, edited by A Kozulin, Boris Gindis, Vladimir Ageyev and Suzanne Miller. Cambridge, UK: Cambridge University Press.

Krause, Kerri-Lee, Robyn Hartley, Richard James, and Craig McInnis. 2005. *The First Year Experience in Australian Universities: Findings from a Decade of National Studies*. Melbourne: Department of Education, Science and Training.

Kruger, Tony, Anne Davies, Bill Eckersley, Frances Newell, and Brenda Cherednichenko. 2009. *Effective and Sustainable University-School Partnerships*. Canberra: Australia: Victoria University School of University.

Kuh, George D. 2008. *High Impact Educational Practices: What They Are, Who Has Access to Them and Why They Matter. Washington, Association of American Colleges and Educators*. Association of American Colleges and Educators 2008 [Accessed 21st June 2013]. Available from
http://www.neasc.org/downloads/aacu_high_impact_2008_final.pdf.

Kuh, George D, Jillian Kinzie, John H Schuh, and Elizabeth J Whitt. 2005. *Student Success in College: Creating Conditions That Matter*. San Francisco: Jossey-Bass.

Kuhn, Thomas S. 1970. *The Structure of Scientific Revolutions*. 2nd ed. Chicago: University of Chicago Press.

Lankshear, Colin. 1997. *Changing Literacies*. Buckingham: Open University Press.

Leontiev, Aleksie N. 1978. *Activity, Consciousness, and Personality*. Englewood Cliffs, NJ: Prentice-Hall.

McLaren, Mary-Rose, and Julie Arnold. 2008a. Kinda-Kinder': An Early Years Literacy and Numeracy Initiative for Higher Education Students In *6th Hawaii International Conference on Education*. Hawaii.

—. 2008b. 'Kinder-Kinda': An Early Years Literacy and Numeracy Initiative for Higher Education Students Paper read at Hawai International conference on Education, January 5-8, at Honolulu, Hawaii.

Paavola, Sami, Lasse Lipponen, and Kai Hakkarainen. 2004. "Models of Innovative Knowledge Communities and Three Metaphors of Learning." *Review of Educational Research* 74 (4 Winter): 557–76.

Pring, Richard. 2000. *Philosophy of Educational Research.* London: Continuum.

—. 2002. "The False Dualism of Educational Research." *Journal of Philosophy of Education.* 34 (2): 247-60. doi: http://onlinelibrary.wiley. com /doi/10.1111/1467-9752.00171/pdf.

Rogoff, Barbara. 1995. "Observing Sociocultural Activity in Three Planes." In *Sociocultural Studies of Mind,* edited by James Wertsch, Pablo del Río Del Rio and Alvarez Alvares. New York: Cambridge University Press.

Schofield, Janet Ward. 2000. "Increasing the Generalizability of Qualitative Research." In *Case Study Method,* edited by Roger Gromm, Martyn Hammersley and Peter Foster. London: Sage Publications.

Seely-Flint, Amy, Lisbeth Kitson, Kaye Lowe, and Kylie Shaw. 2014. *Literacy in Australia: Pedagogies for Engagement.* Milton, Queensland: Wiley.

Sfard, Anna. 1998. "On Two Metaphors for Learning and the Dangers of Choosing Just One." *Educational Researcher* 27 (2): 4–13.

Smith, Liz, Sally Kift, Karen Nelson, Jade McKay, and Marcia Devlin. 2012. "Effective Teaching and Support of Low Socioeconomic Students". Paper read at First Year in Higher Education, at Brisbane.

Stake, Robert E. 1994. "Case Studies." In *Handbook of Qualitative Research,* edited by Norman K Denzin and Yvonna S Lincoln. London: Sage.

Tinto, Vincent. 1993. *Rethinking the Causes and Cures of Student Attrition.* Vol. Two. Chicago: University of Chicago Press.

—. 2012. "Enhancing Student Success: Taking the Classroom Success Seriously." *The International Journal of the First Year in Higher Education* no. 3 (1): 1–8.

Upcraft, M. Lee, John N Gardner, and Betsy O Barefoot. 2005. *Challenging and Supporting the First-Year Student: A Handbook for Improving the First Year of College.* San Francisco: Jossey-Bass.

Van Huizen, Peter, Bert Van Oers, and Theo Wubbels. 2005. "A Vygotskian Perspective on Teacher Education." *Journal of Curriculum Studies.* 37 (3): 267-90. doi:

http://dx.doi.org/10.1080/0022027042000328468.

Vygotsky, Lev. 1978. *Mind in Society*. Cambridge, MA: Harvard University Press.

Wagner, Jon. 1986. "Integrating the Traditions of Experiential Learning in Internship Education." In *Experiential Education and the Schools*, edited by Richard J Kraft and James Kielsmier. Boulder; Colorado: Association for Experiential Education.

Warmoth, Arthur. 2000. *Social Constructionist Epistemology* 2000 [Accessed 11th November 2012]. Available from http://www.sonoma.edu/users/w/ warmotha/epistemology.html.

CHAPTER SEVEN

BECOMING A COMMUNITY OF READERS: ACADEMIC LITERACIES IN THE SOCIAL WORK CLASSROOM

JUANITA CUSTANCE, JOHN FOX AND PAULINE O'MALEY

Introduction

> I'm not sure it has changed/influenced the way I write but it's changed the way I read!

In this chapter we discuss a collaborative project undertaken by two academic language and learning (ALL) specialists and a discipline lecturer within Victoria University's Bachelor of Social Work degree. The project evolved from a desire to embed ALL support within key units of the degree program, partly in response to the university's emerging emphasis on developmental approaches to learning; and partly due to observations that many students were reluctant to take up the traditional support offered outside the classroom. The project sought to encourage the retention of social work students, many of whom are attracted to the interpersonal interactions central to the discipline, but are surprised and sometimes intimidated by the reading and analytic demands that are integral to the course .

Here, we document the initial three semesters of our collaboration and reflect on the cycles of team planning, teaching and consideration of student responses that guided our work. The project evolved as we developed a clearer picture of our students' needs and the work it was possible for us to achieve together. Our experience suggests that focusing on reading early in students' university experience is fruitful, and that students benefit from opportunities to develop explicit strategies for engaging with texts and from the modelling of this engagement by both peers and teaching staff. When this activity is collaborative students participate in a way that allows for an openness about difficulties and a willingness to grapple with and push past them. While we always hoped to engage students in discipline-specific reading and to normalise the challenges inherent in this labour, our expectations were exceeded as together we became a powerful community of readers. This outcome suggests that inter-disciplinary, collaborative work that is dynamic, fluid and responsive can be effective in supporting academic development.

Following a brief description of our project's institutional and theoretical background, in this chapter we outline the key understandings we developed during each of the three semesters' work completed to date. We conclude by reflecting on the elements we believe contributed to this project's success, and note some areas of tension we continue to explore. As our project has evolved in part through conversation with students, we would like their contributions to be heard and have chosen to include their words, garnered from questionnaires and focus groups, in text boxes interspersed throughout the chapter.

Background

> … gives confidence in ourselves, in our abilities.

Social work and ALL

Victoria University's Social Work Unit is founded in critical, anti-oppressive and anti-discriminatory theory, which seeks to promote the transformation of individual lives, and of the broader contexts that produce discrimination, exclusion and oppression (Grace *et al.* 2013). Victoria University is located in the culturally diverse western suburbs of Melbourne, Australia. A substantial number of our students are from non-English-speaking backgrounds. Many come from a low socioeconomic background and may often be the first in their family to attend higher education. The students undertaking the Bachelor of Social Work reflect this broad diversity and include a significant number of international and mature-age students. Our commitment to engaging in critical pedagogy has seen social work staff undertake a variety of educational projects and partnerships designed to support students in their studies (Grace *et al.*

2013). One longstanding partnership has been with the university's Department of Academic Support and Development. The support provided to social work students has included occasional lectures and academic skills sessions delivered within tutorials, but has primarily involved the referral of students for external consultation with ALL advisors. However, the number of students who took advantage of these opportunities, especially for individual assistance even when recommended to do so, was disappointingly low. Just as social work was looking for ways to better support its students, Academic Support was keen to work against a prevailing deficit view of student learning. We understood academic literacy as being deeply connected with the discursive patterns of a discipline in a particular time and place rather than a (grammatical) problem to be fixed in "faulty" students through isolated interventions (AALL 2010). Accordingly we sought to pursue an "embedded" approach to language and literacy development, where ALL could be meaningfully contextualised within discipline areas rather than being addressed externally or added to courses as "bolt-on" packages of generic study skills (Wingate 2006, 458). Embeddedness is a concept that is broadly applied within the ALL field. It is developmentally focused; however the term can be used to describe a variety of practices that range from the creation of discipline-specific teaching material (often writing-focused, such as models of specific assignment responses) to team teaching and input into curriculum and course delivery. Embeddedness is measured by the degree to which ALL development is integrated with the activities that students undertake as a regular part of their course of study (Roberts et al. 2004). The embedded approach we developed can be described as a fully integrated model (Latham 2010) and aligns with the concept of "outreach" (Grace et al. 2011, 2013) in the social work discipline, where the work is situated within a community and seeks to engage participants in their own environment on their own terms. The synergy of these shared interests was further supported by the university's establishment of a Language, Literacy and Numeracy (LLN) Strategy, which introduced educational developers into discipline areas to assist with ALL capacity-building.

The university's LLN Strategy encouraged the adoption of Lea and Street's (1998, 1999, 2006; Lea 2004) academic literacies approach, which is concerned with facilitating the valuing and engagement of students' diverse knowledge and life experiences. Lea and Street characterise the development of academic literacies as going beyond decontextualised study skills or academic socialisation that goes some, but not all, of the way in understanding the actual "discursive practices... and the experiences of participants being socialised through course-related activities"

(Duff 2007, 14). Lea and Street suggest an approach that is concerned with:

> ... meaning-making, identity, power, and authority, and foregrounds the institutional nature of what counts as knowledge in any particular academic context. ... [It] views the process involved in acquiring appropriate and effective uses of literacy as more complex, dynamic, nuanced, situated, and involving both epistemological issues and social processes. (Lea and Street 2006, 369)

In keeping with our shared values, this approach, with its focus on meaning-making at an epistemological level, has been at the heart of our collaborative work. It stems from our observation that students would benefit from a greater focus on explicitly engaging with unit readings and that they would further benefit from the development of reading strategies that would allow this engagement to begin.

Project development

Our project team consisted of a social work lecturer, an LLN educational developer and an Academic Support and Development lecturer. We designed a collaborative team-teaching approach to delivering selected second-year units within the social work program. We focused on these second-year units of study for both practical and pedagogic reasons. The structure of Australia's tertiary sector means it is possible for students to enter degree programs through non-traditional pathways. Many of our social work students gain sufficient study credit by undertaking a vocationally oriented advanced diploma, to enter directly into the second year of the degree course. While there is no doubt that pathway students bring rich, relevant experiences and insightful perspectives (Gonzalez *et al.* 2005) to the course, and indeed that some have undertaken academic work before, it is also clear that many entering in the second year struggle with the reading and writing demands of the academic discipline. Pathway students skip the foundational subjects introduced in the first year. This brings us to what we consider to be a further powerful reason for introducing an academic literacies project in the second year of the degree. In second year students truly begin to grapple with the specific discourses and content of critical social work. They are asked to analyse competing discourses and to consider their ability to enact anti-oppressive theory. Embedding work on ALL development at this point allowed us to pursue an epistemological approach, where we sought to align students' growing awareness of key disciplinary themes with the work of critical analysis and the processes of meaning-making in text.

Students were initially streamed into the team-taught tutorials on the recommendation of the unit coordinator. However, timetabling and other considerations meant that a cross-section of social work students was represented. The coordinator identified students who had either struggled in first year or who were pathwaying into the second year via diploma studies or other recognitions of prior learning processes. Two-thirds of the class were of non-English-speaking backgrounds. Several of the students had experienced extremely disrupted schooling, particularly those who had arrived in Australia as refugees. Most of the students were employed as shift workers, largely in aged care and the disability sector, or had significant personal caring responsibilities. Some students participated across all three semesters, while others moved in and out of the project as their course plans, willingness to participate and personal commitments allowed. Students were advised of the nature of the class and that it may require an extra time commitment.

The units involved were "Social Welfare: History and Current Context" and "Introduction to Social Policy". The former is offered in the first semester of the second year and introduces students to key concepts of the contemporary Australian welfare state, including "need", "wellbeing", "welfare" and the "state", together with some key dimensions of structural oppression. Students are engaged throughout in determining how our humanity is defined and how that informs different ideas of need and welfare. Having been asked to consider their own ideas of humanity and human welfare, students are then engaged in reviewing the historical development of those ideas from the Poor Laws of 17th-century England to contemporary practices in Australia. This unit also explores the forms that welfare has taken in relation to particular communities in Australia, with particular emphases on class, disability, gender, and race. These themes are further explored in the second semester unit, "Introduction to Social Policy", where students are introduced to Australia's political and social policy processes, and to the ideas and actions that found long-standing influential political traditions, such as liberalism, conservatism and socialism, as well as contemporary movements, such as "green" politics. The unit assists students to re-conceptualise "social" issues as "social policy" issues. It emphasises how we can bring about change by becoming aware of policy-making in our own lives and how oppression can be challenged by promoting our ability and obligation to engage in transformative politics on a wider scale.

In all three semesters all of the project team were present in both lectures and tutorials. In the first two semesters, the team members co-delivered tutorials while in the third they split between two tutorial groups comprising the social work lecturer and an ALL specialist in each. In order to accommodate the academic literacies focus, tutorials were extended by an hour each week. Students were made aware that they could meet with one of the ALL specialists individually outside of tutorial time if they requested. Throughout the entire project team members met each week to reflect, share observations, identify learning objectives and plan for the tutorial sessions to follow. The ALL specialists responded to the social work lecturer's draft lecture notes. While we were unsure where the project would take us, our intent was always transformative. Each week we reviewed our course delivery, what we perceived to be the student response, and shared research from ALL, education and social work disciplines that helped us understand the work we were doing. While the social work lecturer considered whether student assignments provided any evidence of a greater critical engagement with the unit content than had been typically seen in previous years, the ALL specialists looked for evidence of changing practices in reading and in using the readings by completing close text analysis of selected student work. We aimed to implement situated responses to problems uncovered during the course of each semester. As a team we reflected on what we felt worked, what didn't and why, as we planned the following week's class. One of the great benefits that emerged for us while undertaking such a praxis inquiry was that the dynamic process allowed for new insights to be integrated into the ongoing project.

Our focus on transformative practice, and in particular on the transformation of cultural practices such as organisational activity, language, discourses and social interactions (Kemmis and McTaggart 1988), echoes the concerns of both critical literacy and critical social work, which seek to challenge existing power relationships by giving voice to those whose ways of experiencing the world are often marginalised, particularly in institutionalised settings (Gonzalez *et al.* 2005). Part of our pedagogical enquiry was to investigate ways of creating a learning space where (to acknowledge Paulo Freire) academic knowledge could be co-produced and collaborative rather than top-down and prescriptive. Accordingly, we were keen to consider how our students were experiencing being in a team-taught tutorial.

Our data was collected from questionnaires and focus groups. At the end of the first and second semesters students were asked for their feedback in class and in independently-run focus groups. During the third semester we introduced three questionnaires that sought to understand students' reading strategies, the area we had come to understand as essential to this group's academic development. Each of the questionnaires was more open-ended than the last. The first questionnaire asked students to nominate which of the introduced reading strategies they were using and to indicate how useful they were. The second questionnaire asked students to reflect on what they had learnt about texts and how they may have applied this understanding in their academic work. The third had four open-ended questions relating to: perceptions of being in the class; the reading strategies that stuck with them; whether they had experienced any change as readers over the semester; and any suggestions for the next phase of the project. In the final week of that semester another focus group was held. This data collection process allowed us to adapt our practice responsively within each semester rather than having to wait until the next.

The Evolving Project

> At first I was very much struggling with the reading as I felt it was too long, hard and complicated. But now with the help of different ideas and techniques given by our tutor it is much easier to know the reading structure and what it is about. I have definitely improved my reading ability.

The first semester

The first semester's focus was on how to structure the team-teaching and embed integrated activities in response to the students' identified ALL needs. Initially we maintained a sharp distinction between the subject content and the academic literacies work. A typical tutorial session involved discussion and class activity based on that week's lecture topic followed by some explicit academic literacies work related to students' assignment development and the teaching team's perception of where the group's general academic literacies needed strengthening (or in some cases establishing). Each tutorial was followed by a team meeting to discuss student responses and develop an activity plan for the following week.

Initially the skills sessions were provided as an optional extra for those choosing to stay for the additional hour. However, attendance was sporadic. Sessions were well attended as assignments drew near, but had only a small number of attendees in the weeks between. Although the ALL specialists were involved in various activities during the traditional tutorial, the discipline lecturer was not allocated time to participate in the skills session and would leave the room at the end of the standard tutorial. We soon discovered that this appeared to signal that the meaningful part of the class was over, and the majority of students would follow. The discussion in our weekly meetings began to crystallise around what we were increasingly understanding as an artificial divide between "content" and "skills", which we were inadvertently reinforcing by our classroom practices. We understood that content and academic literacies were inextricably entwined, and concluded that we needed to reflect this in our tutorial activities. Another mode of integration was needed if we were to overcome this false abstraction between academic literacies and content.

We decided to introduce some of the academic literacies work earlier in the tutorial, as well as look for ways to more seamlessly integrate the discussion of content with academic literacies development. We began looking for ways in which we could work with the knowledge being explored in the content area to scaffold knowledge of academic literacies. As the semester continued, and we drew more heavily on the weekly readings as the most accessible site for both content and academic literacies development, it became increasingly evident, and may be of little surprise to other educators, that students were not engaging with the readings. In response, we designed the last few tutorial activities around small group discussions of sections of the required readings and worked with each group on developing strategies such as identifying textual features like topic sentences and paragraph structure and creating visual representations of texts such as concept maps.

The second semester

I'm understanding the readings. I find myself reading for meaning, and not just reading for the sake of it... I read for meaning now even if it means I read it several times.

We began the second semester with the aim of investigating why students were not engaging with readings and tested strategies that would begin a process of engagement. Although it was clear that students were either not doing the readings or not retaining the key ideas, we were still unclear if this was due to literacy skills, time, contextualisation, or issues around cultural or academic backgrounds.

Our decision to explicitly engage with the readings was driven by our observation of students' poor reading behaviours and influenced by our own reading of Salvatori (2000, 2002) and her notion of grappling with difficulties. She believes grappling with difficulties:

> ... makes it possible for students to make visible, to articulate knowledges and forms of understanding that would otherwise be "consigned to the dark". This enabled teachers to engage them, and in light of them, "to respond" by systematically revising assumptions about and approaches to teaching that put a ceiling on the learner's intellectual capabilities. (2002, 202)

In order to gather some ongoing feedback from students, we agreed that one of the requirements of the first assignment, a group presentation, would be to briefly discuss any difficulties, large or small, the group had encountered with the readings and explain how they had tackled this problem. The assignment required the students to draw links between the relevant week's reading and a specified social security benefit, such as unemployment or parenting benefits. The discussion of difficulties was intended to assist us in gaining some formative understandings of where students were struggling and how we might best respond, as well as help to normalise the labour of reading. The students' honest and reflective response to the task was a welcome surprise and convinced us of the value in pursuing what Salvatori (2000, 81) terms a "pedagogy of difficulty" by encouraging persistence and a willingness to engage with complexities. The first group, largely international students, explained they had had trouble concentrating on a reading about Australian politics because they could not remember the prime ministers of Australia and what their ideologies were. They shared with the class a timeline they had created as a reference to overcome this difficulty, which the rest of the class gratefully took copies of. This set the tone for this section of the presentations (and often saw students snapping photos of each other's examples on the whiteboard). Students were very open about discussing difficulties and supported each other to extend their repertoires of strategies to tackle them (including asking your mum who is "so old" whether she remembers former Australian prime minister Gough Whitlam!).

During this period we implemented tutorial activities that were designed to allow all students to cooperatively engage in discussion and exploration of the required class texts. The

> It is okay to have difficulties when you are reading. How you handle those difficulties is the key.

teaching team made the decision to be open about any difficulties we ourselves encountered and offered sometimes diverging opinions about texts. We established a tutorial routine of small-group reading activities that then opened into a whole-class discussion to encourage the participation of students who may otherwise have remained silent, and to facilitate peer learning and authentic engagement with reading strategies.

We were influenced by van Pletzen's (2006) focus on making the reading experience, both that of the teaching staff and the students, visible, so as to better reveal the assumptions that are made by both educators and students in relation to reading. Van Pletzen (2006, 106) has cautioned that:

> Educators often assume that learners will manage to access the content of reading material or understand the other reasons for which reading materials might have been set, while learners often misjudge educator's objectives and have difficulty understanding how they should approach a text, or what use they are expected to make of it. For each party it is the relative invisibility of the reading process that makes it hard to understand and address the other party's objectives and frustrations.

These activities sought to make visible the ways in which we made meaning, both individually and collectively. During these activities we moved between groups, facilitating discussion not only about the texts, but also about *how* students were reading them: How did they identify the key contentions? What was it in the text that prompted students to draw the conclusions they did? Could they recognise the author's position, particularly in relation to referenced content? Were they convinced by the text's argument and why? In these ways we hoped to model and explicitly encourage students to apply reading strategies that aided the development of critical engagement with course materials.

In order to deliver a scaffolded ALL program it became clear that as part of our weekly meetings we needed not only to set the activities to engage with each week's social work lecture and readings, but also to foreground the language and discourse features that would be highlighted. Examples of these areas of focus included the use of referencing; signal phrases; TEEL structure (topic sentence, explanation, evidence, link); paragraphing;

> The more we read, including perspectives we may not agree with, the more well-formed our own opinions and ideas will be.

genre structure; voice; and rhetorical metaphor. By actively situating ALL within the discourse we hoped to raise students' confidence in their ability to comprehend the language of the discipline and the way that it works to create meaning, and in the process encourage them to connect more deeply with the course content. To further break down the divide between content and academic literacies, the discipline lecturer repeatedly presented the historical development of social policy as an engagement in making meaning and as a history of labouring to identify and apply different ideas about the human condition and human wellbeing. This positioning of content within the history of ideas enabled relevant concepts and events to be presented in the lectures in terms of "grappling" to make meaning in ways that were analogous to the activities then undertaken in tutorials. Some lectures were explicitly presented in the TEEL structure, with an exaggerated highlighting of the question being addressed, the claims being made, and evidence presented in support, so as to demonstrate the centrality and value of language and discourse analysis skills.

Ongoing feedback as to how students were responding to our approach was collected from the responses to our questionnaires and via our examination of their assignments, which we analysed for evidence of the impact of the work we had done. We looked for evidence of

> It's helpful because you can see the different links.

students' understanding of the text being cited by evaluating their ability to make appropriate textual selections, identify authors' claims and then analyse and evaluate claims. At our regular meetings we discussed the insights we gained from the concepts and skills that were being taken up, and those that would benefit from further reinforcement. This knowledge was also useful as we considered what we wished to foreground in our planning for the following semester.

The third semester

> … more aware of bias and motivation/writer's intentions and not accepting everything I read as the absolute truth!

Guided in part by the student feedback, the third semester continued our approach of close engagement with both the content and structure of texts, but with a greater emphasis on drawing out the connections (or indeed disconnections) students were able to identify between the texts and their own experience and cultural understandings. As this semester began in the middle of the academic year, we had a mix of students, some of whom had participated in the "outreach" tutorial in the previous semester and some who had recently "pathwayed" into the course. In order to allow these differences to be accommodated, we allocated these different groups into two distinct "outreach" tutorials, each taught by one ALL specialist with the discipline lecturer. Broadly speaking, similar approaches were adopted in each tutorial, drawing on the same activities, but allowing more time to understand and begin the process of "grappling" for those who were new to the course.

We continued to test teaching strategies that students told us had made a difference to their ability to participate in tutorials, such as providing focus questions for the weekly readings (often excerpts requiring deeper engagement with smaller amounts of text); close readings in small groups then shared and expanded with the class; and the use of visual organisers

> I used to *just* write without much consideration of structure. Now I have structure in mind when I write.

such as concept maps, matrices, webs and graphs for working with difficult texts and unpacking assignment questions. We actively encouraged behaviours that developed learning-community participation, including organisational practices such as giving students opportunities to write on the board and changing the teacher-focused physical space. Students requested that more time be given to considering issues from different cultural perspectives and on the practicalities of developing and linking ideas for assessments. Consequently, much of the third semester's ALL work focused on how reading strategies could be effectively developed to create better writing. Tutorial activities made use of comparative and evaluative graphic organisers so students could experience using these tools to jointly develop arguments and critically appraise material.

While we continued to engage in an ongoing reflective discussion with students about *how* they were learning, we also invited them to provide feedback on their experience of being in a supported tutorial by completing an open-ended online survey, participating in an evaluative forum in the final class and attending a semi-structured interview conducted by an independent researcher. This data is yet to be analysed.

Reflections

While our project continues to evolve, five key themes that emerged from our shared experience are discussed in this section. The first is the importance of normalising the experience of difficulty in academic work. This sits in close relationship with the second theme, the development of a learning community and its importance to both students and staff. Under *Broadening Engagement* we consider our mixed success at trying to be "everything to everyone". Our final themes reflect two external influences we felt had a significant impact on student learning. One of those "external" influences was the individual advisory sessions with the ALL specialists that were available to students outside of class time. Finally, an ongoing impact for both students and the collaborative team, which we detail below, is time and its challenges.

Normalising the challenges of reading

Throughout this project we sought to normalise the challenges of reading in the discipline by making it clear that reading well was not straightforward, but difficult and demanded skill and effort. Conscious of the stigma often felt by those experiencing these difficulties, we presented reading as an "excavation". Drawing on Foucault's (2002) equation of analysis with an archaeological "dig", we reframed reading from some straightforward absorption of information to an endeavour to reveal something that was not obvious, where the effort of revelation required care and effort, and progressed by trial and error. In particular, the analogy was utilised to emphasise that a quick traversal of a text would often miss its significance in just the same way that the treasures of a "dig" might not be readily seen from the surface. We sought to promote a recognition of reading as a promising labour with regard to the academic literacies work of Lea and Street (1998, 1999, 2006; Lea 2004) and their insistence on the value in going beyond "study skills" and "socialisation" approaches.

Within the classroom we combined this contextualised approach to meaning-making with a focus on identifying difficulties and articulating how we all, lecturers and students alike, grapple with and overcome them (Salvatori 2002). This approach helped build a sense of community and aided a shift in the power dynamic, freeing students from the pressure of needing to get it right first time. During tutorial activities we observed them exploring, drawing tentative conclusions, returning to the text and grappling again with ideas, claims and understandings.

As part of our aim to make reading visible (van Platzen 2006) we developed learning activities designed to build efficacy and scaffold students to develop as strategic and confident readers. These activities focused on specific reading strategies, such as: identifying text purpose; establishing focus questions; skimming and scanning; making use of text structure; signalling; and concept-mapping, which were all used as a way into meaning-making. We undertook explicit work on excavating texts: identifying the author's claims and evidence, and then using this as a bridge for students to think about how to build, support and structure their own arguments. For each activity, the teaching staff introduced, modelled and illustrated the strategies through worked examples, and then engaged the students in activities in which they proceeded to apply those strategies themselves. As previously discussed, the presentations, where students described how they overcame any difficulties when reading and when linking their readings to social security benefits, were particularly effective in encouraging this labour and reducing associated perceptions of stigma or shame.

Our focus on doing such explicit work on reading was not on teaching individual reading strategies for their own sake, but to develop strategic readers (Grabe and Stoller 2002). To become strategic readers, students need to develop strategies for reading, do plenty of reading and grappling with difficulties; as well as experience the joy and delight of exploring ideas when reading and in conversations that follow a deep engagement with text. By foregrounding close engagement with text as the vehicle in which to approach academic literacies, we have aimed to ensure that students understand the significance of the texts in their course, are given explicit tools for engaging with these and other texts, build confidence around their own reading strategies and begin to develop their own voice as participants in their academic and professional discourse communities. When we asked what strategies we introduced that students were using and were resonating with them, concept mapping was high on the list. They also nominated contextualising information (by using headings, skimming and scanning, reading more than once, and noting topic sentences and keywords); and revisiting texts for deeper engagement (particularly through the use of guiding questions that were emailed to students each week and small group discussions in the tutorials). The students clearly saw this transformation themselves and reported feelings of empowerment.

> I believe digesting the readings and discussing them as a class has helped me understand the readings better, and using mind maps and dividing up different information into different brackets has helped improve my understanding and organisation skills.

> [I am] doing more research and looking outside the box, i.e. taking things at a broader perspective.

Although we began the second semester hoping to investigate why students were experiencing difficulty with reading, we began noticing a shift in the tutorial dynamic once the discussion of difficulties became normalised. Discussing the problem became the solution.

Becoming a learning community

This "visible grappling" produced more than improved engagement with readings and "strategic readers"; it promoted a sense of community. One of the highlights of this project was the manner in which students collaboratively constructed understandings of key content in tutorials. We saw a diverse group of students begin to engage critically with texts, and move beyond merely attempting to understand the unit content to actively critiquing it. Rather than the tutors' questions being met by silence (eventually broken by a confident high-achieving student), or concern about "correct" answers, responses often began with a student saying they found the point confusing, to which others would offer interpretations or indeed challenges. The learning community that developed as a result of this project provided students with an opportunity to connect theory to their own experiences, while encouraging all of us to recognise and grapple with the frustrations and joys of doing academic work. This emergent approach of embedding academic literacies development within a learning community approach aligns with Lea and Street's (1998, 1999, 2006; Lea 2004) emphasis on epistemology and knowledge as contextualised, contestable and fluid. Students who reported that they "feel so alone at uni" emphasised the impact of this experience; they reported feeling like part of a learning community in this class. As the project evolved, so too did the learning community; trust was built and the commitment to the group increased. Some students reported a change in their sense of responsibilities to the group.

> The sense of community input has been really helpful. It gives us a chance to share what we know as well as learn off others.

> I'm not the only one— [I] feel more open and free no matter how silly it might sound.

> [We] feel bonded—different to other classes.

> [I want] … to be accountable to my group—prepare my readings, make relevant notes… contribute to group discussion.

In this safe environment students began to be more overt about the challenges the work presented and work together to overcome them. They started to become what Wenger (1998, 85) suggests an effective community of practice can become: "a force to be reckoned with". Hager (2008) and Hager and Hodkinson (2009, 2011) use the metaphor of "becoming" to account for a complex understanding of learning as a holistic process that is not just cognitive but also social and embodied. We have found this to be a fruitful concept in thinking about the ongoing project of learning in a learning community. Our experience was that participants in such a learning community "become" together. Hager (2008, 685) suggests "people become through learning and learn through becoming". Such interactional, dynamic aspects of this process have been central in our project. As Hager has acknowledged, community and environment are central to learning. Benesch (2001, 91) makes the character of this dynamic community clear. It is:

> … not based on a notion of hierarchy or induction of novices by experts [but] [i]nstead… founded on a postmodern recognition of difference (Weiler, 1994), of multiple and overlapping identities and goals. Yet, the recognition of difference does not rule out the possibility of shared needs and rights among people who find themselves together temporarily.

This recognition that we are all learners together who can bring our different perspectives to our shared work has been significant in our project.

This experience of "becoming" was not limited to the students. It was also experienced by the teaching staff and, in turn, was an important contributor to building the community. We were all learners in the process, learning from each other in a context where knowledge was constructed and reconstructed within the learning community and we all benefitted by questioning and exploring together.

> I like the interaction between our tutors, especially when they coordinate with each other and teach their technique. It makes the tutorial more active.

Alongside the natural classroom banter and differing perspectives offered by having multiple tutors from different discipline areas in a team-teaching space, the discussion of difficulties presented an opportunity for the teaching team to be more readily accepted by students as participants in a community of academic readers, sharing our own difficulties, strategies and responses to texts rather than being viewed as distant expert instructors and assessors. This interaction involved the teaching staff "grappling" in the classroom with the complexities of the content and language in an open dialogue that was intended to both model the specific skills and promote a deeper appreciation of the labour involved in any complex reading, regardless of the level of one's previous education.

This experience of community and its importance to learning are mirrored in the way we, as a teaching team, developed our own community. Just as the students' shared engagement with the work of reading promoted their shared "becoming" and sense of safety and confidence, so too the weekly planning sessions increased the capacity of the teaching team to "become" more than isolated content specialists. The importance of these regular team meetings to the development of the project and to our understanding of what was possible in the classroom cannot be overstated. The process of team reflection was time-consuming and not without its challenges, notwithstanding the common foundations in critical theory, as previously noted. Meeting together on a weekly basis was crucial in building shared pedagogical practice, clarifying our learning and teaching aims and developing a deeper understanding of each team member's assessment of the tutorials and of student learning. Our common foundations in critical theory assisted us to collaborate broadly, integrate the ALL work and engage in "grappling" with ideas and alternate readings so productively in the tutorials. Our experience aligns with that of Hirst *et al.* (2004, 68) who outline the way in which, in their own collaborative project, their learning "was paralleling the types of academic practices" they were trying to develop in their students. They highlight the importance of human relations within the community, the significance of this in the learning process and assert that one of the major benefits of their workshops was that students reported developing relationships with other students and staff in the learning community.

Broadening engagement

It is important to note that there were variations in the extent to which students participated in the process of "becoming". Whilst students were initially streamed into the team-taught tutorials, timetabling and other considerations meant that a cross-section of students was represented. This included a number of students who appeared to be enrolled in the "outreach" tutorial in order to limit their time on campus (other tutorials ran later in the day).

With this in mind, we sought to construct learning activities that would provide opportunities for all students to further their participation in disciplinary discourse and extend their ALL skills regardless of their existing skill base (Vygotsky 1979, Northedge 2003). Bloom's revised taxonomy (Anderson and Krathwohl 2001) contributed to this approach. The close focus on reading, which included investigations of *how* as well as *what* writers are saying, sought to encourage the less-experienced students to apply and analyse the theoretical content in their essay writing and tutorial discussion, while still leaving space for the stronger students to engage with evaluating and creating rich arguments in their work. However, some students, who the social work lecturer had observed performing at this higher level in previous classes, were disengaged. The emphasis on the readings was frustrating for some who were confident in their ability to express themselves academically and wished to spend more tutorial time in less directed, wider-ranging class discussions. Their engagement in class activities was limited. However, we were surprised by a number of high-performing students who took up this opportunity to engage with the ALL work in class, who provided assistance to their fellow students and who, as we explain in more detail below, sought the advice of the ALL specialists in order to extend their abilities.

> More discussion on lectures, spend too much time on the readings.

How we might address the resistance expressed by some students, perhaps through revised learning activities or a tighter targeting of enrolments into the outreach tutorials, is one of the questions we will continue to explore in future semesters.

Individual sessions

Initially, we felt students might be less likely to access the individual assistance that is offered to students undertaking social work subjects, since ALL issues were being addressed in class. However, rather than rejecting individual advisory sessions, we found students in the shared tutorial came to value the opportunity to meet individually with one of the ALL specialists. Students from the supported tutorials were by far the largest cohort of any students across the university that the ALL lecturers met with for one-to-one assistance. They knew us, and for them it was a logical extension of the work in the classroom. Our impression is that these sessions made a vital contribution to the development of the learning community. They provided opportunities for students to directly deal with ALL issues intensively in a comfortable environment. These sessions allowed the students' strengths and weaknesses to become "visible" in ways that are not possible within the classroom setting because of the greater sense of safety afforded in individual sessions. Crossing the threshold to seeking this assistance—and overcoming whatever obstacles or reservations had previously discouraged them from doing so—formed part of a mutually-enhancing combination of interactions. It appears that the familiarity and comfort experienced in the classroom settings enabled the uptake of those opportunities, which, in turn, reinforced the strengths of the in-class interactions. The extent to which students took up these opportunities, in contrast to their previously low rates of participation, marks the success of the "outreach" objectives of the project.

Students who demonstrated the greatest improvements in their work were those who took advantage of both the tutorial activities and the individual advisory sessions. The extent to which these sessions, as compared with the class activities, contributed to the improvement in the students' academic literacies is uncertain, as of course are factors such as ambition and individual resources. It should be noted that not all students who sought individual sessions or contacted the ALL specialists could be considered to be "struggling" with the work. We can speculate as to why these students approached us, however it remains clear to us that, whatever their motivation, these are students the ALL specialists would not have seen if we had remained outside of the classroom as centrally located learning-support advisors. This surprising shift in seeing more capable social work students access ALL services has been an interesting outcome of this project. Providing outreach support amplified the effect of that support and made it okay for a broad group of students to discuss difficulties and seek assistance.

Time

The second noteworthy external influence concerned the time available for preparation for the classes. Time has been a challenge on several levels. This project has demanded a considerable amount of time from the participating staff, particularly when the time taken up in planning meetings and related communications, and attending lectures, tutorials and individual sessions is taken into account. It takes time to build strong collaborative teams, even where the team share comparable theoretical and pedagogical foundations. For the content staff member it was a matter of dedication to this approach, because this preparation time was not accounted for in workloads. For the ALL specialists a greater time commitment is required to attend lectures, be familiar with the course architecture and be deeply familiar with the course readings. This sort of time commitment on staff members raises issues of sustainability and highlights the need for institutional support

The ability to invest the necessary time is also a key issue for students. Our student questionnaires asked specific questions about reading behaviours; where students did their reading and how much time they spent reading for the unit. The evidence is that many students do not have reading behaviours that are conducive to effective engagement with texts. Several students indicated they were doing their reading on public transport, often not in a sustained way. Many students were doing less than two hours of reading each week and some as low as 20 minutes. A couple of students simply responded that they were not devoting enough time to reading, although another indicated that she was doing way too much! The majority of students indicated they were leaving their reading preparation until a couple of days before the class.

Students are often time-poor and carry numerous roles and responsibilities. As noted in Crisp and Fox (2012) and Cree *et al.* (2009), the typical higher education student is no longer the "traditional student" who is free of conflicting responsibilities and able to consistently prioritise their studies. On the contrary, as others have noted (Abbott-Chapman and Edward 1999; Clegg *et al.* 2006; Crossan *et al.* 2003), the experience of the mature-age and other "non-traditional" student is now very much the norm. This is certainly the case for many of the students who study social work at Victoria University and even more so for those participating in the "outreach" tutorials. Most of them are engaged in significant amounts of paid and unpaid work, including familial responsibilities, in addition to full-time university studies. This played out in their preparation and their attendance. One student explained this poignantly in answer to the question, "what, if any, change have you experienced in yourself as a reader during the semester?"

> Change, really not much, I am still human, struggling with my life, trying to get through my assessments.

Crisp and Fox (2012), having surveyed recent literature regarding the challenges of the transition into higher education, suggest that the impact of "external" demands may push students towards a far more instrumental approach to learning, such that they will be less likely to come to the university and take up services that are not seen as essential elements of their course, such as accessing support and central ALL services. They point to suggestions in the literature that, contrary to the views originally expressed by Tinto (1975, 1987) and since developed in terms of "belonging" or "mattering" (Pittman and Richmond 2008; Rayle and Chung 2007; Read *et al.* 2003; and Yorke 2004), these "external" commitments may now work to dramatically decrease students' opportunities to develop and draw on peer support. As far back as 1999, Abbott-Chapman and Edwards (6) noted that:

> The pursuit of university study is becoming more and more solitary, and less a group activity of a "community of learners"... More students are becoming "disengaged" as pressures of employment, financial problems, family and community commitments take their toll... and so becoming a student becomes more and more "a job of work".

Our impression is that this situation has only escalated since that time. In this context, the standard points of engagement, such as tutorials, assume a greater significance. This "outreach" project is, in part, a response to these pressures. Its success may reflect the increasing importance of these points of engagement, and that they are assuming a greater role in promoting a sense of "belonging" and "mattering" than previously, and, with that, make a comparable contribution to both retention and effective learning.

The project's success, however, needs to work against this increasingly instrumentalist approach to studies. There is reason to believe that the students' reading practices may reflect their endeavours to manage their competing responsibilities and limited time by restricting their engagement with study to those activities that are seen to be directly contributing to their assessment. Whilst this does not rule out questions of whether students prioritise and manage their time appropriately, it does pose difficulties in promoting the allocation of sufficient time to prepare for class and benefit from the learning opportunities that are not obviously or immediately subject to assessment. Future cycles of the project will need to consider the influence of these various factors and what the appropriate responses to them might be.

Conclusion

This project has highlighted for us the value of undertaking an embedded approach to ALL at university, and demonstrated some of the benefits to be enjoyed by participating in the "outreach" tutorials. The students clearly valued the explicit and relevant teaching of ALL skills and the manner in which the normalisation of the challenges of learning promoted a sense of community and shared "becoming". For the teaching staff, the project had many rewards. For the ALL specialists it provided a welcome opportunity to both teach and to learn from each other and our students. Too often the role of ALL is removed from the substance of academic learning and reduced to that of external support. Students are sent to have their problems fixed. We are consulted at crisis points: when assignments are due (or overdue); when difficulties are overwhelming; or when tutors suggest the problem lies with students' grammar, and they are sent to workshops for the essay to be "repaired". Being able to journey with students both in the classroom and by providing one-on-one assistance throughout semester was highly rewarding, not only because of the relationships formed, but because this provided us with greater professional insight and greater opportunity to challenge students to push forward in their studies. Students benefitted from seeing us also struggle at times with material that was less familiar and often outside of our discipline knowledge. For the discipline lecturer the project made a necessary and promising contribution to the teaching of critical social work to a diverse range of students. The successful progression of students in such studies is dependent upon their ability to "grapple", in increasingly challenging ways, with complex theory and complex scenarios, much of which involves substantial amounts of discipline-specific reading. With few students previously accessing external ALL support, sharing the teaching space enabled a more pro-active approach to developing academic literacies, and a greater engagement with those skills by students. Moreover, the location of the ALL specialists in the teaching spaces in units undertaken early in the course supported the often challenging transition into the new disciplinary discourse and practice. Students who, in the lecturer's experience, were most likely to have failed the unit and possibly left the course, demonstrated remarkable progress and an enthusiastic adoption of the key learnings (both in content and academic literacies). Our experience has been of a truly collaborative venture, one that has foregrounded the significance of reading, normalised difficulties, and along the way destigmatised support and promoted a supportive learning community that helped some of our most vulnerable students establish the foundations needed for successful university study.

Nevertheless, there remains a series of tensions within the project. At one level, these are reflected in the time in class given to skill-building and that devoted to the content, and to the delivery of activities that are engaging at different levels of learning and for different cultural backgrounds. At a broader level this involves the time and resources a course, teaching staff and students can devote to building and sustaining a learning community. We believe, in a perfect world, the embedding of academic literacies would be seamless with content, that students of different abilities and experiences would equally benefit from sharing their varied perspectives and that the promotion and maintenance of such a community of learners could be undertaken on a sustainable basis. We strive towards that perfect world! Our project suggests that the development of essential academic literacies, and the building of student confidence and commitment in the process, benefits greatly from making the labour of reading explicit. That labour takes time. Our experience indicates that securing the time necessary for those labours may prove the most challenging task.

Reference List

Abbott-Chapman, Joan, and Janet Edwards. 1999. "Student Services in the Modern University: Responding to Changing Student Needs." *Journal of the Australian and New Zealand Student Services Association* 13: 1–21.

AALL. Association for Academic Language and Learning. 2010. *Association for Academic Language and Learning position statement.* Canberra, ACT.

Anderson, Lorin. W., and David R. Krathwohl (eds.). 2001. *A Taxonomy for Learning, Teaching and Assessing: A Revision of Bloom's Taxonomy of Educational Objectives: Complete Edition.* New York: Longman.

Benesch, Sarah. 2001. *Critical English for Academic Purposes: Theory, Politics and Practice,* Mahwah, New Jersey: Lawrence Erlbaum Associates Inc.

Clegg, Sue, Sally Bradley, and Karen Smith, 2006. "'I've Had to Swallow My Pride': Help Seeking and Self-Esteem." *Higher Education Research & Development* 25 (2): 101-113.doi: 10.1080/072943606 00610354

Cree, Vivienne, Jenny Hounsell, Hazel Christie, Velda McCune, and Lyn Tett. 2009. "From Further Education to Higher Education: Social work Students' Experiences of Transition to an Ancient, Research-Led University." *Social Work Education* 28 (8): 887–901. doi: 10.1080 /02615470902736741

Crisp, Beth, and John Fox. 2012. "Making New Students Feel that They Matter: Promoting Social Inclusion within the University Community", in *Practising Social Inclusion*, edited by Beth Crisp, (ed). Oxford: Routledge,

Crossan, Beth, John Field, Jim Gallacher, and Barbara Merril. 2003. "Understanding Participation in Learning for Non-Traditional Adult Learners: Learning Careers and the Construction of Learning Identities". *British Journal of Sociology of Education* 24 (1): 55–67. doi: 10.1080/0142569032000043605

Duff, Patricia. A. 2007. "Problematising academic discourse socialisation". In Learning Discourses and the Discourses of Learning, edited by Marriott, Helen; Moore, Tim; Spence-Brown, Robyn. Melbourne: Monash University ePress 1.1–1.18. doi: 10.2104/ld07000

Foucault, Michel. 2002. The Archaeology of Knowledge. Translated by A. M. Sheridan Smith. London: Routledge.

Grace, Marty, Angela Daddow, Ronnie Egan, John Fox, Carolyn Noble, Pauline O'Maley, Corinna Ridley, and Doris Testa. 2011. "Blurring the boundaries: A collaborative approach to language and learning support for Social Work students", Multiculturalism Perspectives from Australia, Canada and China Conference, 21-22 November 2011, University of Sydney, Australia,74-80.

Grace, Marty, Rob Townsend, Doris Testa, John Fox, Pauline O'Maley, Juanita Custance and Angela Daddow. 2013. "Student Diversity as Grass Roots Internationalisation in Social Work Education". Advances in Social Work & Welfare Education 15 (1): 120–34.

Gonzalez, Norma, Luis C Moll and Cathy Amanti, 2005. Funds of Knowledge: Theorizing Practices in Households, Communities and Classrooms. New Jersey: Lawrence Erlbaum Associates Inc.

Grabe, William and Fredricka L. Stoller. 2002. Teaching and Researching Reading, Essex, England: Pearson Education Ltd.

Hager, Paul. 2008. "Learning and Metaphors." Medical Teacher 30 (7): 679-686.doi: 10.1080/01421590802148899.

Hager, Paul, and Phil Hodkinson. 2009. "Moving Beyond the Metaphor of Transfer of Learning." British Educational Research Journal 35 (4):619-638. doi:10.1080/01411920802642371.

Hager, Paul, and Phil Hodkinson. 2011. "Becoming As an Appropriate Metaphor for Understanding Professional Learning." In Becoming' a Professional: an interdisciplinary analysis of professional learning, edited by Leslie Scanlon, Dordrecht Heidel Springer. doi: 10.1007/978-94-007-1378-9_2.

Hirst, Elizabeth, Robyn Henderson, Margaret Allan, June Bode, and & Mehtap Kocatepe. 2004. "Repositioning Academic Literacy: Charting the Emergence of a Community of Practice." Australian Journal of Language and Literacy 27(1): 66–80.

Kemmis, Stephen, and Robin McTaggart. 1988. The Action Research Reader (3rd ed.). Geelong, Australia: Deakin University Press.

Latham, Theresa. 2010 "Embedding Literacy" In Teaching Adult Literacy: Principles and Practice, edited by Nora Hughes and Irene Schwab, 344–65. Berkshire, UK: Open University Press.

Lea, Mary, and Brian Street, 1998. "Student Writing in Higher Education: An Academic Literacies Approach." *Studies in Higher Education* 23: 157–172.

Lea, Mary, and Brian Street. 1999. "Writing as Academic Literacies: Understanding Textual Practices in Higher Education." In *Writing: Texts, Processes and Practices*, edited by Christopher N. Candlin and Ken Hyland, 62-81. London: Longman.

Lea, Mary. 2004. "Academic Literacies: a Pedagogy for Course Design." *Studies in Higher Education* 29 (6): 739–56. doi: 10.1080/03075070 42000287230.

Lea, Mary, and Brian Street. B 2006. "The Academic Literacies Model." *Theory into Practice* 45 (4): 368–77.

Northedge, Andrew 2003. "Rethinking Teaching in the Context of Diversity." *Teaching in Higher Education* 8 (1): 17-32. doi: 10.1080/1356251032000 052302.

Pittman, Laura D., and Adeya Richmond. 2008. "University Belonging, Friendship Quality, and Psychological Adjustment during the Transition to College." *The Journal of Experimental Education* 76 (4): 343–61.

Read, Barbara, Louise Archer, and Carole Leathwood. 2003. "Challenging Cultures? Student Conceptions of "Belonging" and "Isolation" at a Post-1992 University." *Studies in Higher Education* 28 (3): 261–77. doi: 10.1080/03075070310000113397.

Rayle, Andrea D., and Kuo-Yi Chung. 2007. "Revisiting First-year College Students' Mattering: Social Support, Academic Stress, and the Mattering Experience." *Journal of College Student Retention* 9 (1): 21–37.

Roberts, Celia, Mike Baynham, Paul Shrubshall, Jessica Brittan,Bridget Cooper, Nancy Gidley, Violet Windsor, Jan Eldred, Sue Grief, Celine Castillino, and Margaret Walsh. 2005. *Embedded Teaching and Learning of Adult Literacy, Numeracy and ESOL: Seven Case Studies.* London: National Research and Development Centre for Adult Literacy and Numeracy.

Salvatori, Mariolina R. 2000. "Difficulty: The Great Educational Divide." In *Opening Lines: Approaches to the Scholarship of Teaching and Learning*, edited by Pat Hutchings, 81–93: Menlo Park, CA: The Carnegie Foundation for the Advancement of Teaching.

—. 2002. "Reading Matters for Writing." In *Intertexts: Reading Pedagogy in College Writing Classrooms,* edited by Margurite Helmers, 185–206. Hoboken: Routledge.

Tinto, Vincent. 1975. "Dropout from Higher Education: A Theoretical Synthesis of Recent Research." *Review of Educational Research* 45(1): 89–125.

—. 1987. *Leaving College: Rethinking the Causes and Cures of Student Attrition*. Chicago: University of Chicago Press..

van Platzen, Ermein. 2006. "A Body of Reading: Making 'Visible' the Reading Experiences of First-year Medical Students." In *Academic Literacy and the Languages of Change,* edited by Lucia Thesen and Ermein van Pletzen, 104–29. New York: Continuum. Vygotsky, Lev. 1978. Mind in Society: The Development of Higher Psychological Processes. Cambridge, MA: Harvard University Press.

Vygotsky, Lev. 1978. *Mind in Society: The Development of Higher Psychological Processes*. Cambridge, MA: Harvard University Press.

Wenger, Etienne. 1998 *Communities of Practice: Learning, Meaning, and Identity.* Cambridge: Cambridge University Press.

Wingate, Ursula. 2006. "Doing Away With 'Study Skills.'" *Teaching in Higher Education* 11(4): 457–69. doi: 10.1080/13562510625106 00874268

Yorke, Mantz. 2004. "Retention, Persistence and Success in On-campus Higher Education, and their Enhancement in Open and Distance Learning." *Open Learning: The Journal of Open and Distance Learning* 19(1): 19–32.doi: 10.1080/0268051042000177827.

CHAPTER EIGHT

STUDENTS SUPPORTING STUDENT LEARNING (SSSL) AND PRACTICES OF EMPOWERMENT

GILL BEST

Programs that see individuals as broken and in need of repair are less likely to create the conditions for success than those programs that assume students are a valuable resource to themselves, their families, communities and society. (Tierney 1997, 13)

Introduction

Students Supporting Student Learning (SSSL) is an umbrella term devised to capture the essence of a suite of student–peer mentoring programs at Victoria University. SSSL has emerged from over 20 years of experience working with students from diverse backgrounds to support their academic needs (Kirkwood *et al.* 2012). The professional context in which SSSL is situated is the Association of Academic Language and Learning (AALL), an organisation created in 2005 to act as a unified body and voice for those in the profession who teach students to develop their academic language and learning skills (Stevenson and Kokkinn 2007). Chanock's (2011a and 2011b) historical review of the association demonstrates that there has been interest and anxiety in Australia concerning university students and their success since at least World War 2. Initially the first AALL practitioners were "employed to remediate deficiencies in growing cohorts of tertiary students and to mediate the problems of non-traditional students in particular" (A78). In other words, there was a focus on remediation, of "fixing up" students. However, many of these early pioneers in the realm of student learning support "soon reframed their role to provide "initiation, not remediation", as Beasley (1988, 50) put it. They saw themselves as interpreters between the cultures of their students and the cultures of their institutions, and they accumulated knowledge about both of these through "close reading" of student writers and their texts" (Chanock 2011b , A78).

Since these early years, ALL staff have responded to supporting students' academic needs in a variety of ways, "scaffolding" the process of student learning (Gibbons 2002; Woodward-Kron 2007). One-to-one consultations are commonly used as a way to provide learning support to students about their writing and are extremely useful for understanding the reasons why students write the way they do and for providing highly customised feedback (Chanock 2002 and Chanock 2007). Courses on study skills which focus on elements of study such as note-taking and essay structuring are also common but are usually taught separately from the content of the discipline (Chanock 2011). This separation of skills from content is considered problematic as it locates academic skills as a side issue rather than integral to student learning and development. Separated skills courses have been described by Bennett, Dunne and Carre (2000) as the "bolt-on" approach and to be avoided (Wingate 2006; Wingate, Andon and Cogo 2011). The alternative preferred approach is to "embed" academic skills into curriculum in order that the skills become not only integrated and visible but also assessable (Wingate *et al.* 2011; Huijser, Kimmins and Galligan 2008). It is a complex process requiring an active partnership between the ALL practitioner and discipline lecturer (Percy and Skillen 2000).

Embedding skills within the curriculum is an example of how the teaching of academic skills and its philosophical underpinnings have shifted from a predominantly remedial approach to one which is developmental, summarised by Huijser, Kimmins and Galligan (2008) as follows:

> ... the development of academic skills is most effective when it is integrated into course design, as this removes it from the deficit model in which students need to seek additional help to overcome "their deficit". Such a model places the responsibility to overcome this deficit squarely on the student, while this paper argues that developing and improving academic literacy and numeracy skills should be seen as a shared responsibility between teachers and students. Learning advisors can play a crucial role in this, as they are in a unique position to mediate between student needs and appropriate course design, especially when they perform a dual role of both learning advisors and academic developers. (34)

The changes in thinking and approaches to the teaching of academic skills have interesting parallels in the changes which have occurred in thinking about student departure from university. Zepke, Leach and Prebble (2006) have referred to two discourses within this literature. The first, sometimes referred to as the social integrationist or assimilationist view, rests on the premise that, in order to be successful, students need to adapt emotionally and intellectually to fit the university's culture. To do this it is deemed necessary for students to separate themselves from friends and family in order to give them a greater chance to assimilate into the culture of the university (Tinto 1988). It is a one-way process in which the student adapts and the university remains static. In contrast, Tierney (1992 and 2000) has argued that universities should be the adapters, adapting to their students in ways which not only acknowledge the range of students' identities present on campus but in ways which ensure they are "affirmed, honoured and incorporated into the organisation's culture" (Tierney 2000, 219). The work done by ALL practitioners to embed academic skills into curriculum is a clear and excellent example of the sort of institutional change called for by Tierney where the focus is on improving the deficits of the unit's design rather than the deficits of the students studying it. But does "embedding" affirm, honour and incorporate students' identities into the university's culture as Tierney also argues it should? Furthermore, as ALL units become increasingly stretched and under-staffed, leaving a widening gap between what needs to be done to support students and what can be done, what else can ALL practitioners do with finite resources to meet the challenges of providing learning support to their diverse student populations? And how can this be achieved in ways which utilise something other than remedial modes of support?

Van der Meer and Scott (2008) have suggested a very specific response to this challenge, arguing that AALL units should shift from a focus on teacher instruction to a focus on what they describe as "peer-learning primacy" (van der Meer and Scott 2008, 72). While they acknowledge that embedding skills into curriculum is a worthy approach, they point out that it "depends to a large extent on the willingness of teaching staff. Also, with changes in teaching staff, successful intervention are (sic) not necessarily future-proof" (73). The authors argue for a shift in usage of staff time in order "to privilege supporting peer-learning activities" (75) so that there is "an intentional lessening of other learning-support activities" (74). They argue for this refocusing on both resource and educational grounds, stating that implementing peer-learning programs will extend the type of support available and is also educationally valid because of the evidence that peer learning works. Indeed, student–peer learning or peer support is a strategy that has been shown to have an impact on student success (Kuh *et al.* 2010; Krause, McInnis and Welle 2003; Falchikof and Blythman 2001; Johnson and Johnson 1999; Topping, 1996). It has its theoretical and pedagogical roots in social constructivism, its central tenet being that the social nature of learning is the key to success. Student–peer learning leverages Vygotsky's (1978) concept of the "zone of proximal development", that is, the difference between what a person can achieve on their own and their potential when helped by a peer (Vygotsky 1978).

At Victoria University, student–peer learning programs have been offered as a form of learning support since 1998. In 2010 this work was formalised through the creation of Students Supporting Student Learning (SSSL). SSSL is conceptualised as the next step at Victoria University in the development of learning-support strategies and systems implemented to assist a large, diverse student population. In a document which proposed the creation of SSSL, McCormack, Best and Kirkwood (2009) stated:

> The proposal argues for introducing a new and powerful agent into the systems for enhancing student learning at VU—student communities of learning driven by Students Supporting Students' Learning programs. Instead of sheeting home responsibility for enhancing learning to over-worked academic staff, marginalised learning advisors, or students as individuals, this proposal focuses on enhancing student learning by enhancing and encouraging learning interactions among students themselves. (3)

But the existence of SSSL programs goes further than merely offering another form of learning support. SSSL programs intentionally place students and their knowledge and understandings of university and the units they study at the front and centre of the learning process. In SSSL programs, students are the knowledge-holders and knowledge-sharers, meaning there is the capacity to open new ways of knowing, where students can be utilised "not as individuals but as a community... it is the talents, skills, experience, generosity, enthusiasm and energy of students themselves that are the most powerful yet under-utilised resource at our disposal in enhancing student learning" (McCormack, Best and Kirkwood 2009, 3).

SSSL programs are, therefore, a very different form of learning support, through which Tierney's (2000) call to honour, celebrate and utilise our students' identities is being actioned. SSSL programs intentionally and actively unlock students' potential for learning by bringing students together to learn with and from each other. The students are regarded as knowledge-holders and the programs are a springboard for knowledge sharing and co-construction, both in relation to the content and skills of units the students are studying or have studied, and in relation to the university's broader systems and processes. The students within the programs have a dual purpose: to impact on student knowledge and understanding and to impact on students' sense of belonging. The former is the initial focus and the latter a highly significant by-product, for it is known that when students feel friendless and disconnected they are more likely to leave university (Hausmann, Schofield and Woods 2007; Hurtado and Carter 1997). In other words, SSSL programs are implemented not only to have an impact on students' academic success but to foster a greater student connection and engagement with the university in general. The development of SSSL programs has been another step in the journey from remedial to developmental modes of learning-support provision at Victoria University. SSSL programs are based on and continue to develop under the influence of Tierney's work, focusing on the collaborative strengths of Victoria University students rather than on students' real or imagined individual academic weaknesses.

The Student Mentors

Students who wish to become student mentors (some roles lead to some students having slightly different titles such as student writing-mentors or student rovers) are generally high-achieving students who apply for a position through a competitive written application and interview process. Their mission is to assist students with their learning and to impact positively upon students' academic, social and emotional wellbeing. To do this effectively and authentically, emphasis is placed on student mentors pushing to the forefront of their interactions with other students the fact that they are students, just like the students they are helping. In communications with student mentors, this is described as "studentness" (Tout, Pancini and McCormack 2013), for it is in their "studentness" where the significance and the power of their interactions lie.

All student mentors in SSSL programs are paid as an acknowledgement of the important contributions their peers make to students' learning and success (Tout, Pancini and McCormack 2013). However, the act of placing students on the university payroll can complicate the ways their roles are perceived and lead to the assumption that the students are merely an extension of the existing institutional workforce, "first-tier service workers accountable to the logic of productivity in the university as a workplace" (Tout, Pancini and McCormack 2013, 5). This assumption is potentially intensified at Victoria University because of the university's strong focus on employing students on campus. Known as "students as staff", this initiative was launched in 2010 (Mitchell and Kaye 2012) as a way to provide on-campus employment to students and in turn to impact positively on students' progress and completion (Pascarella and Terenzini 2005). However, the focus within SSSL programs is not on students "learning to work" but rather on students "learning to learn" and "learning to help others learn". The outcome of a student being employed by the university as a student mentor in the SSSL context has been succinctly described by McCormack, Pancini and Tout (2010) as "learningful work" (41).

The student mentors within SSSL programs are therefore first and foremost employed to be students. Their learning is assisted and developed through interactions, formal and informal, with other student mentors and SSSL lecturers. SSSL staff expertise is utilised to respond flexibly to the student mentors' learning needs in different disciplinary and university contexts. They design, develop and evaluate individual SSSL programs and select, train, teach and support the student mentors. SSSL lecturers teach the student mentors in three main face to face contexts: 1) Student-mentor training sessions; 2) student-mentor development workshops; and 3) through student-mentor observations and feedback. Training is compulsory and occurs across up to three days depending on the type of program. Training reflects the active collaborative nature of SSSL programs and provides students with a theoretical foundation for the roles they are to embark on (Jacobs, Hurley and Unite 2008). Throughout the duration of each program, student mentors participate in weekly half-hour student-mentor development workshops. These are designed to meet the immediate needs of the particular group of student mentors at any one point in time. Content of the workshops is determined based on need as perceived by SSSL staff and also at the request of the student mentors themselves. Student mentors also sometimes facilitate the sessions. Student mentors are observed formally at least twice during a program. Observations vary in length but are usually for 15 minutes. Observations focus on areas of development specified by the student mentors. Notes are taken as a tool to aid later discussion and feedback. Student mentors meet either individually or in pairs (depending on the program type) with the SSSL staff member who observed the session. A discussion is held, focusing on areas of strength and areas the student mentor finds more challenging. SSSL teaching and student-mentor development is not confined to face-to-face support. Student mentors and SSSL staff also communicate via an online platform, posting reflections on their experiences, asking questions, sharing ideas and giving support and encouragement to each other. In addition, student-mentor progress interviews are conducted. These are opportunities for student mentors to reflect on their progress, to raise any issues of concern and to set goals for the future. In addition to the work of the SSSL staff, university counsellors play an important role assisting with the more demanding students that student mentors work with, guiding and advising the student mentors about the psychological and social boundaries associated with their roles.

The SSSL Programs

At Victoria University, the implementation of student–peer learning programs has been an evolving process through which we have learned and continue to learn about what works for Victoria University's students and the Victoria University organisational context. SSSL programs directly target three key regions of engagement necessary for new students to succeed: academic engagement with the unit and its disciplinary content; social engagement with staff and other students; and a wider institutional engagement with the systems, processes and procedures of the university at large. SSSL programs can sit alongside other learning-support approaches as one of a suite of strategies or they can be the main form of learning support provided for a particular area. SSSL programs currently take four main forms, described below. They have been designed and developed according to the specific student cohort needs and the pragmatics of the day-to-day teaching and learning contexts. The program models have evolved from collaborations with a wide number of staff and students in a wide variety of disciplines and contexts across Victoria University since 1998. Care is taken to implement the appropriate peer-learning model that will best suit the specific learning context and student needs. Programs are designed to focus heavily on the collaborative strengths of students working and learning together. For this reason, all SSSL programs are group- and/or team-based. The programs are deliberately designed to create strong and effective teams involving student mentors, student mentees, SSSL staff, unit and course coordinators, librarians and counselling staff. All SSSL programs are evaluated for academic and social impacts.

SSSL programs connected to units of study

There are currently three SSSL program models connected to units of study. In each model those students who have achieved the highest grades in the unit are invited to apply to become a student mentor. Students are selected through a competitive written application and group and individual interview process. All SSSL programs connected to units of study are implemented in full collaboration with the relevant unit lecturer/coordinator. The programs are referred to as Peer Assisted Study Sessions (PASS), Peer Assisted Tutorials (PATs) and Trident.

PASS is the Australian term for an academic-support program utilised internationally and initiated in the US in the 1970s as Supplemental Instruction (SI). PASS sessions are group-based, weekly review sessions facilitated by two student mentors which students attend voluntarily. The focus of each session is determined by the student mentors who have recent experiences of studying the unit and who therefore have insights into what students struggle with from a student rather than staff perspective. PASS avoids a remedial label by targeting units rather than students. Usually, the unit will have one or more of the following indicators of need: high failure rates, low levels of student retention, high student dissatisfaction (Martin and Arendale 1992). Student mentors assigned to PASS design collaborative learning activities each week. These activities aim to review content taught in lectures and tutorials to help students clarify their understandings of key concepts or topics.

The second model of peer learning connected to units of study is known as Peer Assisted Tutorials or PATs. A PAT program is best placed where it is unlikely that the students will attend an additional voluntary program such as PASS (described above). PATs at Victoria University have their origins in a model of peer learning observed by the author at the University of Texas El Paso in the US known as the Peer Leader program. It has been adapted significantly to suit the Australian and Victoria University context. In this model of student–peer learning, student mentors who have studied a unit, for example Chemistry 1, are situated within the usual Chemistry 1 tutorials throughout the semester. This means that unlike PASS, which is a student-only zone, in PATs the student mentor is an additional presence alongside the tutor. Students who have previously studied and excelled in the unit attend the same tutorial on a weekly basis to support students with their academic work and their academic skills. Student mentors function as "model students" of the discipline rather than authority figures and help students deepen their understanding and engagement with the tutorial topics. They act as a bridge between the students and the tutor helping students to feel more confident about asking questions to enable them to understand key concepts or topics. Within a tutorial, a student mentor might help to facilitate group discussion, share experiences of assignment writing, and demonstrate how they approached a particular topic or problem. Exactly what each student mentor will do each session will vary depending on the topics being taught and how the tutorial is designed. Student mentors suggest ideas to the tutor for how they can be of assistance in the PAT and help to create a positive group-learning environment where students feel comfortable to ask questions.

Where feasible and appropriate, student mentors group students together to learn with each other.

SSSL's third model of student–peer learning connected to units of study is known as Trident. Trident is a large-scale student–peer learning program that was created specifically for a first-year engineering core unit but which can be transferred to other units if appropriate. Trident consists of three peer-learning models PASS, and PATs (each described above) and Study Space. Study Space is a dedicated room where students can "drop in" to seek assistance from student mentors. Attendance at Study Space is voluntary. Trident's power to support student learning lies in the links between each of the three peer-learning models available to the students studying the unit. Specifically, when students attend their usual tutorials they are assisted not only by the tutor but also by the student mentor. Student mentors play a key role within the tutorials, not only in assisting students, but in suggesting that students seek more assistance from themselves from the other voluntary elements of the program, i.e. PASS and Study Space.

In addition to SSSL programs which are directly connected to specific units of study are those programs which are "centrally delivered". These are programs that are available to any student who chooses to make use of them rather than being only for the students in particular units. The two centrally delivered programs are the Student Rover and Student Writing Mentor programs. The Student Rover program was established in 2007 to foster and facilitate social and educational engagement within the new Learning Commons areas in Victoria University´s libraries.

> [The Learning Commons] is a learning space that is open—in terms of reflecting the need of students to learn when they have time—often outside the usual university opening time and also reflecting students preference for flexible spaces that can be moulded and modified to suit their preferred learning styles… The Learning Commons is an approach to supporting our students' learning that recognises that we need to take into account the entire learning experience of the learner while at university, not just their time in the classroom. (Gallagher *et al.* 2009, 99)

It was also anticipated that engaging high-achieving students in the public sphere of the Learning Commons would send a positive message concerning the strengths of Victoria University students to the wider student community (Keating and Gabb 2005). Approximately 35 students are currently employed to provide assistance to the students in the Learning Commons at four campuses. Student rovers are not merely another layer of worker within the library but rather they are students offering student knowledge to other students in a student way, based on their own student experiences and learning (Tout, Pancini and McCormack 2013). Student rovers assist students with basic enquiries relating to the use or location of university facilities and resources; they model successful learning behaviours and strategies and refer students to relevant IT, library or learning-support services within and outside the libraries. The student rover selection process reflects Tierney's (2000) call to honour students' identities:

> Students are also selected so that their gender, linguistic and sociocultural backgrounds and study discipline area are roughly representative of the student cohort attending that particular Learning Commons. (McCormack and Dixon 1997, 2)

The second centrally delivered program is the Student Writing Mentor program which was implemented for the first time in 2011. The Student Writing Mentor program has its origins in the long-standing tradition in US universities of providing Writing Centres which are staffed by students trained to be peer writing tutors (Topping 1996). Hughes, Gillespie and Kail (2010) found that students who had been "peer writing tutors" gained "a new relationship with writing; analytical power; a listening presence; skills, values and abilities vital in their professions; skills, values and abilities vital in families and in relationships; earned confidence in themselves; and a deeper understanding of and commitment to collaborative learning" (Hughes *et al*. 2010, 14). At Victoria University the emphasis, as with the other SSSL programs, is on student writing-mentors being expert students rather than expert writing tutors. The student writing-mentors are students who like writing and who have learned about the challenges and joys of academic writing during the course of their studies and who wish to take on a role to assist other students with their writing development. The student writing-mentors work in the Writing Spaces, which are spaces based at two campus libraries. Assistance is provided on a "drop-in" basis each week across each semester. Student writing-mentors assist students with their academic writing by talking with students about their written assignment drafts, making constructive comments and offering strategies for improvement. The work of the student writing-mentors is based upon the tenets of other SSSL programs whereby student mentors work as facilitators to improve student learning in a student-centred way.

In addition to the above SSSL programs is the Senior Mentor program, which was introduced in 2008 (and extended to include a senior rover in 2012). Senior mentors are a key part of the SSSL staff team and bring a vital, energetic student perspective and energy to the work of SSSL. These senior student mentoring positions are available for students who have previously been student mentors in an SSSL program and who are looking for ways to become more involved in SSSL. Students apply for the positions through a competitive written application and interview process. Senior mentors work for 10 hours a week during semester. Outside semesters and exam periods, these hours are increased to 20 hours per week. There are currently three senior mentors and one senior rover in any one year. Senior mentors bring a vital student perspective to SSSL programs. They gain an overview of student–peer learning programs at Victoria University which in turn helps them to take an active part in the planning, design and evaluation of individual SSSL programs and in the recruitment and interviewing of student mentors. Senior mentors also play a highly significant role in acting as a bridge between SSSL staff and student mentors. They share their experiences and insights of their own student-mentoring experiences and offer advice and guidance. As with the other SSSL programs the senior mentors are engaged in "meaningful work" (McCormack, Pancini and Tout 2010), gaining insights into the inner workings of the large organisation in which they study.

Conclusion

SSSL programs mobilise students in the core business of the university, student learning, and in turn impact on student belonging and success. The programs are uniquely placed, not only to extend the reach and type of student learning support available, but to do so in ways which acknowledge and utilise students' diverse social, economic and linguistic backgrounds. By placing students at the centre of the process of student learning across the university, students are empowered to regard themselves as actors rather than passive recipients in their learning. For those of us fortunate enough to work closely with the students in student-mentor roles, the energy, commitment and enthusiasm they show are palpable. One hopes this is a direct result of their identities being utilised, affirmed, honoured and celebrated.

Reference List

Beasley, Vic. 1988. "Developing Academic Literacy: The Flinders Experience." In *Literacy by Degrees*, edited by Vic Beasley, Gordon Taylor, Brigid Ballard, Hanne Bock, John Clanchy and Peggy Nightingale. Milton Keynes: SRHE & Open University Press.

Bennett, Neville, Dunne, Elisabeth & Carre Clive, B. 2000. "Skills Development in Higher Education and Employment". *The Society for Research into Higher Education.*

Chanock, Kate. 2011a. "A Historical Literature Review of Australian Publications in the Field of Academic Language and Learning in the 1980s: Themes, Schemes, and Schisms: Part One." *Journal of Academic Language & Learning* 5 (1): A36–A58.

—. 2011b. "A Historical Literature Review of Australian Publications in the Field of Academic Language and Learning in the 1980s: Themes, Schemes, and Schisms: Part Two." *Journal of Academic Language & Learning* 5 (1): A59–A87.

—. 2002. Problems and Possibilities in Evaluating One-to-one Language and Academic Skills Teaching. In *Academic skills advising: Evaluation for Program. Improvement and Accountability,* edited by J. Webb & P. McLean, 199–221. Melbourne: Victorian Language and Learning Network.

—. 2007. "Valuing Individual Consultations as Input into Other Modes of Teaching." *Journal of Academic Language & Learning* 1(1): 2007, A1-A9.

Falchikov, Nancy and Margo Blythman (2001) *Learning Together: Peer Tutoring in Higher Education* Psychology Press.

Gallagher, Adrian, Amanda Pearce, and Robin McCormack. 2013. "Learning in the Learning Commons: The Learning Commons at City Flinders and St Albans Campuses." In *Learning Spaces in Higher Education: Positive Outcomes by Design,* edited by Radcliffe, David, Wilson, Hamilton, Powell, Derek and Tibbetts, Belinda 99-106. St Lucia, Queensland University: University of Queensland.

Gibbons, Pauline. 2002. *Scaffolding Language, Scaffolding Learning: Teaching Second Language Learners in Mainstream Classroom.* Portsmouth, USA: Heinmann.

Hausmann, Leslie, Janet Schofield, and Rochelle Woods. 2007. "Sense of Belonging as a Predictor of Intentions to Persist among African American and White First-year College Students." *Research in Higher Education,* 48 (7): 803–39.

Hughes, Brad, Pauline Gillespie, and Kail Harvey. 2010. "What They Take with Them: Finding from the Peer Writing Tutor Alumni Research Project." *Writing Centre Journal* 30 (2):12–46.

Huijser, Hendrick, Lindy Kimmins, and Linda Galligan. 2008. "Evaluating Individual Teaching on the Road to Embedding Academic Skills." *Journal of Academic Language and Learning* 2 (1): 23–38.

Hurtado, Sylvia., and Deborah, Faye Carter. 1997. "Effects of College Transition and Perceptions of the Campus Racial Climate on Latino College Students' Sense of Belonging." *Sociology of Education* 70: 324–45.

Jacobs, Glen, Maureen Hurley, and Cathy Unite. 2008. "How Learning Theory Creates a Foundation Fo Si Leader Training." *Journal of Peer Learning* 1 (1): 6–12.

Johnson, David W, and Roger Johnson. 1999. *Learning Together and Alone: Cooperative, Competitive and Individualistic Learning.* Boston: Allyn & Bacon.

Kirkwood, Keith, Gillian Best, Rob McCormack, Dan Tout. 2012. "Student Mentors in Physical and Virtual Learning Spaces". In *Physical and Virtual Learning Spaces in Higher Education: Concepts for the Modern Learning Environment*, edited by Mike Keppell, Kay Souter, and Matthew Riddle.

Keating, Shay and Roger Gabb. 2005. *Putting Learning into the Learning Commons: A Literature Review.* Post Compulsory Education Centre, Melbourne, VIC: Victoria University.

Kuh, George, Jillian Kinzie, John Schuh, and Elizabeth Whitt. 2010. *Student Success in College: Creating Conditions That Matter.* San Francisco: Jossey-Bass.

Kuh, George, Jillian Kinzie, Jennifer A. Buckley, Brian K. Bridges, and John C. Hayek. 2006. "What Matters to Student Success: A Review of the Literature." In *Commissioned Report for the National Symposium on Postsecondary Student Success: Spearheading a Dialog on Student Success.* https://www.ue.ucsc.edu/sites/default/files/WhatMattersStudentSucces s%28Kuh,July2006%29.pdf

Krause, Kerri-Lee, Craig McInnis, and Cindy Welle. 2003. *Out-of-class Engagement in Undergraduate Learning Communities: The Role and Nature of Peer Interactions.* Association for the Study of Higher Education Conference, 13-16 November, Portland, Oregon, USA. *Refereed conference publications*

Martin, Deanne and David Arendale. 1992. "Supplemental Instruction: Improving First Year Student Success in High Risk Courses." The Freshman Year Experience: Monograph Series 7. University of South Carolina.

McCormack, Rob, and Julie Dixon. 2007, "Rovers At the Border: The Double Framing of Student Rovers in Learning Commons." Paper presented at the 30th HERDSA Annual Conference: Enhancing Higher Education, Theory and Scholarship, Adelaide, SA, July 8-11.

McCormack, Rob, Geri Pancini, and Dan Tout. 2010. "Learningful Work: Learning to Work and Learning to Learn." *International Journal of Training Research* 8 (1): 40–52.

McCormack, Rob, Gill Best, and Keith Kirkwood. 2009. Students Supporting Student Learning: A Proposal for Supporting Student Learning. Melbourne, VIC: Victoria University.
http://snap.vu.edu.au/sites/default/files/documents/SSSL%20Concept%20Paper%202010%20.pdf

Mitchell, Gaon and Judy Kay. 2012. Leveraging Work Integrated Learning through on-campus Employment – A University-wide Approach. In Proceedings of the Australian Collaborative Education Network (ACEN) National Conference Deakin University, Geelong.

Pascarella, Ernest and Patrick Terenzini (2005) *How College Affects Students: Volume 2*. San Francisco, CA: Jossey-Bass.

Percy Alisa and Jan Skillen. 2000. "A Systematic Approach to Working with Academic Staff: Addressing the Confusions at the Source". In *Sources of Confusion: Proceedings of the 2000 Language and Academic Skills Conference*, edited by Kate Chanock, 224–56. La Trobe University, Melbourne: Melbourne, Vic.

Stevenson, Marie, and Beverley Kokkinn. 2007. "Pinned to the Margins? The Contextual Shaping of Academic Language and Learning Practice." *Journal of Academic Language and Learning* 1 (1): 44–54.

Tierney, William. 1992. "An Anthropological Analysis of Student Participation in College." *Journal of Higher Education* 63 (6): 603–17.

—. *Power, Identity and the Dilemma of College Student Departure* 1997 [1 November 2013]. Available from
http://www.usc.edu/dept/chepa/pdf/ power.pdf.

—. 2000. "Power, Identity, and the Dilemma of College Student Departure." In *Reworking the Student Departure Puzzle*, edited by John M Braxton, 213–34. Nashville, TX: Vanderbilt University Press.

—. 2002 "Parents and Families in Precollege Preparation: The Lack of Connection between Research and Practice." *Educational Policy* 16: 588.

Tinto, Vincent. 1988. "Stages of Student Departure: Reflections on the Longitudinal Character of Student Leaving". *Journal of Higher Education* 59 (4): 438–55.

Topping, Keith. J. 1996. "The Effectiveness of Peer Tutoring in Further and Higher Education: A Typology and Review of the Literature". *Higher Education* 32 (3): 321–345.

Tout, Dan, Geri Pancini, and Rob McCormack R. 2010. "Student Rovers in the Learning Commons: Facilitating Places for Learner

Engagement". Paper presented at ACEN 2010 National Conference. Work Integrated Learning (WIL): Responding to Challenges, Curtin University of Technology, Perth, WA, 29 September –1 October.

—. Pancini, Geri, and Rob McCormack, (2013) "Using Mobile Peer Mentors for Student Engagement: Student Rovers in the Learning Commons". *Higher Education Research & Development.* doi:10.1080/07294360.2013. 841645
http://dx.doi.org/10.1080/07294360.2013.841645

van der Meer, Jacques, and Carole Scott. 2008[a]. "Students' Experiences and Perceptions of Peer Assisted Study Sessions: Towards Ongoing Improvement". *Journal of Peer Learning*, 2 (1): 3–22.

—. Jacques, and Carole Scott. 2008[b]. "Shifting the Balance in First-Year Learning Support: from Staff Instruction to Peer-Learning Primacy." *Australasian Journal of Peer Learning*, 1: 70–79.

Vygotsky, Lev. 1978. *Mind in society: The Development of Higher Psychological Processes.* Cambridge, MA: Harvard University Press.

Wingate, Ursula. 2006. "Doing away with 'Study Skills', *Teaching in Higher Education*, 11(4): 457–469.

—. Nick Andon, and Alessia Cogo. 2011. "Embedding Academic Writing Instruction into Subject Teaching: A case study". A*ctive Learning in Higher Education.* 12 (1): 69–81.

Woodward-Kron, Robyn. 2007. "Negotiating Meanings and Scaffolding Learning: Writing Support for Non-English Speaking Background Students". *Higher Education research and development* 26 (3).

Zepke, Nick, Linda Leach, and Tom Prebble. 2006. "Being Learner Centred: One Way to Improve Student Retention?" *Studies in Higher Education Volume* 31 (5): 587–600.

ABBREVIATIONS

AALL	Association of Academic Language and Learning
ABSTUDY	Aboriginal study allowance
ABS	Australian Bureau of Statistics
ACER	Australian Council for Education Research
ACSF	Australian Core Skills Framework
ALL	Academic Language and Learning
ALTC	Australian Learning and Teaching Council
AM	Acquisition Metaphor
AQF	Australian Qualifications Framework
ARC	Australian Research Council
ATAR	Australian Tertiary Admissions Rank
ABEC	Bachelor Education Early Childhood/Primary
ABED	Bachelor of Education (P-12)
CAE	College of Advanced Education
CALD	Culturally and linguistically diverse
CCLT	Centre for Collaborative Learning and Teaching
CFU	Core Foundation Unit
CHAT	Cultural–Historical Activity Theory
DEEWR	Department for Education
ESL	English Second Language
FYHE	First Year in Higher Education
FYE	First-year Experience
HE	Higher Education
HECS	Higher Education Commonwealth Scheme
HEPPP	Higher Education Participation and Partnership Program
ICT	Information and Communication Technology
ITAS-TT	Indigenous Tutorial Assistance Scheme Tertiary Tuition
LC	Victoria University Learning Commons
LLN	Language, Literacy and Numeracy
LMS	Learning Management System
K&K A	Knowing and Knowledge A
MOOC	Massive Open Online Course
MSLE	Monitoring student learning engagement
NESB	non-English-speaking background
NTEU	National Tertiary Education Union
PASS	Peer-assisted Study review Sessions

PAT	Peer-assisted Tutorials
PELA	Post-Entry Language Assessment
PST	Pre-service Teacher
PM	Participation Metaphor
QUT	Queensland University of Technology
RTS	Return to Study
SES	Socioeconomic Status, as measured by the Australian Bureau of Statistics
SES	Student Experience Survey
SEU	Student Evaluation of Unit
SSSL	Students Supporting Student Learning
TAFE	Technical and Further Education
TEEL	Topic sentence, Explanation, Evidence, Link
T & L	Teaching and Learning
VCE	Victorian High School Certificate
VE	Vocational Education
VET	Vocational Education and Training
WIPCE	World Indigenous People's Conference on Education

CONTRIBUTORS

Dr Gill Best, Senior Lecturer, Coordinator, Students Supporting Student Learning (SSSL), has worked at Victoria University since 1991. She holds a PhD from Victoria University titled "First-year University Students and their Parents: Conjoint Experiences of University". For many years she taught academic skills and language support to hundreds of students via one-hour consultations, taught academic skills workshops and embedded skills into curricula. From 1998 she experimented with student–peer learning, creating a myriad of different programs to suit a wide variety of contexts. In 2010 this work culminated in the creation of Students Supporting Student Learning (SSSL) and a suite of programs which has been tried and tested to work for our students and our organisational context. Gill considers SSSL to be an exciting transformative system of learning support for Victoria University students and a key to unlocking and developing the talents and knowledge of Victoria University's socially, culturally and linguistically diverse student population. It is the students' energy and vitality and their willingness to help other students learn that are the foundations of the success of the programs and which "make her get up in the morning".

Juanita Custance is Lecturer in Academic Support and Development at Victoria University. Her teaching career spans secondary, vocational, and higher education, beginning with community projects in literacy development and inclusion in Australia and USA, which focused on developing skills through engagement in project activities. Juanita brings this experience, that literacies are most meaningfully developed through activity rather than via "top down" instruction, to her academic work, where she has developed and delivered literacies programs in areas as diverse as engineering, multimedia, art and design, sport coaching, exercise science, humanities, hospitality and the social sciences. She holds a Postgraduate Diploma of Teaching (University of Melbourne), a BA in Applied Linguistics and English Language (University of Melbourne) and is currently undertaking research for her Master's degree at the Graduate School of Education, University of Melbourne in using cultural–historical activity theory (CHAT) to investigate embedding English language and literacies development within discipline-specific learning contexts. She has longstanding interests in multicultural communications, globalisation, and equity issues. In 2013 Juanita received the Victoria University Vice-Chancellor's Citation for Excellence in Higher Education Learning and Teaching.

Dr Julie Fletcher is Lecturer in Foundations within the College of Arts at Victoria University. Herself a "non-traditional" student, Julie returned to study as a single parent of three, and completed her studies while raising children and also working as a sessional academic. She holds a BA with majors in social theory, politics and literature (University of Melbourne), BA (Hons) (University of Ballarat), and completed her PhD within the Faculty of Arts and Education at Deakin University. Her PhD thesis, "Witnessing Tibet: Life Narrative as Testimony in the Tibetan Diaspora" examines rights-based political action in the transnational Tibetan refugee community. Julie's research and practice interests in first-year transition and the non-traditional student have their origins in her own experiences, her deep commitment to human rights and social justice, and many years of teaching increasingly diverse first-year students. She has completed research on equity and access: *Way to Go: Strategies to Increase Access to University for Young People from Low Socioeconomic Backgrounds* (2007) with Kim Toffoletti, Lyn McCreddin, and Lynne Alice at Deakin University, and first-year experience and retention: *A Preliminary Investigation into Student Attrition* (1996) with John McDonald at the University of Ballarat.

Dr John Fox holds a doctorate in social theory, a Masters in Social Work (RMIT University), a Masters in Social Policy and Human Services (RMIT University), and Bachelor degrees in law and jurisprudence (UNSW). He has lectured in social work at Victoria University since 2007 and is responsible for teaching units in social welfare, legal context, and social policy. With a keen interest in poverty, John works to promote a better recognition of the significance of the body and material world in social theory, social policy, and social work. His doctorate undertook a genealogical review of Marx's theory of species being, and demonstrated a greater role for dialectical and material approaches to the body and the balance of the material world than previously considered in the scholarly literature. He continues to research ways in which bodily experience can reveal the limitations of, and suggest alternatives to, dominant ideas of humanity and social interaction, with a current research focus on the works of Theodore Adorno and recent post-humanist theory. His teaching in the early units of the social work course looks to realise the unique opportunities available in the transition into higher education to deeply probe and begin to reconstruct, in dialogue with students, different, and more inclusive, ideas about a good and just human life.

Dr Andrew Funston holds a BA (hons) MA and PhD from the University of Melbourne. His doctoral study (2012) investigated the higher education transitions of students at one of Australia's newer universities. Andrew is a course coordinator in the College of Arts at Victoria University. Prior to becoming an academic Andrew worked for the Victorian State Government in arts and youth policy fields. He wrote a report for the government on the training levels of the rock music industry and went on to establish in 1986 with Linda Carroll *The Push*, a statewide non-profit youth organisation which still operates today. For the Communications Law Centre Andrew researched young people's use of mobile phones with Kate MacNeill (1999). For the Foundation for Young Australians Andrew researched disadvantaged young people's access to the internet with Meg Morrison (2000). He also researched ICT use by children from separated families with Katie Hughes (2006). In 2012 he published *Non-traditional Students Making their Way in Higher Education: An Australian Case Study* (Youth Research Centre, University of Melbourne). Andrew has recently contributed a case study on in-depth interviewing for a collection on qualitative research methods for SAGE (forthcoming in 2014).

Dr Miguel Gil holds a BA (Universidad de Navarra), a MA Prelim. (La Trobe University), PDipl Translation (Victoria College), MA (Monash University), and PhD (La Trobe University). Miguel has gathered a wide range of experience in the field of retention, transition and first-year student experience, first as a retention officer at Edith Cowan University (2004–10) and currently as a Transition and Retention Coordinator at Victoria University for the College of Arts and Education. His involvement in this area and his close contact with academics and student services professionals has afforded him a realistic perspective of the challenges and opportunities surrounding the transitioning of students into and out of their studies. Miguel is currently completing research work into the graduate attribute of "global citizenship". He is also working on a book titled *Academic Writing in Context*, addressed to beginning students who want to make sense of academic writing in the wider context of academic culture. In parallel, Miguel has been focusing on intellectual history, largely in connection with the Enlightenment and its impact on the formation of a new type of knowledge regime. He is taking this interest further by looking into a social and comparative characterisation of the role of intellectuals in transitioning societies.

Dr Gwen Gilmore holds a PhD in Education (Exeter, UK), a Master of Education Administration and Diploma of Second Language Teaching (Massey University, NZ), a BA and Diploma of Teaching (Canterbury University, NZ). Gwen is a lecturer in literacy and student retention at Victoria University. She coordinates core units in the first year of the Bachelor of Education P-12 course, a Diploma of Education Studies pathways course and teaches units in the Master of Education. Her doctoral study (2010) was titled "Inclusion and Professionalism: Reducing Fixed-Term Exclusions in a South-West Secondary School. A Cultural–Historical Activity Theory Study of a Disciplinary Inclusion Room" and contributes to her wider research expertise in the field of cultural–historical activity theory (CHAT and AT) in the context of developing improved knowledge of teacher-education settings with reference to literacy learning and student retention. She is building on her knowledge and principles of inclusive education to examine pre-service teacher identity in relation to diversity, to consider how an appreciative inquiry approach offers a more specific lens to develop the principles of social justice and how integrating a cohesive academic literacy into core units can positively engage staff and students in university settings.

Dr Michael Hallpike has taught in the Liberal Arts program at Victoria University since 2005. He has also lectured courses in the history of modern political thought and in political philosophy at La Trobe and Melbourne universities. His PhD (La Trobe University) is an inquiry into the institution of the university, combining social and political theory with historical sociology. His current research concerns relationships between imperial formations and systems of knowledge. Dr Hallpike has played a leading role in cross-faculty collaborative curriculum design in a number of areas at Victoria University. He was co-designer of an award-winning legal writing course; he participated in the cross-faculty development of a discipline-linked unit (Writing Sociology) in Community Services; he was a co-designer of a highly successful new diploma (the Diploma of Education Studies); he has convened two communities of practice (COP) at Victoria University (the Language & Learning COP and the Legal Discourse COP); and he was Statewide teacher representative on the Steering Committee for the most recent reaccreditation of the Liberal Arts course.

Dr Pauline O'Maley is an educational developer in the Department of Academic Support and Development at Victoria University. She works with staff and students in the College of Arts; her particular interest is in exploring ways to make discipline-specific academic literacies explicit. She enjoys working with lecturers to explore enabling and sustainable ways to build learning communities. Pauline has a PhD from Queensland University of Technology; her doctoral research focused on approaches to diagnostic assessment of adult literacy students. Pauline has an abiding interest in second-chance education and positive transitions.

INDEX

critical literacies, 21
    in the social sciences, 180–85
critical pedagogy, 220
critical social work, 222
criticality, 25
Crosling, Glenda, 193
Crossan, Beth, 238
cultural capital, 68, 106, 121, 193,
    205
cultures, 18, 185
    cultural identity, 91
    insiders and outsiders, 185
curriculum, 14, 15, 32, 157
    co-curriculum, 32, 43
    core curriculum, 15
    curriculum design, 44
    embedding skills, 24
    experiential, 22
    inclusive, 25
    multicultural, 21
    multidisciplinary, 18
    re-imagined, 18
    renewal, 36, 37
    transformations, 78
    writing accross the curriculum,
        36
curriculum design, 3, 19, 20, 25, 43
    foundation units, 15
    holistic approach, 130
Cuseo, Joe, 38, 42, 49, 53, 152, 193,
    207
Custance, Juanita, 22–23
Daddow, Angela, 115
David, Miriam, 69
Davidson, Kristy, 212
Dawkins, Peter, 28, 49, 53
Deakin University, 43
deep engagement with text, 232
deficit approach, 3, 6, 7, 8, 15, 33,
    107, 111, 112, 192, 221, 246, 247
desynchronisation, 70
Devlin, Marcia, 19, 25, 68, 84, 85,
    87, 93, 97, 145, 146, 154, 193
Dewey, John, 189
disciplinary discourse, 109, 236

discourses
    academic discourses, 47, 83,
        113–17
    counter-discourse, 18
    justice, 7
    specialist, 18
diversity, 3, 194–95
    life stories, 131
Domingo, Robert, 145
Drew, Sue, 37
dual sector, 31, 58, 59, 150
Duff, Patricia, 222
early intervention strategies, 157
Eberly, Charlene, 160
Eckersley, Bill, 201
Edith Cowan University, 40
Edward, Janet, 238
Edwards, Anne, 190, 196
Edwards, Daniel, 28, 159
Edwards, Janet, 239
Egea, Kathy, 160
Egege, Sandra, 149, 160
embeddedness, 221
embedding skills, 247
engagement, 17, 20, 21, 22, 24, 25,
    36, 44, 48, 51, 56, 58, 93
    AUSSE Australasian Survey of
        Student Engagement, 49, 92
    community, 71
    engagement with texts, 238
    monitoring. *See* MSLE
        (Monitoring Student Learning
        Engagement)
    MSLE (Monitoring Student
        Learning Engagement, 58
    ontological, 123–26
    ontological engagement, 18
    operational/ontological, 117–21
    patterns of student engagement,
        96
    political engagement, 79
    shared engagement, 235
Engeström, Yrjo, 190
equity, 6, 7, 18, 26, 36, 59, 72, 189
Ernst & Young, 45
Evans Commander, Nanette, 82